THE
Jewish Festivals

THE
𝕵𝖊𝖜𝖎𝖘𝖍 𝕱𝖊𝖘𝖙𝖎𝖛𝖆𝖑𝖘

*A Guide to Their History
and Observance*

HAYYIM SCHAUSS

Translated by Samuel Jaffe
Foreword by Harold S. Kushner

SCHOCKEN BOOKS   NEW YORK

Library of Congress Catalogue Card Number:
62-13140
ISBN: 0-8052-0937-9

Printed in the United States of America

2 4 6 8 ['96] 9 7 5 3 1

To
the memory of
my parents

Contents

FOREWORD

BY HAROLD S. KUSHNER

Samson Raphael Hirsch, the leader of modern Orthodoxy in nineteenth-century Germany, once remarked, "the Jew's calendar is his catechism." Jews absorbed the central ideas of their faith not by studying them systematically but by celebrating the weekly Sabbath and the annual cycle of festivals, and gradually absorbing the lessons they conveyed.

Every spring, Jewish families would gather for a Seder meal. They would eat matzo and bitter herbs, and a child would ask the Four Questions. By means of those repeated rituals, over the course of years the family members would become familiar with the story of Israel's bitter enslavement in Egypt and God's deliverance of the people into freedom. The centrality of the Exodus story was underlined by the *Kiddush* prayer over a cup of wine to welcome each Sabbath and festival, proclaiming the occasion "a reminder of our exodus from Egypt."

Fasting on Yom Kippur, the Jew would learn of a God who made strenuous demands of us but left a door open for repentance and return. On Sukkot, he would be reminded that gratitude is the first and most indispensable element of a religious life. And on Hanukkah and Purim, the Jew would hear about a God who helps the weak triumph over the strong and the deserving win out over the wicked.

For the reader who would seek to understand the messages of the Jewish holidays and thereby understand the basic precepts of Judaism, there is no better way to begin than by reading Hayyim Schauss's classic work, *The Jewish Festivals*.

Published nearly sixty years ago, it continues to impress the reader with its accessibility and erudition.

Schauss's approach to the festivals is both historical and developmental. He describes a holiday's Biblical origin and mode of observance, then goes on to tell how different ways of celebrating evolved in the post-Biblical period, necessitated by the destruction of the Temple, the end of the sacrificial system, and other changing circumstances. He then typically offers a description of the holiday in an East European *shtetl*, with an occasional glimpse at "exotic" non-European communities. He offers us both the rabbinic-legal guidelines for the holiday and the folk customs bordering on superstition that attach themselves to it. At his best, Schauss paints unforgettably vivid portraits of Jews thronging the Temple of Jerusalem in the first century, or East European villages stopping all work to celebrate a *yom tov* in the eighteenth century.

Reading these chapters, one not only gains much information. One also learns something about the religious creativity of the Jewish people. Never content merely to do what their forefathers had done, Jews were always pouring "new wine into old bottles," inventing new forms and customs to supplement the traditional ones, attaching new meanings to forms that were in danger of slipping into obsolescence. Reading Schauss, one sees how what were originally agricultural festivals took on a historical-theological significance for a people who no longer worked the land: Shavuot evolved from an offering of the first fruits and grains to a celebration of the giving of the Torah. The lighting of the Sabbath candles, originally a functional necessity, became a way of inviting the presence of God into our homes on Sabbath eve. (Some scholars would insist that the Pilgrim festivals—Pesach, Shavuot, and

Sukkot—were both natural and historical even in the Biblical period.)

The book has its limitations. It can be distracting, if understandable, for a book originally published in 1938, to find the Jewish homeland referred to as Palestine and to see Hebrew terms transliterated in the East European, Ashkenazic pronunciation. While his grasp of history is generally impeccable, when Schauss refers to Jewish observance in his own time (admittedly the 1930s were a low point of Jewish observance), his comments have the antiquated air of a sixty-year-old magazine article. Thus he tells us that "even Orthodox Jews keep their shops open on the Sabbath" and "the observance of (the fast day) Tisha B'Ov is definitely on the decline, even among professing Orthodox Jews." Perhaps an accurate account about the demoralized, Depression-ridden Jewish world of the thirties, but not true today.

But Schauss's major limitation is his insistence on describing rather than explaining or evaluating. He describes the Yom Kippur ritual of the scapegoat in Biblical or Second Temple times, but never tells us *why* Jews did it. What psychological need did the scapegoat meet as part of Yom Kippur? For that matter, what did Yom Kippur mean to the Jew who fasted and prayed for atonement? What did Purim mean to the vulnerable Diaspora Jew who read the story of Queen Esther amid noise and merriment? Beyond a comment on the restorative power of the Sabbath, one looks in vain for any guidance from Schauss on these matters.

The Jewish Festivals is an indispensable introduction to the ideas and values contained in holiday observances. It should be the first book read on the subject, but it should not be the last. After reading Schauss to learn *how* a Jew celebrates, the reader

should go on to a guide that will explain what it all means, and
what it can mean today. But Schauss, ever vivid, learned, and
comprehensive, remains the place to start.

APRIL 1996

THE
Jewish Festivals

i. Sabbath – IN ANCIENT TIMES

Its Beginnings... The origin of the Sabbath is obscure, as are the beginnings of all other festivals. Only this much is certain, that the Jewish Sabbath did not originate in Babylonia, as some Assyriologists asserted.

We know from the inscriptions of the ancient Babylonians that certain days of a certain month or months were distinguished from the other days of the month. These were the seventh, fourteenth, nineteenth, twenty-first, and twenty-eighth days of the month. These days were related either to the phases of the moon, or to the sacred number seven. The nineteenth day was also distinguished because, added to the thirty days of the previous month, it totaled forty-nine, seven times seven. On those days, it is told in an inscription, the king is not to eat meat roasted on coals, nor any food touched with fire; he is not to change his clothes, ride in a chariot, or discuss affairs of state. Neither shall the priest reveal an oracle, or the physician treat the sick.

These days were not called Sabbaths, nor did they have any relation to the Jewish Sabbath. To begin with, they were not days of rest, but days on which, because of certain primitive beliefs, it was considered unlucky to work. Secondly, the entire folk was not enjoined to guard against labor on those days, but only certain people—the king, the priest, the doctor. Thirdly, the day had nothing to do with a seven-day week that ran throughout the year, as among the Jews; these were only certain days of the month, and not of all months, but only of a certain month.

The Jewish Sabbath has no relation to these days of the Babylonian calendar. What we must consider, however, is the day of the full moon, known as *Shabattum*, which is designated as an unlucky day, in which one must appease the gods with sacrifices.

Even to this *Shabattum* the relation of the Jewish Sabbath is weak and dubious. For the Assyriologists do not know the meaning of the word *Shabattum*, and we are not in any way certain that there is any relationship between the two words, despite the similarity in sound.

Then, too, there is no proof that the Jewish Sabbath had anything to do with the full moon. The fact that the New Moon and the Sabbath are so often coupled in the Bible is no proof whatsoever that Sabbath signified full moon. The New Moon and the Sabbath came regularly throughout the year and they could, therefore, be coupled even though the Sabbath referred to the week and not to the month.[1]

The scholars are, therefore, divided regarding the origin of the Sabbath. One group contends that the Sabbath was originally, among Jews, one day of the month, the full moon, like the Babylonian *Shabattum*. It was only later that the Jews discarded the observance of this day, being opposed to anything which had to do with the worship of the stars. On the other hand, the Jews introduced the seven-day week, with the seventh day as a day of rest, and transferred to this day the name Sabbath.

A second group of scholars contends that the Jewish Sabbath never had any relation with the Babylonian *Shabattum* and the phases of the moon, but was, from the beginning, even from the days of Moses, instituted on the seventh day of the week as the day of rest.[2]

Even those scholars who contend that the Sabbath was

originally related to the full moon concede that the Sabbath we know, the Sabbath of later times, of the seventh day of each week, was an original Jewish creation.

In addition to the fact that the Sabbath was not related to the moon, but was the seventh day in a week which ran throughout the entire year independently of the month, the motive behind the Sabbath was genuinely Jewish. In the Babylonian *Shabattum* the motive for observance was the superstition that it was unlucky to work on that day because of the phase of the moon; the Jews introduced into the Sabbath a humanitarian motive. Even in the oldest laws of the Pentateuch Jews are enjoined to work only six days of the week and to rest on the seventh, "that thine ox and thine ass may have rest, and the son of thy handmaid, and the stranger, may be refreshed." [3]

The Sabbath, as a day of rest in each week, was thus a genuinely Jewish institution. Moreover, in its further development, the Sabbath traveled its own unique Jewish path. The New Moon could scarcely be accommodated in the Jewish religion and lost its status as an official festival. The Sabbath, however, continued to grow in significance and importance until it became one of the very fundamentals of Judaism.

In the Days of the First Temple...From the meager sources available regarding the Sabbath in ancient days, when the Jews still had their own kingdom in Palestine, it seems that the Sabbath was more than a day of rest; it was also a day of joy and celebration. [4]

We read in the writings of those days that it was an ordinary thing to wend one's way to the "man of God," riding a donkey, and taking a servant along. This is done even in harvest time. Apparently, work in the fields is stopped on that day, and even a servant can be spared for the trip.[5] Only some of the people travel to the "man of God," but Jews come *en masse* to the sanctuary. The Temple in Jerusalem is crowded. To keep order, two-thirds of the royal bodyguard are on duty on that day in the Temple; the rest of the week only one-third of the king's bodyguard serves in the Temple, the others being on duty in the royal palace. The Sabbath was thus the fitting day for the priest Jehoiada to carry through his *coup d'etat* against Athaliah and to put the young prince Jehoash on the throne.[6]

Since work is halted and Jews go to the sanctuary to celebrate the day, commerce is also stopped. The prophet Amos condemns the grain dealers, who can scarcely await the passing of the New Moon and the Sabbath, so anxious are they to practice their commercial knavery.[7]

This, approximately, is the picture we have of the Sabbath in those very old days, when both kingdoms, Judah and Israel, still existed. It was a festival on which there was a cessation of daily work, and people assembled in the sanctuary to celebrate the day. The strict rest of later days was not yet a part of the Sabbath; it was a day when people took trips throughout the land; a day when the pious chief priest in Jerusalem executed a *coup d'etat*. It is very possible that this condition was changed in the later period of the Jewish kingdom. It may be that even then, in the period prior to the Babylonian exile, the Sabbath began to grow in significance and that there was a demand in some Jewish circles for a stricter observance of Sabbath rest.

At any rate, beginning with the Babylonian exile, we find the Sabbath attaining a new significance, and a deeper spiritual content.

In the Babylonian Exile... The Sabbath attained a higher state of development among the exiled Jews in Babylonia, and it was these exiled Jews who enforced on Palestine their Sabbath, with its stricter observance and its universal rest.

It is easy to explain why the Sabbath assumed a different character during the Babylonian exile. In the days of the independent Jewish kingdom the three great festivals of the year, Pesach, Shovuos, and Sukkos, were still joyous revelries, closely connected with the village life of the peasants, as will be expounded later. In the face of these three festivals the Sabbath could not play a great role. As far as festive joys were concerned the Sabbath could not vie with them. But in exile these great festivals also became holy gatherings of the congregation, days of rest, of sacred earnestness and spiritual elevation. The Sabbath could very easily measure up to such types of festivals. Moreover, the Sabbath could appropriate some of their significance for itself. For there was never any local revelry connected with the Sabbath. From the very beginning, the Sabbath combined in its observance the aspect of rest as well as the aspect of joy.

Thus, the observance of the Sabbath fitted the circumstances and the spiritual needs of the Jews of Babylonia. Living as they did in a strange, non-Jewish environment, and trying to maintain their national existence in these strange surroundings, the Sabbath, like circumcision, became a mark that distinguished them from their non-Jewish neighbors. The Jews in Babylonia did not possess the outer means of worship through which they could find favor in the eyes of God and become one with Him. They had no sanctuary, and no sacrifices could be offered on the altar. But precepts such as circumcision and the observance of the Sabbath could be observed even in exile. Therefore, the Jews observed them with greater fervor than before. These precepts attained a new significance. They became a substitute for sacrifices; they became the very first precepts of Judaism, the main symbols of the Jewish religion.

Ezekiel, the prophet who lived among the exiled Jews in Babylonia, ascribed to the Sabbath an abstract, religious significance. "I gave them My Sabbath, to be a sign between Me and them, that they might know that I am the Lord that sanctify them." [8] Observance of the Sabbath is thus, according to Ezekiel, the sign that distinguishes Jews from non-Jews. This thought of Ezekiel, together with his phraseology, we meet also in the Priestly Writing, one of the sources from which the Pentateuch was composed, according to modern, critical investigation of the Bible. Just as circumcision is, according to the Priestly Writing, the sign by which God made a covenant with Abraham, so the Sabbath is the external sign by which God made His eternal covenant with Israel, through Moses at Mount Sinai. Even God Himself submitted to the law of the Sabbath and rested on the seventh day when He created the world. Jews must therefore observe the Sabbath, the holy day, and be a holy people and guard themselves against the practices of the heathen peoples about them.[9]

But the Jews profaned the Sabbath, says Ezekiel, meaning that the Jews in Palestine, in the time of the independent kingdom, did not observe the strict Sabbath rest. The Jews in Palestine, about a century after the Babylonian exile, did not as yet know of the strict Sabbath of the Babylonian Jews.

Nehemiah narrates, in his memoirs, that when he came to Jerusalem from Susa the second time, he found that the Jews in Judah were very lax in their observance of the Sabbath. In some parts of the land they continued their usual agricultural labors on this holy day. In Jerusalem they did cease their labors because they celebrated; it was a fine day for marketing and the peasants brought wine, grapes, figs, and many other products to sell in Jerusalem. Phoenician merchants brought fish and other wares to sell in Jerusalem, taking advantage of the fine marketing possibilities on a day when people had leisure to buy.

Nehemiah first admonished the leaders for permitting this to go on; he told them that the destruction of Jerusalem came because the Jews of former days did not observe the Sabbath. After admonishing them he gave strict orders that the gates of the city were to be shut tightly at twilight on Friday, and were not to be opened again till the end of the Sabbath. He did not trust the local officials to enforce this, however, but sent his own servants to see that no merchandise be brought into Jerusalem. When some merchants came and remained outside the walls of the city, Nehemiah gave them such a drastic warning that they left and did not dare to return. To safeguard the reforms he had instituted he ordered Levites to be ready to make their way to the gates every Sabbath and see to it that nothing that could possibly profane the Sabbath be allowed to enter the city.[10]

The strict Sabbath rest became incorporated into the laws of the Priestly Code, which the Jews had adopted at the Great Assembly and had sworn solemnly to observe in all future generations. The Sabbath became the holy day of the Lord, a day of complete rest and cessation from all work.[11] For profaning the sacredness of the Sabbath the Priestly Code prescribed the penalty of death.[12] The observance of the Sabbath and safeguarding it from profanation became so fundamental to Judaism that an anonymous prophet of this epoch declared it the very first and most important symbol for worshiping God and accepting Judaism.[13]

In the Days of the Second Temple...The institution of the Sabbath was based on two motives. There was the humanitarian motive, rest not only for all men, but even for the ox and the ass. The other motive was religious; Jews refrained from work and sanctified the seventh day in order to be a holy people of a holy God.[14]

In accordance with these two motives the Sabbath developed simultaneously along two lines, the restrictive and the spiritual. On the one hand, the laws and regulations of the Sabbath grew immensely in number and ever stronger became the restrictions against all forms of labor. On the other hand, the Jew did not feel the rigor of the Sabbath laws. Hand-in-hand with the growing rigorous, external rest of the Sabbath, an inner rest, a spiritual elevation, and a liberation from the every-day chores of the week were experienced on this sacred day. The simultaneous development of the Sabbath along these two lines is already expressed in the biblical writings of the earlier days of the second Temple. On one hand, the Priestly Writing of the Pentateuch prescribes the death penalty for gathering sticks to make fire on the Sabbath. On the other hand, an anonymous prophet of that time calls for observance of the Sabbath as a delight, not as a burden.[15]

In the course of time the Sabbath became the day on which the Jew expressed his religious feelings and expanded intellectually; the day which he devoted to religious instruction and education. At the same time that the Sabbath became such a significant institution among the exiled Jews in Babylonia, the institution of the synagogue also arose and attained a great significance. Both institutions, the Sabbath and the Synagogue, complemented each other very well. The Jew was given the opportunity of spending the Sabbath in the synagogue, to hear the reading and translation of a section of the Torah and a portion of the Prophets, and to hear the preacher re-interpret it in his sermon. This character of the Sabbath as a day of religious study became still stronger when the institution of the *Bes ha-Midrosh*, House of Study, devoted expressly to the theoretical study of the Torah, grew up.

The Sabbath became still more beloved and engraved on the hearts of Jews when Antiochus Epiphanes prohibited its observance under penalty of death. Devout Jews allowed themselves to be killed rather than to cease observing the Sabbath. Mattathias and his colleagues decreed that for defensive purposes profanation of the Sabbath was allowed. It was difficult, however, to draw a strict line of demarcation between offense and defense, and Jews in later times were on many occasions defeated because of the Sabbath observance.[16]

There were among the Jews certain groups and sects for whom the Sabbath had only a rigorous and ascetic character. No fire or light was allowed on the Sabbath, even when that fire or light was kindled before the Sabbath. One was scarcely allowed to stir or move on the Sabbath. During the days of the second Temple sects and groups which observed this rigorous Sabbath included the Samaritans, the Essenes, and, probably, the Sadducees; in later times the Karaites were added to these sects. Among the Pharisees, however, and that means among the great majority of the people, the Sabbath never assumed this one-sided, rigorous character. It is true that the Pharisees increased the prohibitions of work on the Sabbath down to the most minute detail, but, on the other hand, they eased, in many respects, the rigor of the Sabbath rest and preserved the character of the Sabbath as a day of delight and joy. They did more than permit the burning of lights on Friday night; they declared it a precept. They permitted walks of two thousand cubits in any one direction on the Sabbath and, provided food had been placed at that point on the day before, the place was considered an abode and a further walk of two thousand cubits was allowed. If it was a question of succoring the sick, of saving an endangered life, breaking the law was allowed. There were many such moderations of the rigorous Sabbath rest, for the Sabbath was given to the Jews, not the Jews to the Sabbath, said the Pharisees.[17]

Thus the Sabbath became, among the Jewish masses who followed the teachings of the Pharisees, a wonderful gift from Heaven, from God to Israel. The pleasures of the Sabbath are one-sixtieth of the delights of the world to come; on the eve of the Sabbath God gives man a special soul, and with the passing of the Sabbath it is taken away from him, to mention only a few of the sayings of the Talmud regarding the Sabbath.[18]

The Sabbath of the Pharisees not only put its stamp on all of Jewish life, but also influenced greatly the life of all civilized humanity. With no other religious idea or institution have the Jews influenced the world as much as with the Sabbath, a seventh day as a day of rest in each week.

ii. $\mathfrak{Sabbath}$ = IN ITS DEVELOPMENT

At the Beginning of the Common Era... The Jew carried the thought of the Sabbath in his mind during the entire week. Food delicacies acquired on the other six days were put aside for the Sabbath. Thursday was the market day on which Jews of the farms and villages of Palestine brought their produce to town, and merchants displayed and sold their wares. But the climax of the preparations for the sacred Day of Rest came on Friday. It was a day of hurry and bustle for all. It was considered a great merit to do work on Friday in preparation for the Sabbath. The Jews were so occupied on Friday, preparing for the Sabbath, that they were certain that the prophet Elijah would not appear with his message of redemption on Friday.[19]

All Jews, rich and poor, baked *challos*, Sabbath loaves for the Sabbath. People sometimes ate stale bread during the rest of the week, but on the Sabbath they wanted the best, and the Jews, like the orientals of today, liked their bread fresh from the oven.[20]

In order to assure against profanation of the Sabbath the Jews added the late Friday afternoon hours to the Sabbath. In Jerusalem a priest, standing on a high tower of the Temple, blew a trumpet as a signal to put away all work and to begin the Sabbath rest. In all other cities and towns of Palestine the sexton of the community ascended the roof of an elevated house, usually the synagogue, at the required time, and blew six blasts on the trumpet at intervals. At the first blow of the trumpet the Jews in the fields about the town put down their work; those who worked closer to town did not rush from the fields, but waited for those who worked further out, and all marched into town together. The shops, however, were still open; they closed at the second trumpet call. The third blast was the signal at which the pots were taken from the stoves and wrapped in various materials to preserve their warmth. The third blast was also the signal for kindling the Sabbath lights. The devout, who wore phylacteries all day long, removed them at this signal. Then came an intermission, followed by three successive blasts, thus heralding the sacred Sabbath rest. The sexton was not allowed to carry the trumpet down from the roof; he left it there until the next night, when he used it to signal the end of the Sabbath and the resumption of work.

On the Sabbath, one wore special Sabbath clothes. Better and tastier meals were eaten; it was a precept to eat three Sabbath meals. The Sabbath, however, was celebrated with more than better clothes and food: the study of God's Torah played a great role on God's sacred Day of Rest.

The Sabbath, in general, thus attained its peak in the first two centuries of the Common Era, the age of the *Tannaim*, as the Jewish teachers and sages of that period were called. However, there were no Friday night services as yet. This most beautiful part of the Sabbath observance developed somewhat later in the age of the *Amoraim*, as the sages of the Talmud from the third century on were called, and it did not attain its highest peak until much later, at the very threshold of modern times.

In the time of the *Tannaim* there was no Friday night service in the synagogue, for *ma'ariv*, evening prayer, was not a community service at that time, but an individual prayer, and there was no exception made on Friday. Each man said the evening prayer by himself, some adding a few words about the sanctity of the Sabbath.

The entire family was united at the evening meal late on Friday afternoon, just after the last signals of the trumpet, while it was still light. There were religious brotherhoods that ate together, these meals playing a great role in their lives. The diners reclined as they ate, according to the custom of the period. After the meal they recited the benediction. By that time it was usually dark. It was then that *Kiddush*, the prayer of sanctification of the Sabbath, was recited by the head of the group, over a glass of wine.

After the meal people went to the House of Study to listen to lectures on religious topics. The children also went to school. But they did not learn new lessons. They just reviewed the lessons which they had learned during the week.

Later it became customary to hold communal services in the synagogue on Friday night, and to recite *Kiddush* in the synagogue then. We know that this was the custom in Babylonia, in the time of the *Amoraim*. In Babylonia wine was not so readily available as in Palestine, and the custom of reciting *Kiddush* over other beverages, or even over bread, was introduced. Another innovation of that time was the reciting of *Kiddush* at home before the meal, because by the time they returned from the synagogue the Sabbath had already arrived.

The Sabbath was inaugurated with the first Sabbath meal on Friday night, and leave was taken of the Sabbath with the third Sabbath meal. This third meal was, in the time of the *Tannaim*, started while it was still day. Darkness came toward the close of the meal, when a blast was blown on the trumpet as a signal that the Sabbath was over. A light was brought in and a benediction recited over it. After the meal a container of odorous spices was carried in on a bed of coals, the spices sending their fragrance throughout the room (the regular custom of those days), and a benediction was recited over it. At the end, the benediction over the meal was recited; thus associating it with the benediction of *Havdoloh*, division between sacred and profane, in which leave was taken of the Sabbath.

This was also changed in later times. Jews ceased eating the third meal at the end of the Sabbath, that meal being eaten earlier. Moreover, eating during the twilight hours of the Sabbath, before *Havdoloh*, was forbidden.[21]

In the Middle Ages...During the Middle Ages the Sabbath was, for the Jew, the island of rest in a surging sea of persecution. It was the day on which the prince, who through the craft of a witch had been transformed into a dog, was again beheld in his once handsome features, according to the description of the poet Heine.

Friday was the day of cleaning and scouring in preparation for the Sabbath. On Friday night even the humblest dwelling was transformed into a palace of rest and spiritual joy. The cover that graced the table was heavily embroidered, even in the poorest of homes. In the wealthier homes a seven-branched candelabrum was suspended from the ceiling over the table; it was lowered and lighted on Friday night, and drawn up again after the Sabbath.

The approach of the Sabbath was announced by the beadle of the community; it was also his duty to awake the members of the congregation for prayers on the morning of the Sabbath. Every morning he went from house to house, knocking on the doors with a wooden mallet; on the Sabbath, however, he used his fist.

Life in a Jewish home of several centuries ago was full of tenderness and piety. The relationship between man and wife was tender and true, as was the relationship between parents and children. This spirit was evidenced especially on the Sabbath and festivals.

On Friday night, after all work had been put aside, the entire family gathered about the father, the head of the house, and presented a picture of hominess and warmth.

After evening prayers the father blessed his children, and the rabbi gave his blessing to all the youth of the community. The father blessed his children again after the *Havdoloh* benediction.

The picture of a well-to-do Jewish home of the fifteenth century on the Sabbath has been preserved for us by a non-Jewish writer who wrote a description of the home of a wealthy Jew in the German town of Regensburg.

He describes a large room, paneled in costly woods, finely carved, and richly bedecked with hangings. This room was the temple of the master of the house, in which he observed the ceremonies of the Sabbath.

A crimson-red tablecloth covered the round table in the center of the room, and above it hung the seven-branched candelabrum, glistening as if it had just come out of the foundry, and lighted with seven candles. The dining-table, specially decorated for the Sabbath, bore heavy silver cups, and about the table stood high backed chairs, decorated in gold and upholstered in silk. In a recess stood a massive silver wash-basin, where all washed their hands before coming to the table, wiping them afterwards with costly linen towels.

The high-point of all this picture of wealth and luxury was the table itself, bedecked with flowers and covered with Sabbath delicacies, centering about a crystal wine-flagon. On the side were sofas covered with cushions of down, and a cabinet filled with precious objects and antiques.

That is the picture of a rich Jewish home of five hundred years ago. But even the poorest Jew made his home as splendid as possible on the Sabbath, and he, too, saw that the three Sabbath meals were served in his home. The third meal, however, was eaten quite early in the day, and in the short winter days this meal was eaten directly after the second meal, as a form of dessert.

After the Friday evening meal the entire household sat about the table and sang *z'miros*, table songs, in honor of the Sabbath. The *Pay'tonim*—the liturgical poets of the Middle Ages—not only enriched the Sabbath prayers with their poetical insertions but they also created hymns and poems to sing at the table.

Everyone sought to have a special guest with him at table on the Sabbath. A pious Jew naturally sought to have with him a student from the Talmudic academy, or some other learned Jew. It was the custom to arrange for the invitation of poor Jews by the householders of each town. It was also the custom to ask the guest to pronounce the benediction after the meal. If the guest were a learned man it would be the good fortune of the household to hear from him a novel interpretation of a portion of Torah. And nothing could give a Jew of those days greater joy than an original exposition of the Torah.

The afternoon of the Sabbath was devoted to promenading, usually to the stream. People gathered in groups to talk politics, one Jew arguing for one of the ruling princes, another for his rival. There was much study of the holy books, but there was ample reading of secular literature.

The adults spent much time on the Sabbath in the synagogue and in the *Bes ha-Midrosh*, but the youth spent much time in play. Each ghetto had a community dance-hall for weddings, and on Sabbath afternoon there would be gatherings in the dance-hall for sociability and for dancing. Boys and girls would play with nuts, rolling them off a board. There was also some chess playing; it even became a custom to use special silver chess pieces on the Sabbath.

The most desired food for the Friday evening meal was fish and, like other Jewish delicacies, it was highly spiced with pepper and garlic. Broiled poultry was also a great delicacy, especially goose.

In Germany it was the custom among Jews to bake special cakes for the Sabbath, which were called *pastetten*. Jewish children were very fond of this cake, and it was one of the reasons that they welcomed the coming of the Sabbath. There is a story told of those days regarding a Jewish child who fell into the hands of robbers. When Friday night came and no *pastetten* were served the child cried so bitterly and so loudly that his screams brought help and he was saved.[22]

At the Threshold of Modern Times...The most beautiful part of the Sabbath observance, the ceremony of *Kabbolas Shabbos*, the greeting of the Sabbath on Friday, just before evening prayers, is of recent origin. It was first introduced at the end of the sixteenth century; it evolved at that time among the Kabbalists, the religious mystics of Safed, of whom the greatest and most influential was Rabbi Isaac Luria.

The Talmud tells that certain Palestinian *Amoraim* of the third century would dress themselves in Sabbath clothes on Friday evening and say, "Come, let us go out and meet the Sabbath Queen," or "Come, bride; come, bride!" The Kabbalists in Safed took this personification of the Sabbath as bride and queen literally. They would go, late Friday afternoon, in a procession outside the town to greet the queen and bride Sabbath; they sang certain Psalms and they would end with, "Come, bride; come, bride!"

Many Jewish poets of that period composed poems greeting the Sabbath as a bride. One of these songs, "L'choh Dodi" (come, my friend [to meet the bride]), composed by Solomon Alkabetz, one of the circle of Kabbalists in Safed, became famous because it had the approval of Rabbi Isaac Luria.

Under the influence of the Kabbalists of Safed this ceremony of greeting the Sabbath with Psalms and the song of Solomon Alkabetz was introduced in all Jewish communities. As a remembrance of the procession of the Kabbalists outside the town it became the custom for cantor and congregation to turn about at the last stanza of the song and face the door of the synagogue, as if they expected the royal bride, the Princess Sabbath, to come in to her beloved groom, Israel.

With the introduction of this ceremony the beauty and the poetry of the Sabbath reached its peak, which was retained through the seventeenth and eighteenth centuries and, in eastern Europe, practically to the present day.[23]

iii. 𝔖abbath ꞊ IN MODERN TIMES

In Eastern Europe...It is only Thursday, and already the pre-Sabbath atmosphere is felt in the community. People rush to the market early to buy poultry and fish for the Sabbath. Late on Thursday evening the women knead the dough for the *challos*, the Sabbath loaves. On Friday they are up before dawn to heat the ovens. There is much work to be done, and, in addition, it is a great religious merit to rise early on Friday to prepare for the Sabbath.

When the oven is ready the housewife forms plain or braided loaves from the dough which she kneaded the night before. First, however, she performs the ceremony of "taking *challoh*," taking off a piece of dough, reciting a benediction, and throwing it into the burning stove, as a remembrance of the precept of setting apart the first of the dough as a gift to the priest. While the dough burns she recites a *t'chinoh*, a meditative prayer, in which she prays to God that He accept the piece of dough as a sacrifice on the altar; that He give her the means to feed her beloved children; and, that in His great mercy, He protect her from worry and hardship.

Friday morning is distinguished from all other mornings of the week by reason of the warm buns served fresh from the oven. The children eat the buttered buns and go off to the *Cheder*, the Jewish religious school. Even the *Cheder* is different on that day. School is open for only half the day and is devoted mostly to chanting the section of the Pentateuch and the portion of the Prophets for the Sabbath.

By noon-time the children are through with *Cheder* and

they have quite a few hours, nearly half a day, for mischief. No regular lunch is served. Very devout Jews do not eat at all from morning to evening, in order to enjoy more fully the Sabbath meal at night, and thus earn greater merit.

The town assumes, from the afternoon on, a unique Friday appearance. The stoves flame high with their fires, burning now to heat the *cholent*, the dish cooked on Friday and kept warm in a closed stove until the next day. But the stoves are heated for *cholent* only in some of the homes, for whoever has a large enough stove accommodates a few of his neighbors. On the hearth of the stove the pots and pans stew and simmer with the Sabbath food. From every Jewish home the smoke rises black, in sooty pillars to heaven.

The men lend a hand, but it is mainly the women who are rushed and occupied. A board for noodles is set on the table and the housewife rolls and cuts, making noodles for soup and pudding. Business is brisk in the food shops. Women rush in and out, from home to shop and back again. This woman is short of sugar, that one needs flour, a third a bit of pepper for the stuffed fish, and traffic in and out of the shops is heavy.

Later in the afternoon there is quiet and peace. The food for the Sabbath is already cooked. The *cholent* is put into the oven and the stove is sealed with clay to keep the heat in. A jar of hot water is set in a recess in the stove, built especially for this purpose, for warm foods and drinks on the Sabbath. Belated Jews rush home from the bathhouse, their faces shining and ruddy.

Elderly, devout Jews are already seated in the synagogue, clad in their Sabbath finery, chanting the Song of Songs. Soon the beadle goes through the streets, calling at the top of his voice, "Into the Synagogue!"

One by one the stores close, in rapid succession. The houses are spic and span. The pots and pans have been removed from the stoves, the fires no longer flame. Father, mother, and children are busy washing, combing, and dressing for the Sabbath. Every moment the stillness grows deeper; the atmosphere becomes more peaceful and Sabbath-like in each nook and corner of the house. The Sabbath approaches slowly with soft quiet tread, and spreads a sacred peace over all Jewish homes.

The polished candlesticks, of which there must be at least two, stand on the table. In richer homes they are silver, but brass is more usual. The mistress performs the ceremony of lighting the candles, one of the very few precepts which apply especially to women. She puts the candles in the candlesticks, lights them, covers her eyes with her hands, and recites the benediction with her eyes closed. Then she looks at the candles and recites the *t'chinoh* for the occasion. She prays to God that she may see her children in health and honor, that they may grow up good and pious Jews, with hearts open to an understanding and appreciation of the Torah.

The table is covered with a white tablecloth. At the head of the table lie the two *challos*, covered with a finely embroidered cloth. The men of the family are still in the synagogue, greeting the Sabbath Queen in song and prayer.

They come home from the synagogue. "Gut Shabbos," "Gut Shabbos," they greet and answer one another. The house is imbued with a spirit of rest and family bliss. Father and sons walk back and forth in the house, singing *Sholom Aleichem* (Peace be with ye, ye ministering angels, etc.). This is a greeting to the two angels which the Highest King, the King of Kings, sends to accompany every Jew from the synagogue to his home on Friday night. The master of the household then recites the last chapter of Proverbs, beginning, "A woman of valor, who can find? For her price is far above rubies," thus serenading the mistress of the house.

The family seats itself at the table. Quite often the master brings a guest home with him from the synagogue, some poor wayfarer passing through the town. The *Kiddush* is recited. Gefilte fish, noodle soup, carrot pudding (*tsimmes*), and poultry are served. *Z'miros*, table songs, are sung between courses and after the meal.

The dining and the benediction are over. The master chants the portion of the Pentateuch for the week. He chants it three times, twice in the original Hebrew and once in *Targum*, the old Aramaic translation. The mistress, weary from the day's toil, sits with a stool beneath her feet and reads the *Ts'enoh Ur'enoh*. This is a paraphrase of the Pentateuch, parts of the Prophets, and the five scrolls, interwoven with Midrashic tales and interpretations, published in Yiddish in the seventeenth century and the most popular folk book of the last centuries.

The younger people read folk tales or go out walking, but not for long. All are weary from the work of the day and they go to bed early.

On Sabbath morning all is quiet in the town. The shops are closed, and trade is at a standstill. All the food needed for the day had been prepared the day before. All are free to go to the synagogue early. There are devout Jews who rise Saturday at dawn and go to the *Bes ha-Midrosh* to study Torah hours before the regular services commence.

The service is long, and sometimes, when an itinerant cantor with his choir comes to town, the services are still longer. They eventually end and all return home. Again *Kiddush* is recited, designated this time *B'rochoh*, benediction. Breakfast and dinner are eaten practically together, the main feature of the dinner being the *cholent* and *kugel* (pudding). There is much singing during the meal.

The afternoon passes. People promenade for a while through the town; the children are tested on their learning; most people take a Sabbath nap. And then on to the *Bes ha-Midrosh* to study.

Study is conducted in groups, separate ones for Bible, Mishnah, Talmud, and other important branches of Jewish lore. The youth wander about or play games. The time is thus occupied till *Minchoh* (afternoon prayers). Often *Minchoh* is postponed until later, to allow a *maggid*, a preacher, passing through the town, to deliver a sermon. A small community has a rabbi but cannot afford a resident preacher and must depend on these itinerants.

After *Minchoh* the third Sabbath meal is eaten, generally a dairy meal, kept for warmth in the recess of the stove, but by this time of the day it is cold, or, at best, lukewarm.

It is about this time of the day that sadness and sorrow begin to be felt—the Sabbath Queen is soon to leave. This feeling becomes deep and pronounced in the synagogue between *Minchoh* and *Ma'ariv*, the evening prayers. All of the men of the town are gathered there. One lamp, still burning from the night before, hangs over a long table near the entrance; around it stand a large group of men, sadly chanting from the Psalm, "Happy are they that are upright in the way, who walk in the law of the Lord." [24] The melody is a mournful one and clutches at the heart. A blanket of fear descends on all, especially on the children. There is a popular belief that the sinful souls are given rest during the Sabbath and are driven back into the flaming *Gehenna* as soon as the Sabbath is over.

This fearful atmosphere is terminated by the slap of the

sexton's hand on the *bimoh*, a signal for *Ma'ariv* services. These always come late, in order to prolong the sacredness of the Sabbath.

At the same time the mistress of the house, at home, waits until she sees three stars together in the sky, the sign that the Sabbath is over. She then recites the famous and beautiful *t'chinoh*, beginning,

> "God of Abraham, Isaac, and Jacob,
> Guard Thy people Israel in Thine arbor;
> The beloved Sabbath is departing. . . ."

She lights a candle and exclaims: "A good week, a full week, a fortunate week, on us and on all of Israel. Amen."

"A good week," is the greeting the men also give as they come home from the synagogue. The ceremony of *Havdoloh* is then begun. For this there must be two candles, placed together. Some use a braided candle made for this purpose. One of the children holds the candles and is urged to hold them as high as possible. "You'll get a tall bride, then," a boy is told, or "You'll get a tall groom," if the child is a girl. The master of the house pours a glass of wine or beer, lets it overflow onto the table, and says, "A full week." He recites certain sentences from the Psalms and then the benediction over the beverage. He cups his hands and scans his fingernails while reciting the benediction over the light as if to make use of it. Some also recite a benediction over a spice box. Finally the master recites the *Havdoloh* benediction, to the One Who distinguishes between the sacred and profane, and sips the beverage. Only the males get a taste of the beverage. It is believed that if a woman drinks of the *Havdoloh* glass she grows a beard. The master dips the candles in the liquid that spilled on the table, thus putting out the light. Some people also put this liquid on the eyes, as a cure for weak sight. Now all sing *z'miros* for the departure of the Sabbath, most of them centering about the prophet Elijah, the forerunner of the Messiah.

A fourth meal is then prepared, some tiny bite, called *M'laveh Malkoh*, the farewell to the Queen Sabbath. The house still has traces of the Sabbath spirit about it. It is as if a dear and beloved guest has just departed, but her presence is still felt, and consolation comes from the fact that she will soon reappear.

After this meal all sit about, idly chatting, and telling tales and legends—of the prophet Elijah, of Solomon and the Queen of Sheba, of Alexander the Great, of Don Isaac Abrabanel and the expulsion from Spain, and even of Napoleon's march on Moscow.

The women do the ordinary household tasks, but they neither knit nor sew.

In Western Europe and America... This is a picture of Sabbath rest in a town in Lithuania a generation ago, among *Misnagdim*, the opponents of the *Chassidim*, the sect that arose in Poland in the eighteenth century. The Sabbath was observed, with some differences in liturgy, but with still more fervor, among the *Chassidim* who, a century ago, constituted nearly half the Jewish people. However, the Sabbath led its ideal and idyllic existence through the nineteenth century and practically to the present day only in Eastern Europe. It was not so in Western Europe and America, in those countries which experienced the technical revolution of the nineteenth century.

The rigorous Sabbath rest, which Ezra and Nehemiah introduced in Palestine in the fifth century, B.C.E., could be preserved until the nineteenth century only because the economic, social, and cultural circumstances under which Jews lived were favorable to it.

In ancient times, during pre-Christian and early Christian centuries, it was easy for Jews to observe the Sabbath. In Palestine there was no obstacle. It was also possible for the Jews in the Diaspora, since observance was no hindrance to their economic life; the non-Jews had no weekly day of rest whatsoever and the Jew could easily make up what he lost by resting on the Sabbath, especially since work hours were not limited then, as they are now.

When the non-Jews became Christians and adopted the Jewish idea of a Sabbath, transferring it to Sunday, Jewish merchants and craftsmen profited still more. The observance of Sunday was not forced on the Jew; on the contrary, Sunday was the best day for trade, since the non-Jews came from the villages and countryside and gathered in town.

Added to this, the Jews, until the beginning of the nineteenth century, lived in ghettos and were politically, socially, linguistically, and culturally isolated from the surrounding world. Their Sabbath did not conflict with Sunday, nor in general with the social and civic life of their neighbors.

Beginning with the nineteenth century, however, all this was changed. The new technical inventions revolutionized trade and industry and opened opportunities that previous generations could not imagine. The entire economic life assumed new form in Western Europe and America. The Jews emerged, politically and economically, from their isolation and were drawn into the current of the new stream. The Jew, culturally and linguistically, began to fall under the influence of his non-Jewish environment. Culturally as well as economically there developed a common intercourse between Jews and non-Jews. In addition, there came the *Haskalah*, the movement of enlightenment among Jews, which shook to its very foundations the old and dogmatic forms of Jewish religious life. In the face of general Sunday observance the Jew could not observe the Sabbath.

It was thus that Sabbath observance was weakened in the nineteenth century. For about twenty-three hundred years, from the time of Ezra and Nehemiah, the Sabbath stood as fast and firm as a rock, until it was washed away by the mighty waves of the new economic life of the nineteenth century. Not only among religiously indifferent Jews, but even among orthodox Jews the strict observance of the Sabbath was left to a stubborn, self-sacrificing circle. Nowadays even Jews who, in general, live according to the orthodox code keep their shops open and work on the Sabbath. It is a not infrequent occurrence in small orthodox congregations in America that there are no *Kohanim*, descendants of the priestly caste, to pronounce the ancient priestly blessing on holidays. If the only *Kohanim* present work on the Sabbath they consider themselves unfit to perform this ceremony. It has become customary for such *Kohanim* not to pronounce the priestly blessing.

The only Jewish group that tackled the Sabbath problem and that sought ways and means of changing many of the rigorous, out-moded traits of the Sabbath rest, and to adapt the old Sabbath into the new circumstances of the life of the Jews of the nineteenth century, were the Reform Jews. But even they found no solution. The radical solution of some extremists, the transferring of the Sabbath to Sunday, did not find many adherents in Reform. There are Reform congregations that hold services on Sunday morning, but these are not meant to supersede the Sabbath. Such services are designed only for those who find it impossible to attend on Saturday.

New Forms of Sabbath Observance Today...Although the Sabbath, in its old traditional form as a day of complete cessation from work, is not and cannot be observed today, there has arisen, in recent years, a desire, a yearning, in many Jewish circles, for observance of the Sabbath with new forms, more in keeping with present modes of life.

In many congregations late Friday night services, after the evening meal, have been introduced. Women and children, as well as men, take part in these services. Huge candles are kindled on the altar, the *Chazan* recites *Kiddush*, a choir sings *L'choh Dodi* and other traditional Sabbath melodies. A sermon is delivered by the rabbi. Many other traditional Sabbath observances, varying with individual congregations, have been introduced into these late Friday night services. In many congregations special Saturday morning services for children have been introduced.

There is also a revival of the use of the "House of Study" in a new form, either in the synagogue or in an adjacent room, where forums and round table discussions on Jewish life and culture are held. In some circles, the institution of *Oneg Shabbat* (Delight in the Sabbath) has been introduced from the new Jewish life in Palestine. Men and women come together on Friday night or Saturday afternoon, for spiritual edification and intellectual enjoyment.

Here and there, a revival of the old *M'laveh Malkoh* (accompanying the Sabbath Queen on her departure for the week) custom is observed, in a new form. People gather late Saturday night, partake of refreshments, listen to cultural discourses, and create a truly Jewish atmosphere and spirit.

Thus, Sabbath observance is being revived in our own day, retaining the old spirit but introducing modern forms, so to say putting old wine into new bottles.

Sabbath Delicacies...The white Sabbath loaf, together with the fish—and, wherever obtainable, the wine—are the main features that distinguish the Friday night meal. We have already learned that in ancient times Jews baked bread on Friday for the entire week, thus insuring fresh bread for the Sabbath. These loaves of white bread are called, by Jews in Slavic countries, *challoh* (plural: *challos*). *Challoh* means a loaf of bread and also refers to the priest's share of the kneaded dough. Since the destruction of the second Temple the piece of dough is thrown into the fire.[25]

This ceremony was incumbent upon the woman when preparing the dough on Friday, and she observed it as carefully as the lighting of the candles. The word *challoh*, which originally designated this piece of dough, was thus transferred to the entire Sabbath loaf.

The oblong loaves of twisted Sabbath bread are called *berches*, also *barches*, by German Jews. Scholars are of the opinion that this name is derived from the old German goddess of vegetation, *Berchta*. The German woman of the early Middle Ages baked braided loaves for this goddess and called them by her name. The Jewish woman also baked such loaves for the Sabbath and called them by the same name. The German Jews also have another name for the Sabbath loaves, *taatscher*, or *datscher*, from the French *tarte* (German, *torte*), meaning twisted cakes. Among the Persian Jews also the loaves are called *challos*, but the *S'fardim* have no special name for the Sabbath loaves.[26]

In America, where the Sabbath is so little observed, the *challoh* is nevertheless very popular with Jews. There can still be found pious women who bake their own bread on Friday. Most of the women, however, buy the loaves in the bakery. One of the signs of a Jewish neighborhood is the display of *challos* in bakery windows on Friday. The custom of serving two loaves of bread with the Sabbath meal originated from the ancient custom of serving a loaf of bread with each cooked dish. On ordinary days only one cooked dish was served, and, therefore, only one loaf of bread. But on the Sabbath two such dishes were served, each with its own loaf of bread. It thus became traditional to serve two loaves of bread with the Sabbath meal.[27]

The custom of eating fish on the Sabbath, like the Sabbath loaf, is old in origin. Many scholars are of the opinion that the popularity of fish as a Sabbath food is because fish was regarded as a symbol of fertility. Whether or not this is so, the fact remains that Jews were always eager to eat fish on the Sabbath, even in Talmudic times.[28]

The main feature of the Sabbath midday meal is the *cholent*, with its adjunct, the *kugel*, cooked food kept warm overnight in a sealed stove. As far back as the time of the second Temple it was the custom for Jews to keep the Sabbath food in materials that retained heat. Adding heat on the Sabbath is forbidden, not the retaining of it.

Many explanations are given for the name *cholent*, which is quite old. The most plausible one is that it is derived from the old French word *chald* (now *chaud*), meaning warmth. This became *schalet* among German Jews, and *cholent* among Slavic Jews. It is also certain that the dish originated in the Rhineland, where such a large Jewish settlement existed in the early Middle Ages. From there the name spread to all Ashkenazic Jews and, in Eastern Europe, it became changed to *cholent*.[29]

Lighting the Candles...As far back as the beginning of the Common Era, lighting the candles signified the inauguration of the Sabbath. Because of this it attained religious sanctity. The reciting of the benediction over the candles is, however, a product of post-Talmudic times. As late as the twelfth century, it had not yet been accepted by all Jewish communities. It spread, however, and was later accepted by all, becoming one of the main features of the ceremonial of greeting the Sabbath.[30]

During the Middle Ages there arose a controversy among the rabbis as to which was to come first, reciting the benediction or lighting the candles. If the woman recites the benediction first, she thus accepts the presence of the Sabbath and is not allowed to kindle a light. On the other hand, if she lights the candles first there is another complication, for a benediction cannot be recited after the precept is fulfilled. A compromise was accepted: the woman lights the candle first and then recites the benediction, with her hands shielding her eyes against the light of the candles.[31]

Havdoloh...As previously stated, at the beginning of the Common Era the benediction of *Havdoloh* over a glass of wine and the smelling of spices were a matter of course, practiced as part of the third meal eaten on the Sabbath. In the course of time, however, the custom changed; the smelling of spices after a meal was discontinued. A new interpretation was given the custom, therefore, during the Middle Ages. It became related to the "additional soul" that each Jew is supposed to possess on the Sabbath. The spices, it was said, were a means of reviving the spirit when the extra soul leaves at the end of the Sabbath.

The departure of the Sabbath assumed, in time, a foreboding character. The belief was spread that demons are more powerful on Saturday night, especially Lilith, the mother of demons. To this was added the belief that the outgoing of the Sabbath was the hour when the lost souls go back to Gehenna. An atmosphere of fear thus surrounded Saturday night and many curious customs were attached to it and to the *Havdoloh* ceremony.[32]

It was considered dangerous to drink water before *Havdoloh*. On the other hand, it was propitious to draw water from the well directly afterward. Women must not drink of the *Havdoloh* beverage. The glass must be filled to overflowing as a symbol of a full and prosperous week. Such an explanation would be acceptable if it were the custom to fill the glass just to the very brim. But this was not the case, since the liquid must spill over the sides of the glass. It had nothing to do, originally, with a full glass and a full week, but with something quite different, with the pouring of the wine. It originated in the belief, among Jews and other peoples, that spilling wine was a safeguard against evil spirits, that they can be bribed with a bit of wine. This also explains why wine is spilled at the ceremony under the wedding canopy. It is no doubt also the explanation for the spilling of wine from the glass when the plagues are enumerated on Pesach eve. It was considered dangerous to pronounce a calamity without taking some safeguard; therefore the wine is spilled as the plagues are enumerated, thus guarding against harm.[33]

In some regions, as previously stated, it is customary to spill a bit of wine on the table to extinguish the *Havdoloh* candles after the ceremony, then to moisten the eyes and to say the verse of the Psalm: "The commandment of the Lord is pure, enlightening the eyes." [34] This is a superstitious precaution against weak eyesight.

Despite the gloom that the departure of the Sabbath brought with it, it had also a bright and joyful aspect. As previously stated, the belief was current that Elijah would not appear on Friday, and certainly not on the Sabbath. As soon as the Sabbath departed, however, one could expect him to arrive and announce the coming of the Messiah. It is for this reason, then, that since the early Middle Ages z'miros have been sung on Saturday night with the coming of Elijah as the theme.

The eating of the fourth meal after the departure of the Sabbath is an old custom. There was a controversy in the Talmud as to whether the Friday night meal was to be included in the three meals to be eaten on the Sabbath. If it is not to be included, then a fourth Sabbath meal must be added. This fourth meal survived as the M'laveh Malkoh, the farewell to the Sabbath Queen. It was also designated as the meal of King David. The connection with David is explained because of a Talmudic tale about his death. According to this legend King David asked a question of God, "Lord, make me to know mine end, and the measure of my days, what it is." [35] To which God answered that he would die on the Sabbath. Therefore, at the end of each Sabbath David held a feast, since he was assured of a week's life.[36]

Sambatyon, the Sabbath River...Of all the beliefs and legends that arose regarding the Sabbath, none has played as great a role as the legend of the Sabbath river, Sabbation, which later became Sambatyon.

In the time of the destruction of the second Temple a tale was told, in various versions, about a wonderful stream, that flows not regularly, but periodically. According to one version, the stream was dry for six days of the week, and flowed on the seventh; according to another version it flowed for six days and was dry on the seventh.[37]

This was the basis on which the colorful phantasy of the *Sambatyon* legend was built.

Originally the story dealt with a natural phenomenon; even though the flow was not regular, it was still a natural river. And the seventh day on which it either flowed or was dry, according to the version told, was not designated the Sabbath. Jews tied up this seventh day, eventually, with the Sabbath and used it as an argument for Sabbath observance in the time of Caesar Hadrian, after the suppression of the Bar Kochba revolt, when the observance of the Sabbath was strongly forbidden.[38] In later versions the stream of water was changed to a stream of rocks and gravel.

During that time, when the Jewish imagination had built up the legend of the Sabbath river, there also arose a legend regarding a fortunate Jewish people that was not scattered over the world in the midst of unfriendly peoples, that did not suffer, and was not persecuted and insulted. It inhabited a distant, unknown land, where it had a strong kingdom and led a peaceful and secure existence. This Jewish folk was the ten lost tribes, the tribes that had lost their great kingdom, the kingdom of Israel, one hundred and thirty-six years before the destruction of the first Temple, before the downfall of the smaller kingdom of Judah. Other Jews, in their imagination, saw in this fortunate Jewish folk not the ten tribes, but the descendants of Moses. For God had said to Moses: "And I will make of thee a great nation." [39] These

Jews believed that God had literally accomplished this and made a great nation of Moses' children.

The two legends were merged and became one. Where would the lost tribes or the descendants of Moses, as the case might be, have their kingdom? Naturally, beyond the *Sambatyon*. No fierce enemy could approach them there. The miraculous Sabbath river poured forth a stream of rocks and gravel with such speed and power, that nothing could cross it or withstand it. On the one day on which the stream rests, on the Sabbath, a heavy fog descends over it and none can approach it.

This Jewish story of the miraculous *Sambatyon* became a theme for many legends in life and literature from oldest times down to the present day, not only among Jews, but also among Christians and Mohammedans.[40]

v. ✠esach – ITS ORIGINS

Introduction...Pesach, usually called Passover, is first in the calendar of Jewish festivals. It is the greatest of Jewish festivals. For over two thousand years it has been more than *a* holiday; it has been *the* holiday, the festival of redemption.

In addition, Pesach is the oldest of Jewish festivals. Jews observed it in the most ancient of times, in the days when they were still nomadic shepherds in the wilderness.

Pesach is the Jewish spring festival. It begins on the eve of the fourteenth day of the Jewish month Nisan. Originally it was a seven-day festival and is so observed today in Palestine and among Reform Jews, with only the first and seventh days as days of rest. Due, however, to the unsettled state of the Jewish calendar in olden times the festival was extended to last eight days amongst Jews not resident in Palestine. The full holiday, with cessation of work, is observed only the first two and the last two days of the festival. The four intervening days are semi-holidays.

A Festival of the Shepherds...Pesach was not always the holiday that we know today. Generation after generation came and went, epoch upon epoch of Jewish life passed by, and each contributed its strivings and ideals, its hopes and emotions to the festival before it became the great holiday of deliverance and freedom.

Festivals change and develop in accordance with various modes of life and periods of history. Holidays usually start as nature festivals and are observed in that season of the year when nature itself changes, and the ceremonies attending the holiday grow out of these manifestations of nature. Later, however, when men reach a higher cultural level, they give a deeper spiritual meaning to the festival and the old ceremonies assume a new symbolic significance.

It is, therefore, true that a holiday is always older than the interpretation which is given to it. First comes the custom, the ceremony, the observance; no interpretation for them is needed or sought. The ceremony explains itself. Later, after a long time passes, need is found for an interpretation of the festival and its rites. So, Pesach was originally a nature festival, an observance of the coming of spring. Later, as time went on, it became a historic and national holiday, the festival of the deliverance from Egypt, and it thus assumed a newer and higher meaning.

Pesach as a spring festival is very old. Jews observed a spring festival long before the deliverance from Egypt.[41] The beginnings of Pesach carry us back to those pre-historic days when Jews were still tribes of shepherds wandering in the desert. Wherever they found pasturage for their herds, they pitched their tents and grazed their flocks. In the month when the kids and lambs were born, the month that ushered in spring, they observed a festival at full moon (the fourteenth to the fifteenth day of the month). Every member of the family took part in the observance of this festival, which was featured by the sacrifice of a sheep or goat from the flock. The sacrifice occurred just before nightfall, after which the animal was roasted whole and all members of the family made a hasty meal in the middle of the night. It was forbidden to break any of the bones of the sacrificial animal or to leave uneaten any part of it by the time daybreak came. One of the chief ceremonies attendant upon the festival was the daubing of the tent-posts with the blood of the slain animal. It was clear to these primitive shepherds why certain ceremonies were commanded and other practices forbidden. They knew that observance was an antidote to plagues, misfortunes, and illnesses, and that it was an assurance of good luck and safety for the coming year. Similar beliefs, customs, and fetishes were prevalent amongst other peoples, too.[42]

These primitive nomads knew why the sacrifice that was so hastily eaten and the festival with which it was connected were called *Pesach*. It was not till a long time later that the meaning of the word was lost and a new interpretation given to it.[43] To this day we cannot be certain what the word meant originally; neither can we be certain of the details of the ceremonies and rites that accompanied the observance. We do know, however, that the celebration was held at night and that morning brought with it the end of the festival.[44] We also know that the ceremony was not tied up with any sanctuary or priesthood; it was a family festival, conducted by the head of the family.

A time came when the Jews ceased to be nomads and settled in Palestine. But even then they did not forego observing the spring festival of the shepherds which they had brought with them from the desert. It was observed, naturally, in the rural districts only, in those sections where there were still shepherds who made a living from their flocks. There were more shepherds in Judah, in the south, than in Israel, where the land was more fertile and the inhabitants gained their main livelihood from tilling the soil.

An Agricultural Festival...The Jewish peasants of Palestine, those who lived by tilling the soil, had another form of spring festival, one related to the cutting of the grain, which they called "The Festival of Matsos" (Unleavened Bread). The grain harvest began in the spring with the cutting of the barley and ended with the reaping of the wheat, a season that lasted about seven weeks.

Before the start of the barley harvest, the Jews would get rid of all the *sour dough* (fermented dough used instead of yeast to leaven bread) and the old bread they possessed; everything, in fact, connected with *chomets*, the leaven of the last year's crop. We cannot know for certain, by now, what was the origin of the removing of all sour dough and the eating of unleavened bread. It was probably regarded as a safeguard against an unproductive year.[45] In later years the Jews created a new interpretation for this old custom, just as they evolved a new meaning for the Pesach eve ceremonies.

The real importance of the holiday, however, centered in the ceremony of the *omer*, the first sheaf of newly cut barley that was offered to the priest on the first day of the harvest as a sacrifice, as a gift to God. For, all people, in those days, had the belief that everything that man used belonged to the gods and they must, therefore, offer the best of everything, the very first, to these gods as a gift.

There was more than just this one seasonal, agricultural festival observed by the Jews in Palestine. In addition to the "Festival of Unleavened Bread," they also observed the "Feast of Harvest" (Shovuos) and the "Feast of Ingathering" (Sukkos).[46] These three occasions were the greatest and most festive holidays of the year and were always observed in a sanctuary. In those days Jerusalem was not yet the only holy spot in Palestine; temples were situated in many parts of the country. In addition, there were holy sites known as "high places" in many small towns and villages. These were hills considered holy by the Canaanites. When the Jews settled in the land, they also used these hills as places of sacrifice and worship. The Canaanites served their gods, the *baalim*, in these "high places"; the Jews used the same spots to serve their God. The "high places" were open to the sky and on each one was a stone slab which was used as an altar for sacrifices; each one also contained a sacred stone (*matsevoh*) and a sacred tree (*asheroh*), objects which were taken over by the Jews. The services on these "high places" were performed by a priest, who was not only the most learned member of the community and its spiritual leader, but who also acted as the judge in settling all disputes of the region.

The village generally stood on the slope of the hill, within easy reach of the "high place" on top of the hill. At the coming of a festival, the entire village would make its way to the "high place" and there offer its sacrifices; they would then hold a huge feast of the meat of the sacrificial animals, singing holy songs and dancing religious dances. All were joyous and merry. In fact, holy services in the sanctuaries were called "eating before God" and "being merry before God."[47]

Pesach and Shovuos were the seasons for the grain harvest, the time of the year when there was much work to do in the fields, and it was difficult for the Jewish peasant to leave his home and travel to a great sanctuary in a large center. He could do this only at Sukkos, the autumn festival, when he had finished his work and the produce of his field and orchard was stored away; therefore he observed the Feast of Unleavened Bread generally at his local "high place." It is not hard for us to picture the simple, joyous scene on that occasion; we can see festive Jewish peasants from hilly Ephraim or from the Valley of Jezreel, winding up the hill in a joyful procession, bearing the *omer*, the first sheaf of barley, to the "high place." The priest takes the sheaf and, chanting prayers and blessings, waves it over the altar, symbolically giving it to God.[48]

We must thus bear in mind that Pesach and the Feast of Unleavened Bread were originally two distinct festivals, observed at the same time. Pesach was the older holiday, the one the Jews brought with them from the desert; the Feast of Unleavened Bread was newer, instituted only after the Jews had settled in Palestine and become farmers. Both were spring festivals, but the Feast of Unleavened Bread was observed by the entire community gathered in a holy place, while Pesach was celebrated in the home as a family festival.[49]

A Day of Deliverance...Holidays are closely bound up with the life of a people and with their spiritual culture. In the course of time when the life of the people changes, then the festivals of that people also change and assume a new character. The ceremonies and rites, to a great extent, remain but they take on new meaning. They are interpreted differently, given symbolic values, and in this way become something almost entirely new.

This has happened with all festivals, ceremonies, and customs, as it happened to Pesach. Jewish culture and Jewish life evolved and changed during the early centuries that the Jews spent in Palestine. Newer and higher conceptions and ideals arose and, in time, the Jews forgot the meaning and spirit of the old customs and ceremonies of Pesach and the Feast of Unleavened Bread. Above all, the idea of observing nature and the harvest festivals ceased to appeal to the Jews. They had a much greater desire to observe, in the spring of the year, a holiday with a historic background, a festival that would represent symbolically the social and spiritual strivings and ideals of the day. In answer to this desire they began to emphasize Pesach as the festival of the deliverance from Egypt.

This transition came very easily. The memory of the exodus from Egypt burned brightly in the minds of the Jews, and with it the memory that it was in the first spring month of the year that they had left the land of the Pharaohs. The re-living of that great event in the dawn of Jewish history became the chief motive for the celebration of the spring festival. Spring, the time of liberation for nature, and the idea of human freedom seemed to fit very well together; in this way Pesach became the festival of the freedom of the Jewish people, its deliverance from slavery, and its awakening to a new life.

All the customs and ceremonies which were bound up with Pesach and the Feast of Unleavened Bread were then re-interpreted and became associated with the deliverance from Egypt. *Pesach*, for instance, was declared to mean "passing by or over"; and the holiday was called by that name because God passed over the Jewish homes when he slew the first-born of Egypt. The quickly baked *matsos*, according to the new interpretation, were eaten because the Jews were in such a hurry to get out of Egypt that they had no time to leaven their bread and bake it properly. The bitter herbs eaten on Pesach eve were declared to be reminders of the bitterness of the Jewish lot in Egypt. Even the fruit salad of the Pesach night, the *charoses*, was in later times bound up with the deliverance; it was considered symbolic of the mortar mixed by the Jews when they were slaves in Egypt.

These new interpretations were intended for a new generation, to whom the old ceremonies lacked meaning. And one of the foremost problems in those days of change was that of enlightening the new generation, making clear to the young son the symbolic meanings which the old ceremonies had assumed, for the children were entirely strangers to the customs handed down from the old days. "And it shall be when thy son asketh thee in time to come, saying, 'What is this?' that thou shalt say unto him: 'By strength of hand the Lord brought us out from Egypt, from the house of bondage.' " [50]

It was in this way that Pesach and the Feast of Unleavened Bread were joined together, and two distinct spring festivals became one historical holiday, a symbol of the striving of the people toward national freedom. But, since the festival was still bound up with the family, or, at most, the village community, it could not yet become a great national holiday. It was only later, when Pesach was observed by all Jews in one place, in one great sanctuary, that it gained national importance.

This happened in the last few decades before the destruction of the first Temple, in the time of Josiah, King of Judah. Israel, the great Jewish kingdom of the north, was no more. All that remained was Judah, the smaller kingdom of the south. In the reign of Josiah there was a strong progressive party, seeking to reconstruct Jewish national life and establish it on a new basis of justice and right. Sweeping reforms were instituted. One of the most outstanding was the elimination of all the "high places" because Jerusalem was declared the one sanctuary for all the Jews. Sacrifices were forbidden anywhere else and only Jerusalem was to be the goal of the pilgrimages made at holiday time. The festivals, therefore, lost their local character and became national observances that united all Jews in the one holy place, the Temple in Jerusalem.

Through this reform, the Pesach ceremonial took on almost a new character. Since it was forbidden to make the Paschal sacrifice anywhere but in the Temple at Jerusalem, it was impossible to smear the blood of the sacrificial lamb upon the doorposts of the houses. In general, the observance lost its ancient weird character. The Book of Kings tells us truly that such a Pesach as was observed in the eighteenth year of the reign of Josiah, the year in which the reform was instituted, had not been celebrated since the Jews settled in Palestine.[51]

We cannot be certain how long a time passed before the Jews accepted these reforms in practice and ceased to offer the Pesach sacrifice in their own homes. Nor can we be certain how long it took for Pesach and the Feast of Unleavened Bread to become as one festival. But we do know that the importance of the festival grew and that it became, in time, the greatest Jewish national holiday. Sukkos remained the most festive and most joyous of the holidays, but Pesach attained the greatest national importance.

The Greatest Jewish Holiday... The highest point in the evolution of Pesach came in the last century of the second Temple, when the Jews suffered from the heavy oppression of the Romans. It was during this period that the Messianic hope flamed up, and in the minds of the Jews the deliverance of the future became bound up with the first redemption in Jewish history: the deliverance from Egypt. Jews had long believed that in the deliverance to come, God would show the same sort of miracles that He had performed in redeeming the Jews from Egypt.[52] This belief gained added strength in this period of Roman occupation and oppression. Jews began to believe that the Messiah would be a second Moses and would free the Jews the self-same eve, the eve of Pesach.[53] So Pesach became the festival of the second as well as the first redemption; in every part of the world where Jews lived, especially in Palestine, Jewish hearts beat faster on the eve of Pesach, beat with the hope that this night the Jews would be freed from the bondage of Rome, just as their ancestors were released from Egyptian slavery.

The ritual of the Pesach eve had, by that time, developed to rich proportions and was entirely different from the spring festival of the Jewish shepherds of old. The great Greco-Roman civilization ruled almost the entire known world and influenced the Jews to observe their holiday in a richer, more luxurious fashion. They adopted the wine and the soft sofas and the other luxuries that in those days were part of a feast. Jews still partook of the meat of the sacrificial lamb, but not in haste, as the Samaritan sect does to this very day; they ate leisurely and reclined on the softest of cushions.

The Pesach ritual at that time was a compromise between the Pesach of the very old days that was observed in the home, and the Pesach that followed it, the holiday that was observed only in the Temple. Observance, therefore, was divided into two main parts, and was celebrated in two different places, the Temple and the home. In the afternoon of the day before Pesach, the sacrificial animal was slaughtered with elaborate ceremonies in the Temple; it was then taken home, roasted, and eaten in groups, with ceremonies that are almost identical with the Seder observed by Jews today. Outside of Jerusalem the offering of sacrifices was not allowed and Pesach eve was observed in the home, in the family circle, and in the synagogue. In some places, however, it was customary to eat roast lamb, though no sacrifice was offered.

vi. Pesach = IN TEMPLE DAYS

Pilgrims in Jerusalem...At no time in its long and varied history was Jerusalem as beautiful and as thickly populated as in the years preceding the destruction of the second Temple. In addition to the permanent dwellers, the three great festivals would bring countless pilgrims from near and from far, from every country to which Jews had wandered.

It is estimated that Jerusalem, at that time, had a permanent population of close to one hundred thousand and that this was more than doubled by the pilgrims who came for the holidays, especially at Pesach.[54] No matter in what corner of the world Jews lived, Jerusalem was a holy place to them, and the greatest wish of each and every Jew was to enter the inner court of the Temple at least once in his lifetime and to pray to God, to the accompaniment of the holy music of the Levites. At no other time of the year did so many pilgrims descend upon Jerusalem as at the season of Pesach, when nature newly carpeted the brown earth with green, and the fields of Judah seemed a tapestry of flowers gleaming and glistening in the sun.

Jerusalem was never so crowded as during the Pesach holiday. Every inn was filled to overflowing, and whoever had a bit of room in his house made it available to the visiting pilgrims, never accepting any payment. It was customary, however, for the pilgrims to offer their hosts the skins of the animals they had sacrificed in the Temple.[55] Many of the pilgrims set up tents in the squares and open places of the town, living there during their entire pilgrimage. Jerusalem was so crowded at this period that the very fact that everybody was able to find accommodations somehow, somewhere, was declared to be one of the miracles of God.[56]

These thousands of pilgrims did not form a single, homogeneous group; they were as varied as the world and as full of color. There were Jews and Jewish converts from every country of the known world, from Syria and Asia Minor, from Babylonia and Medea, from Cyprus and Greece, and from Egypt and Rome. They did not speak the same language; those from Mesopotamia and thereabouts spoke various dialects of Aramaic; most of the Jews who came from the west spoke Greek. There was, too, a great difference in the outward appearance of these pilgrims. Side by side one would see poor Jewish peasants who had traveled from various districts of Palestine on donkeys, and rich Jewish merchants or bankers that had arrived from distant lands by boat.

All these pilgrims did not come to Jerusalem solely because of pious motives. Many merchants arrived laden with wares, ready to do business, for a holy city that attracted so many pilgrims offered a fine opportunity for sale and barter. Jerusalem was a ready market, even during ordinary times. There was always trade in cattle and other live stock, which were needed for the sacrifices, and in raw materials and finished products of all kinds.

Jerusalem was an especially fine sheep and cattle market before Pesach, for so many animals were needed for the Pesach sacrifices. There was also a large sale of the spices needed for Pesach eve. Most of the cattle came from the immediate neighborhood, but the spices were, in the main, imported from Mesopotamia. Long camel trains from Mesopotamia, laden with spices and herbs, were a common sight at this time of the year.[57]

Preparations for Pesach...Jerusalem is crowded with people and tumultous with their noise. A steady succession of pilgrims pours into the town from every side and through every gate. Further confusion is caused by the near-by peasants, driving their cattle and sheep to market. The Roman Procurator has already arrived from Caesaria, with additional soldiers to guard against any possible uprising during that period. He is quartered in Herod's Palace, which is more than a dwelling, being built like a fortress, encircled by a high wall, studded with soaring towers.

It is early morning. The morning services have been completed in the Temple and the worshipers have left the synagogues. The market place, a broad street that stretches its way through the entire town, is now filled with people. Both sides of the thoroughfare are lined with booths, stands, and tables. Everything is on sale here, whatever the eye can see or the heart long for. Look! There are cakes made from wheat grown on Mount Ephraim! And there, fish from the depths of Lake Kinnereth! A third sells wine and a fourth calls to the passers-by to purchase spices and condiments for the Pesach feast.[58] Here is a booth offering for sale jewelry and adornments which are the fashion in Alexandria and Rome, and there is a street merchant offering a syrup pressed from grapes. One dealer offers golden adornments for the head, a specialty of the goldsmiths of Jerusalem, and he calls, "Buy golden *Jerusalems* as a souvenir of the holy city." [59]

Not an inch of space is wasted. In front of the houses and between the booths and stands sit tradesmen, using the street as their workshop. A tailor sits cross-legged and sews fringes on a coat; opposite him sits a shoemaker repairing the torn sandals of a pilgrim; a blacksmith stands nearby, hammering away on the handle of a sword.

Each of the little side streets that lead off the market street has its particular trade. There is the street of the butchers and the street of the wool-combers; each little street has its specialty. But the big street, the really interesting street, is the great market place. Every moment it becomes more crowded and noisy, and the scene becomes more varied and exciting. The buyers, the sellers, and the idlers crush and jostle each other for space. Here comes a group of pilgrims from Alexandria, dressed in Grecian garments and speaking Greek to each other. In contrast, a group of pilgrims from Galilee, very pious Jewish peasants from the north of Palestine, follow them. Their voices are heard high above the tumult of the market place, and by the Galilean dialect of their Aramaic speech it is recognized where they are from.

Perhaps the greatest noise and the greatest crowds are in the cattle market near the Mount of the Temple. Sheep and goats are sold there by the thousands. Poor Jews bargain over the prices of the animals; the richer pilgrims do not deign to bargain and so pay higher prices for their sacrifical animals.

It is, however, not enough just to buy a sheep or goat in order to be ready for Pesach eve. The sacrificial animal is not eaten alone, but in groups that are made up in advance, for one man cannot eat an entire animal and it is forbidden to leave any part of the animal for the next day. So Jews rush about making arrangements to form a group or to become part of one. A group cannot consist of less than ten people, for it takes at least that many to eat an entire sheep at one sitting. But some Jews form huge groups, numbering so many that each member can get no more than a mere taste of the sacrificial animal, a piece no larger than an olive, entirely too small to satisfy one's hunger. It is customary, then, for such a group to slay another animal, an additional festive offering, called *chagigoh*. This animal is always useful. Unlike the official sacrifice, which had to be eaten before dawn, the *chagigoh* may be held for a second day.

The Morning Before...Thousands of priests and Levites are gathered in the Temple. There are twenty-four divisions of them on duty throughout the land and, generally, there is only one division present in Jerusalem to take care of the Temple service. However, during the three great festivals, when there are so many people in town and so many animals to be sacrificed, all divisions come to Jerusalem.

The *chomets*, the bread and sour dough, is cleaned out of the houses. The night before, by the light of oil lamps, every corner is searched and every bit of *chomets* removed. All the people in Jerusalem wait for the official signal to burn the *chomets*. This signal is given by the priests in the Temple who use two disqualified loaves of the thanks offering.[60] These loaves are placed on top of the outside colonnade of the Temple. As long as these two loaves are in view, *chomets* may still be eaten. When one loaf is removed, the people cease eating *chomets*. When the second loaf is removed, then the people begin to burn their *chomets*.

But this system of signals is not sufficient for all of Jerusalem and another is arranged. Two kine are set to plowing the earth on top of the Mount of Olives and as long as both are attached to the plow, *chomets* may still be eaten. The unhitching of one is a signal to cease eating *chomets* and the removal of the second is a sign to burn *chomets*.

Midday...The spirit of the holiday has permeated every nook and cranny of Jerusalem. By now all have ceased working; even the tailors, the shoemakers, the haircutters, and washers have finished the last piece of work for the pilgrims.

Thousands of Jews march through the town, this one with a sheep, that one with a goat, riding high on his shoulder. All direct their steps to the Temple, to be among the first to offer their Pesach sacrifice. The regular afternoon sacrifice at the Temple is offered an hour earlier than usual and at about three o'clock the people begin the slaughtering of the Pesach sacrifice.

The ritual is repeated three times. When the court of the Temple is filled with the first comers, the gates are shut. The Levites blow the ceremonial *t'kioh*, *t'ruoh*, *t'kioh* (a threefold blast) on their trumpets and the sacrifice begins. The owner himself slays the animal. The priests stand in rows, bearing aloft gold and silver trays, each metal borne by a different row of priests. They perform their share of the ritual and the Levites stand on a platform and sing *Hallel*, Psalms of praise for holidays, to the accompaniment of musical instruments. The elaborateness of the ritual and the singing and playing of the Levites add dignity and beauty to the scene, and the Jews gathered in the court are filled with devotion and piety.

The first section files out of the court and the second section files in. The same ritual is performed again. It is repeated once more for the third and final section. Members of the third section are called "Lazybones." [61]

The entire ceremony and ritual is carried on in a comparatively quiet and orderly manner. Once, in the time of the famous Hillel, there was such a surge and crowding at the sacrifice of the Pesach that an old man was crushed to death, but that never happened again. So orderly is the crowd that all three sections have finished in less than two hours, and the priests are left alone to clean up the court.

Towards Evening...Thousands of Jews rush from the Mount of the Temple through the streets of Jerusalem, each bearing on his shoulder the sacrificial animal wrapped in its own skin.[62] All are busy and expectant, preparing themselves for the great night of the year, the night of redemption.

Darkness descends on the holy city. Everywhere sheep and goats, spitted on fragrant pomegranate wood, are roasting in the clay stoves which stand in the courtyards of the homes. These stoves are called Pesach-ovens and are movable; should there be heavy rain they are carried into the house.[63] The groups are now gathering. Relatives and friends assemble from near and from far. Every large room is a meeting-place for a group. Nobody is omitted. The poor are invited to the homes of the rich and a spirit of brotherliness, of national unity, binds all together at the feast. All are partners: masters and slaves, men and women, the aged and youthful. All are dressed in white, festive clothes, much adorned and bedecked. The women, especially, wear jewelry in honor of the occasion. The Babylonian women are easily differentiated from the native women, since they wear brilliantly colored garments; the Palestinian women, however, wear only clothes made of bleached linen.

The celebration begins. All is quiet in the streets. The full moon moves over the flat roofs of Jerusalem and bedecks everything in silver. In the homes people lounge on sofas placed around the room. The left hand rests on soft cushions, the right hand takes food and drink from small, individual tables set before each feaster. One sits at the head of the room and leads in the ceremonial observance. First a glass of wine mixed with water is taken. Then the right hand is washed and all partake of lettuce dipped in a tart liquid. Then the sacrificial animal is served and is eaten with matsoh and bitter herbs, dipped in *charoses*, a mixture of ground nuts and fruits in wine. Then begins the second part of the ceremonial of the evening; the reciting of the story of the festival, and the discussion of the ceremonies that go with it. A second glass of diluted wine is drunk and the son of the household asks why this night is different from all other nights. His father answers him with excerpts from the Bible telling about the deliverance from Egypt and then explains the meaning of the sacrificial lamb, the matsoh, and the bitter herbs. All listen to him with great attention and devotion. And when he starts to sing *Hallel*, they all join in loudly. They conclude with the benediction for redemption and are filled with the hope of immediate deliverance from their enemies and the removal of the foreign governor and his foreign soldiers from the holy city.

It is now quite late in the night. The third and fourth glasses of wine have been finished and the feast, with its attendant ceremonies, is over. The older members of the group, however, still recline on their sofas and relate and interpret the story of the Exodus. Here and there a member of the group nods, or falls fast asleep. Some of the younger element would like to celebrate further, but their elders restrain them. After eating the sacrificial animal, no entertainment is allowed, such as is common after ordinary feasts. The feasters must satisfy themselves with going from one group to another, greeting and hailing friends. Once more the streets of Jerusalem are filled with promenading Jews, natives and pilgrims side by side. Many of them are on their way to the Mount of the Temple, for the Levites now open the gates of the Holy House [64] and Jews spend the rest of the night there, praying and singing hymns of praise to God.

vii. Pesach = UNUSUAL OBSERVANCES

Change of Emphasis...After the destruction of the second Temple, the custom of making the Pesach sacrifice was, of course, discarded. But Pesach did not lose its status as a great national holiday. The celebration, however, was exclusively in the home. In some places Jews still partook of roasted meat on that night, exactly as they had done before the destruction of the Temple, in certain places outside of Jerusalem. But in general, only a reminder, a symbol of the Pesach sacrifice, remained. It was customary in those days for two main courses to be served at festive banquets of the rich, and these two courses were served at the Pesach feast of every Jew. But after the destruction of the second Temple, these two courses were interpreted as reminders of the Pesach sacrifice and the *chagigoh*, the second or supplementary sacrifice. These two courses usually consisted of a piece of roasted meat on the bone, and a roasted egg.

The holiday still remained for Jews the festival of redemption. The freeing of Jerusalem from foreign rule became the main item in the Messianic hope after the destruction of the city by the Romans, and Rabbi Akiba therefore added a prayer to the benediction for redemption in which was expressed the hope of the Jew to live long enough to observe Pesach in a new, free Jerusalem.[65]

Far from declining through the destruction of the Temple, Pesach now attained still greater importance as the anniversary of the deliverance from the first exile and as the model for delivery from the last exile. The ceremonial of Pesach eve was made even richer and fuller. Jews would sit till late in the night, repeating and discussing the story of the Exodus; often the coming of dawn found them still gathered discussing the miracles of the occasion. The plagues visited upon the Egyptians grew and grew from the original ten to hundreds. The Jews spoke of Egypt but they meant Rome. They spoke of the discomfiture of Pharaoh and the Egyptians, hoping at the same time for the identical plagues to be visited upon the Roman emperor, his governors, and his soldiers, who had laid waste the holy city, destroyed the Temple, and spilled oceans of Jewish blood.

In the main, the basic rite of the Pesach eve ceremonial stayed the same as it had been in the days of the second Temple. But the ritual for the evening became more set and formalized. In the course of time various items of the ceremony were removed and others added. We shall discuss this further when we speak of the customs and ceremonials of Pesach. It is enough to say here that the Jews of the Middle Ages celebrated the holiday almost as it is observed by the Jews of today.

The Festival of Fear... The ceremonial remained the same, but the attitude during the Pesach festival changed in the latter part of the Middle Ages. A new and evil force came from the outside and left its imprint upon the old spring festival and observances, making of it a time of fear for all Jews, a time of horrible visitations, a time of terror and panic in the Jewish sections. At that time the Church had the peoples of Europe completely under its control. Fanatical priests and dark forces of reaction continually fanned hatred against the Jews and spread the wildest charges against them. The most horrible of these was the blood libel.

The blood libel began to spread in the thirteenth century, and countless numbers of Jews perished as a result. Due to the ignorance and superstitious beliefs of the masses of those days, the blood libel became bound up with Pesach, especially with the Pesach eve ceremonial. It was charged that Jews killed Christian children to get blood for the baking of matsos.

Pesach was, therefore, a time of great fear for the Jews of the Dark Ages. It was so easy to spread a rumor that Jews had murdered a Christian child; there were many cases where some individual enemy of the Jews would plant the body of a dead Christian child in a Jewish home and give the signal for a raid on the Jewish quarter on Pesach eve. Such an event is described in Heine's historical romance, *The Rabbi of Bacharach*.

This superstition that Jews use Christian blood at Pesach is not entirely a thing of the past. We, of this generation, have memories of such charges in various European countries, and to this day there are Jewish enemies who spread this accusation of the Middle Ages in the very heart of Europe.

Even in America, only a few years ago, in Massena, New York, the rabbi of the town was questioned on the blood ritual libel when a little girl happened to disappear. The girl was found unharmed the next day, and the mayor, the instigator of the questioning, made a public apology.

*The Marranos Observe It...*At the end of the European Middle Ages there was evolved a notable method of observing Pesach among the Marranos, the secret Jews of Spain and Portugal. These Marranos were entirely separated from Jews and from Jewish life. They had no Jewish books, and the only book on which they could draw for rules of Jewish life was the Latin Bible of the Catholic Church. Basing their ideas about Jews and Judaism on this one book, their conception of Jewish life became an entirely false one. They tried to live not as the Jews of their day did, but as the Jews of the time of the Kings and the Prophets. They knew nothing of the development of Pesach through the ages; they practiced the Pesach described in the Bible.

The question arises: How did these Marranos, who had no Jewish calendars and no contacts with other Jews, know when to observe the various Jewish festivals? Actually, they did not; they reckoned the Jewish holidays by the calendar in general use, applying the Jewish days to the secular month. Thus they observed Yom Kippur on the tenth day after the New Moon of September and Pesach at the full moon of March. When the spies of the Inquisition discovered these observances, the Marranos of Spain advanced the dates of the festivals, observing Yom Kippur on the eleventh day following the New Moon of September and celebrating the Seder (the ceremony of Pesach night) on a Pesach eve that came sixteen days after the appearance of the New Moon of March, instead of fourteen days.

On this sixteenth day they would bake their matsos; on the two preceding days which, according to their curious Jewish-secular calendar, were really Pesach, they ate neither bread nor matsos. There was no ceremony of the burning of the *chomets*. Instead they burned a piece of the dough prepared for the baking of the matsos. In the evening they observed a secret Seder in their homes, eating an entire roast sheep, all the participants wearing their traveling shoes and bearing staves in their hands, exactly as described in the Bible. There were even Marranos, those of Mexico, who followed the old biblical injunction to smear the blood of the sheep on their doorposts.

One noteworthy custom grew up among these Marranos: the custom of beating the waters of a stream with willow branches, which they interpreted as a reminder of the separating of the waters of the Red Sea. It is interesting to note that to this very day the Jews of Morocco make their way to a stream on the last day of Pesach and there recite prayers and blessings. It is possible that this was an old Spanish Jewish custom and that the Marranos took it over and added to it the ceremony of the willow branches which rightly belongs to Sukkos. That holiday they could not observe at all, since one of the requirements of the festival is to sit in booths in the open.

The Pesach of the Marranos is not entirely a thing of the past. There are, to this very day, Marranos in Portugal who still observe Pesach in the manner just described.

The Samaritans and Falashas... The Marranos observed ancient forms of the Pesach ceremonial because they were forcibly separated from the Jewish life of their time and were forced to seek instructions from the books of the Bible. External conditions forced the Marranos to return to a primitive form of observance. There are, however, in our own day, groups of Jews that never came in contact with the masses of the Jewish folk; they never had anything to do with those Jews who are the bearers of Jewish history and Jewish life. They, therefore, observe Pesach exactly as it was observed two to three thousand years ago. Such Jews are the Samaritans of the city of Nablus in Palestine, and the Falashas of Abyssinia.

Modern historical research has proved that the Samaritans are not descendants of the heathen colonists settled in the northern kingdom of Israel by the conquerors of Samaria, as was once assumed. Nor are they to be identified with Nehemiah's opponents of the Persian period. Actually, the Samaritans of today are a small and poor remnant of an old and great Jewish sect that appeared in Palestine about the beginning of the Greek period. They form the oldest Jewish sect in existence. They were always strongly religious Jews who believed in one God and strictly observed the Law of Moses. The only religious books that they possess, however, are the Pentateuch and Joshua. They never recognized the books of the Bible beyond Joshua as holy. Moreover, they denied the sanctity of Jerusalem. They believed that Shechem, the present Nablus, was the holy city and that the holy mountain was not Zion, but Mount Gerizim. They built a temple on top of that mountain, which was later destroyed by the Hasmonean king, John Hyrcanus. The Samaritans and the Jews became blood-enemies who hated and despised each other, just as in later years the Karaites and the Rabbinic Jews hated each other.

In the days of the second Temple almost the entire central part of Palestine, between Judah and Galilee, was thickly populated with this Jewish sect of Shechem; there were also many followers of the sect in southern Syria and in other eastern lands. Today, however, there are barely two hundred left; [66] they speak Arabic and inhabit a special quarter in Nablus. They have a synagogue there and a High Priest, who is their teacher and spiritual leader.

These two hundred Samaritans observe Pesach to this day on Mount Gerizim, in a manner that other Jews ceased practising thousands of years ago. The custom of offering sacrifices has died out with the Samaritans, except on the fourteenth day of Nisan, when they offer the ceremonial Pesach sacrifice.

Exactly as do other Jews, they clean the *chomets* out of their homes the night before Pesach eve, according to their calendar which closely resembles the Jewish. The next day they make the pilgrimage to Mount Gerizim and there set up their tents, one for each family, outfitting them with furniture and utensils. There, on the slope of the hill on whose top once stood their temple, they observe Pesach, living there for the entire festival.

A study of their ceremonies and observances during the festival is of special interest to us, because they practically duplicate the rites of the Jews of the very old days. What certain knowledge we have of Pesach and its rites dates only from the last century of the second Temple; of what happened before there are no exact records. We can learn much about the holiday, however, from the observances of the Samaritans of today; they are for us a living record and monument of the old life lived by the children of Israel on the Mount of Ephraim.

Much of the Pesach that was observed in the days of the second Temple is still unknown to the present Samaritans. They know nothing of the use of wine, of the *charoses*, of eating the sacrificial animal comfortably from a table, of reclining at one's ease, and of many other observances, because these customs came into Judaism in the latter part of the second Temple days, after the Samaritans had already separated from the rest of Jewry.

The main ceremonial in the Pesach observance of the Samaritans is the sacrifice of a sheep and eating it at night, in great haste, together with matsos and bitter herbs. They begin the preparation for the feast late in the afternoon. The Mount of Gerizim becomes a center of activity. All the males of the sect are gathered there, dressed in white, festive clothing, stoking the fires in two huge pits, the one for the roasting of the sheep, the other for the burning of the offal and all the remains after the feast. A huge cauldron of hot water is also ready.

Half an hour before sunset the ceremony starts. The High Priest leads the assembled congregation in silent prayer; the worshipers fall to their knees, their faces toward the peak of the hill, the spot where their temple once stood. The High Priest raises his voice and all join him in a series of chanted prayers.

Exactly at sunset the High Priest faces westward and reads that portion of the Pentateuch which orders the slaughtering of the Pesach sacrifice.[67] About twelve or fourteen of the younger Samaritans busy themselves, meanwhile, with preparing the sacrificial animals. They form a circle about the pit of fire, holding the lambs between their legs, and as the High Priest utters the words, "And the whole assembly of the congregation of Israel shall kill it at dusk," they utter a benediction and throw the lambs, throats to the pit, where they are slaughtered by two ritual slaughterers. Six or seven sheep are slaughtered. An extra animal is available, should a physical defect be found in one of the sacrificial animals.

The slaughtering is a signal for general rejoicing. Greetings are exchanged in the oriental manner; the participants kiss one another, first on the right shoulder, then on the left.

This ends the first part of the ceremony. The second part, which takes place late at night, is the roasting of the animals. First, the bodies must be cleaned and spitted and prepared for roasting. The fire made for the offal burns and smokes as the insides of the animals are cast therein.

At about ten o'clock the High Priest issues forth from his tent and orders the roasting of the sheep. Six or seven men bear the spitted animals on their shoulders and the High Priest leads them in prayer; then all the sacrifices are cast into the pit together. The bodies are covered first with leaves and grass and then with caked mud. For three hours the roasting process goes on, the Samaritans meanwhile passing the time in prayer or in talk. Some go to sleep; but most of them rest on their cots, for rest is needed so that the participants will feel fresh and ready for the third part of the ceremony, the eating of the sacrificed animals.

At one in the morning all are awake and ready. Hands and feet are washed and white garments donned. With girded loins and with staves in their hands, they gather in one assemblage. The roasted animals are in baskets and placed upon the earth. Matsos and bitter herbs, that were gathered on the Mount, are placed on the sheep and later portioned out by the High Priest. When all is ready, the Samaritans form groups about the sacrificed animals and, after uttering the prescribed blessing, fall upon the roast meat, pulling it hastily to pieces with their hands. Portions are brought to the women and children in the tents. Everybody eats rapidly and in twenty minutes all that is left is a mound of bones, which are thrown into the offal pit together with the baskets and utensils that were used and with any matsos that happen to be left.[68] Matsoh is not prepared in advance for the entire festival. The Samaritans bake a fresh supply every morning.

The burning of the remains does not, however, end the ceremony. The Samaritans stay awake till dawn, reciting prayers.

There is still another Jewish sect that makes the ceremonial Pesach sacrifice: the black Jews, the Falashas, of Abyssinia. Who these Falashas are we do not know for certain, nor do we know what percentage of Jewish blood flows in their veins. There are some who claim that the Falashas are Jews who intermingled with the Africans. Others, however, contend that the Falashas are African natives who, a long time ago, became converted to the Jewish faith. Their Judaism is based on the laws and practices of the Bible, which they read in an Ethiopian translation, and they observe, therefore, only the old biblical holidays and festivals, according to the laws laid down in the Pentateuch. They gather in their synagogue on the fourteenth day of Nisan, before sundown, and in the name of the entire community, an animal is sacrificed and eaten according to the laws of the Bible, to the accompaniment of chanted prayers. They also clean their homes of *chomets* and prepare special dishes and utensils for Pesach.[69]

Dramatic Presentations...The Jews of the Caucasus region observe Pesach night sitting on the ground, dressed in their festive best, with a spear and sometimes a pistol by their sides. The women adorn themselves with jewelry of all kinds and the young girls weave flowers in their hair. The most interesting part of their Seder, however, is the dramatic presentations acted there. These are introduced when that part of the services is reached which states that in every generation each Jew must feel as if he himself was redeemed from Egypt. The *Chacham* (the rabbi), who leads the services, thereupon wraps a piece of matsoh in an old cloth, places it upon his shoulder and paces off four cubits, saying, "In this way our forefathers went out of the land of Egypt, their kneading-troughs, bound up in their clothes upon their shoulders." [70] He makes quick gestures at the same time to demonstrate the haste with which the Jews left Egypt.[71]

The young men, meanwhile, go to another room and choose one of their number to play the part of the fugitive

Jew who has just returned from Jerusalem bringing word that the redemption is near. The others clothe him in rags, place a sack on his shoulder, put a staff in his hand, and send him out. In a short time a knock is heard at the door. There stands the masqueraded youth, begging for permission to enter. The following conversation takes place:

"Who are you and what do you want?"

"I am a Jew and I wish to observe Pesach, our time of deliverance, with you."

"How are we to know that you are a Jew?"

"I wear a four-cornered garment with fringes."

"Anybody can put one on. What other proof have you?"

"I have not cut the corners of my hair. See my side-curls."

"That is not enough, either. If you are a Jew, why do you travel so late at night? Don't you know this is a festival?"

"I come from Jerusalem, the holy city; the road is long and filled with obstacles. Everywhere our enemies await us; like an iron wall they stand between you and me in an effort to keep me from celebrating the festival with you."

The masquerader breaks into tears. Those in the household still make no move to admit him. They remain silent and deep in thought; occasionally one sighs deeply. Suddenly the leader of the services gives a sign and the masquerader is admitted. He stands amongst them with a sword by his side, a belt girt about his loins, a staff in his hand, and a sack on his shoulders. His sandals are roughly soled and his clothes are covered with dust.

The household suddenly becomes joyous and the masquerader is showered with questions: "What is happening in Jerusalem, the holy city? How fare our brothers? Is the Messiah coming soon to free us from exile? Have any omens appeared pointing to our redemption?"

The traveler tells them of Jerusalem, of the sages and saints that live there, of the fields and villages that surround the city, of the mountains and holy graves; and he assures his listeners that the sages of the city have seen signs which point to the coming of the Messiah, who will shatter the iron wall that keeps them from entering the holy city. They listen with rapt attention and at the conclusion they raise their hands high and, sighing deeply, call out again and again, "Amen: So be His will."[72]

The Jews of Morocco are also fond of dramatization on Pesach eve. After the reciting of the Seder services, every male in the household slings a rod and pack over his shoulder. They rush out of the house and run up and down the street, shouting, "In this manner our forefathers went out of Egypt, their kneading-troughs bound up in their clothes upon their shoulders."

These Moroccan Jews carry away with them from the Seder a piece of the *afikomon*, the matsoh saved for the end of the meal. They carry it as a safeguard on ocean voyages and throw it into the waters in time of storm, claiming that it has powers to calm the sea.

The last day of the festival is visiting day. The congregation makes its way to a stream on that day and offers prayers. Toward evening the people go in groups from house to house to say farewell to the holiday and to wish each other a happy year. The day after Pesach they march outside the town and recite blessings over the trees.[73]

Between Purim and Pesach...It is the day after Purim, yet one already feels that Pesach approaches; Pesach is in the air. Housewives are already buying the raisins needed for the wine, hops for brewing the mead, and are pickling beets for the Pesach *borscht*. People are having long discussions with the tailor about new clothes and with the cobbler about new shoes for the children. These are the preliminaries which give way to feverish excitement around the first days of Nisan. The wine and mead are being clarified and bottled; not a woman in town has a moment of spare time. Pesach is almost upon us!

But the greatest excitement is in the matsoh bakeries, where matsos are being baked for the entire town. There are three or four of them and every one is working fast and furiously. The matsos made here are not for sale; each Jew brings his own sack of flour and pays the owner to bake matsos for him.

Two kinds of matsos are baked, classified according to the degree of their *kashrus*, of the care taken to ensure that they are ritually correct for the Pesach festival. One type is the regular matsoh which the Jews of the town bake to eat throughout the festival. No special credit goes to a man for eating matsoh throughout the festival; one is not allowed to eat bread and must, therefore, eat matsoh. There is, however, a second type of matsoh; it bears the name *matsoh shel mitsvoh* (the matsoh of the precept). The Jew is enjoined to eat a *k'zayis* (size of an olive) of this matsoh on Pesach eve at the Seder, and a special blessing is recited. This *matsoh shel mitsvoh* is specially prepared and baked with greater care than is given the ordinary matsoh. It is guarded not only during the baking; from the time the grain is cut it is continually watched so that no trace of dampness comes near it. It is therefore called *matsoh sh'muroh*, guarded matsoh, or, for short, *sh'muroh*.

Most householders get only enough of this special matsoh to serve at the two Seders, the first two nights of the festival. During the rest of Pesach ordinary matsoh will be eaten by all except the rabbi. He is so pious that nothing but *sh'muroh* is used in his home during the entire festival.

There is fearful excitement in the bakery in which the *sh'muroh* is being baked in the last few days before the holiday. Every motion is made with the thought that it is being done for the *matsoh shel mitsvoh*. The rabbi stands like a general on the battlefield, giving orders; and he sees that every participant pronounces the words, "For the sake of the *matsoh shel mitsvoh*," as he does his part of the work.

The water handler pours the water into the flour and calls out, "For the sake of the *matsoh shel mitsvoh*." The kneader rolls the dough and calls out, "For the sake of the *matsoh shel mitsvoh*." The shearer cuts off length after length of dough to the tune of "For the sake of the *matsoh shel mitsvoh*." The rollers move their rolling-pins over the dough, flattening it, calling as they roll, "For the sake of the *matsoh shel mitsvoh*." The stipplers take the flattened dough and perforate it in straight lines, calling out, "For the sake of the *matsoh shel mitsvoh*." The Hebrew words come from the tongues of the male workers with ease since they all know some Hebrew. The women, however, are not versed in Hebrew. They find it difficult to repeat such a long phrase, and it sounds garbled and unrecognizable. The men laugh and the women blush;

they say it thereafter quietly, barely moving their lips. And through it all the rabbi gives orders, correcting workers and watching carefully. It is no small responsibility, this baking of the *sh'muroh*.

There are, of course, poor Jews who have not the means to bake their own matsos and to prepare everything necessary for Pesach. But they are cared for. The rabbi, together with two of the more well-to-do members of the community, go from house to house several weeks before Pesach and gather *mo-os chittim* (money for wheat to bake matsos, as the fund is called). There is no difficulty in collecting this fund. All who do not receive from it have to give to it. That is the custom from olden times and all observe it.

For the Jewish children, rich or poor, this is the happiest time of the year; everything is so exciting and engrossing. In addition, beginning with the first day of Nisan, school is open only half a day. And even this half-day is not as tedious as usual, for one learns all about the festival. Study centers about the *Haggadah*, the book of services for Pesach eve, and the teacher explains it with long interpretations of every detail of the book; often he illustrates a passage with a parable from the Preacher of Dubno.[74] And what could be more engrossing than that?

These are days of freedom for the Jewish lad, days filled with longing and expectation. Indoors one is on the threshold of Pesach; outdoors on the threshold of spring. The nights are still cold, but the sun shines with increasing warmth during the day and the winter's mud slowly dries up. Mild winds caress the skin, harbingers of spring. They bring the joyful message of a world becoming youthful and green.

Who could stay at home on days like these? The lads wander about and their mothers are glad to have them out of the way. It is still too early to wander into the forest; there the snows and swamps of winter still linger on. But they wander to the stream to see if the water has overflowed the banks, or they play games with nuts in some dry spot, generally the courtyard of the synagogue.

The pre-Pesach excitement reaches its highest pitch the last few days before the holiday. The housewives ask the men to assist as they wash, scour, whitewash, and shine. Everything is being cleaned and aired. The *chomets* of the long, cold winter is being cleaned away to make way for Pesach.

Shabbos ha-Godol...The Saturday before the festival is known as *Shabbos ha-Godol*, the Great Sabbath. It is a Sabbath, but different from other Sabbaths, in that the holiday waits on the threshold, ready to enter and take possession. In the synagogue a portion of the *Haggadah* is recited, and just before the afternoon services, the rabbi gives his holiday sermon. He begins with a long and complicated argumentation on the laws relating to *chomets;* from this he proceeds with a dialectic discussion of Moses and Pharaoh; of the exodus from Egypt and the crossing of the Red Sea; he concludes, perhaps, with a new interpretation of a difficult passage in the Song of Songs, or with a new moral evolved from "A Kid, A Kid." The congregation listens intently, figuratively eats up his words. But, the youngsters are not interested. What need have they of Pesach sermons when they have the very taste of Pesach in their mouths? For, at noon that day they ate pudding made of matsoh-meal, prepared in honor of the day.

The Search for Leaven...It is the night before Pesach eve. Now comes the ceremony of searching for leaven. It is an ancient custom to search for the last bits of *chomets* on the thirteenth day of Nisan. But how is one to find *chomets* in a house that is washed and clean, that the housewife has scoured for weeks? Still the ceremony must be held and the head of the household must recite his benediction for the occasion. Benedictions must not be pronounced in vain, so the housewife obligingly places pieces of bread in various corners of the house, the number generally being ten.

When the master returns from the evening prayers he at once sets about the task of searching for *chomets*. He holds an old wooden spoon in one hand and the feathers of a goose in the other. Possibly, instead of the feathers, he uses a few willow twigs that he saved from last Sukkos especially for this occasion. He pronounces the benediction and begins the search for bread; obligingly the housewife walks ahead of him with a candle and directs him to the spots and corners where she planted bits of bread; the children follow after, observing every move with curiosity. Eventually the father has all the bits of bread gathered in the hollow of the wooden spoon, wrapped in cloth and bound with thread. He hides it all away to be burned on the morrow.

The Day Before Pesach . . . Everybody rises early on the day before Pesach. Prayers are held much earlier than usual and the earliest risers are the first-born males. It is an old custom that these first-born must fast on the day before Pesach. They can be exempted from this fasting only upon attendance at a religious feast, such as at the completion of the study of a tractate of the Talmud. So, immediately following the early morning services in the synagogue, a study circle in the Talmud or Mishnah is in session in order to hold such a religious feast, and thus to release the first-born from the prescribed fast. The study circle is seated at a long table and one of their number reads the last portion of a treatise of the Talmud. The finishing of a volume of Talmud is always an occasion for celebration, and all attending partake of cake and brandy. Most of those in attendance are first-born males.

All rush home after the services, to eat the last meal at which bread may be eaten. The housewives then heat their stoves, and certain metal pots are placed in the stove to make them kosher for Pesach. Some over-pious women even cauterize the needle they use for sewing up the stuffed *derma*, to make certain that no *chomets* clings to it. Some even scour and make kosher the latch of the door.

The rabbi's home is as crowded as a fair, with Jews who wish to sell him their *chomets*. After Pesach it is forbidden to use any *chomets*, belonging to a Jew, that was left over from before the holiday, even as fuel for the stove. However, it is permitted to use left-over *chomets* belonging to a non-Jew. So a legal fiction is perpetrated, whereby the rabbi acts as an agent and "sells" all this *chomets* to a non-Jew. In every town there is a certain non-Jew who has the option on the "buying" of all the *chomets* in the possession of the Jews of the town at Pesach. It is understood, of course, that some commission for the transaction must be left with the rabbi, and that the non-Jew will later repent of the transaction.

By ten in the morning there is a roaring fire in the big stove in the *Bes ha-Midrosh*, the House of Study, which is close to the synagogue, and the beadle goes through the town calling, "Burn your *chomets*." From all streets come boys and men, bearing in their hands the bound-up spoons that were hidden away the night before, to be cast into the roaring fire.

The men go to the public bath to bathe before the midday

meal. They may eat, on that day, neither bread nor matsoh. (Matsoh must be a new food when served at the Seder in the evening.) So the meal consists of potatoes, fish, and other such neutral foodstuffs.

Afternoon...Each house is clean, without a trace of *chomets*. The dishes in ordinary use have been packed away and new dishes take their place. Everything bears the spirit of the festival and of spring. The housewife and the older daughters are busy preparing the food for the evening feast. The children are sent to bring the *charoses*, the mixture of ground nuts and fruits in wine, needed for the Seder. Some pious individual prepares enough *charoses* to supply the entire town, and as the children get theirs, they leave behind some change which their mothers gave them for the purpose. The money is donated for educational and charitable enterprises.

The sexton goes from house to house, selling *matsoh sh'muroh* to each family. All is now ready for the evening.

The men come home from the evening services. *"Gut Yom-Tov!"* (a happy holiday). The greetings fly back and forth. The home is filled with light; the attitude of the entire household is festive. The table is ready, set with oriental grace. Memories of an ancient day hover over it. The master of the house seats himself on a sofa bedecked with white cushions; he sits with the freedom and airs of a king. Modest charm and a peaceful, festive joy shine in the face of the housewife. The entire family sits about and the Seder, the prescribed Pesach eve service, begins.

The Seder...Using the chant and the translations taught him by his teacher, the youngest son asks the traditional four questions as to the meaning of the evening and the customs of the occasion. His father answers him, beginning with "We were slaves to Pharaoh in Egypt," and continues the service in the *Haggadah*, the family accompanying him and chanting with him.

The first part is finished. Then comes the second part, the main feature of which is the eating of certain foodstuffs with appropriate blessings. The feast ends with the eating of the *afikomon*, the half-matsoh that the master hid beneath a cushion at the very start of the Seder, and guarded closely throughout the service, for one of the children tried to steal it away from him. Should the child succeed, then the father must offer him a gift before he returns it. When there is no child present, the master's wife will sometimes steal the *afikomon* and demand a present.

Then comes the third part of the Seder, consisting of various prayers and songs. One of the main features is the pouring of a cup of wine for Elijah, then the door is opened so that he may enter and drink. The youngsters, meantime, fall asleep. But the rest of the family continue to sit about and sing the old folk songs of the *Haggadah*, "Who Knows One," and "A Kid, A Kid."

The Pesach Days...The eight days of the festival pass by as a sweet dream. Matsoh and beet soup, dumplings and pancakes are eaten and eaten; the children play games with nuts. Sometimes tragedy enters a household. A seed of grain is found in a pot! The pot is carried to the rabbi, who ordains it as *chomets* and declares that not only man, but no living being may eat out of it. Sadly the dumplings or puddings are carted far from the house and destroyed.

And who can keep seeds of grain from blowing in the wells? Every day the sexton calls out in the synagogue that the water of this one's or that one's well cannot be used for the holiday. By the last day of the festival there is barely one well that is not defiled.

The Evening of the Last Day... The Pesach utensils and dishes are packed away and the ordinary ones are brought out again. The bakers prepare their ovens for baking bread. Before any bread can be obtained, however, all the matsoh that was left over, is eaten, though from regular dishes.

The non-Jew to whom the *chomets* was sold before Pesach is already seated in the rabbi's home. As usual, he tells the rabbi that he has repented of his contract and asks what he can do with such a large amount of wares and where he can get the money to pay for them. The rabbi kindly relieves him of his contract and the non-Jew goes on his way, happy that the amount he left, originally, as a deposit, has been returned to him twofold. The *chomets*, having been in the possession of a non-Jew during Pesach, can now be used by the Jews.

Pesach in America—the Family Festival... Pesach has had a long history and has had many evolutions in the course of its career; but it retains to this day one quality it possessed from the very beginning of time. It is a family festival. Here, in America, Pesach is the holiday which unites all members of the family and brings them together at one table, at one joyful feast. Children, grandchildren, brothers and sisters, nephews and nieces, all gather to observe the holiday in the same festive spirit. It makes no difference whether a family is observant or not, whether they recite the *Haggadah* or not; they come together, enjoy the festive spirit of Pesach eve, and feel brotherliness and warmth in the atmosphere of the united family.

The Baking of Matsos...We have already referred to the prohibition of *chomets* and to the two kinds of matsoh used at Pesach: *Matsoh shel mitsvoh*, which must be eaten at the Seder on Pesach eve; and the ordinary matsoh eaten during the remainder of the festival because the eating of *chomets* is forbidden.[75]

In olden times matsos were enormously thick. In Talmudic times there was a controversy as to whether the matsos could be thicker than the breadth of four fingers. (There was no question as to the legality of matsos up to that measurement.) Matsoh at that time was baked by three women, one to knead, one to roll, and one to bake. Such matsoh, to be edible, had to be baked fresh daily. A point of controversy, therefore, arose as to when to bake matsoh if the day before Pesach came on Saturday; whether to bake it on Friday, or on Saturday evening, just before the Seder.

In the Middle Ages the thickness of the matsoh was limited to the breadth of one finger. As time went on, the matsoh became thinner and thinner and, at the same time, crisper. Thin, crisp matsoh could be prepared in advance for the entire festival.

There was a time when it was customary, in some quarters, to make figured matsos. Such matsoh was not regarded as strictly correct and kosher because of the extra time it took to make it. (The longer the dough stands about, the greater likelihood is there of fermentation.)[76]

It is a precept carried over from olden days that the water

used in the making of matsos must be drawn beforehand and kept in a utensil overnight. There was a belief that the sun, setting at night, went under the earth and heated the water in the depths of the wells, making the water tepid and more likely to ferment the dough in which it was used. Thus, keeping the water overnight cooled it and made it safe to use.

There is an old custom known as early as the fourteenth century, which is worth mentioning. Jews would heat the ovens used in the baking of matsos with the willow branches used at the Sukkos festival of the past year; that is, with something that had previously been hallowed.[77]

The process of baking matsos was revolutionized with the invention of the matsos machine, which came about a half-century ago. At first there was a great controversy about the *kashrus* (ritual correctness) of matsoh made with a machine. But technical progress scored a victory here as everywhere else, although there are still, isolated, over-pious Jews who eat only matsoh made by hand.

The flour of which the matsos are baked is made from wheat. There were, however, in previous generations some super-pious Jews who ate only matsoh made from barley flour. It is likely that this custom is still prevailing here and there. Among the Karaites, the use of wheaten flour for matsos is strictly forbidden, barley flour being compulsory.

We may infer from this that matsoh made from barley flour was the older form, that wheaten matsos were an innovation and, therefore, not acceptable in some super-conservative circles. The preference of some super-pious Jews for the inferior matsoh made from barley flour may also be due to the fact that matsoh is referred to in the Bible, as "the bread of affliction."

The Seder...In the course of time the Seder, or Haggadah as the ceremonial of Pesach night is called by the S'fardic Jews, became a religious institution, prescribed, with an exact set of written regulations. But this ritual, which is for us today out of the ordinary and antiquated, was at one time the ordinary procedure at a festive meal in upper, aristocratic circles. It was customary, in those days, to partake of a feast while reclining on sofas, the left hand supported by soft cushions, with a small table at every sofa from which food was served. The menu started with a glass of wine and a toast appropriate to the occasion, after which it was customary to wash one hand and then to eat a bit of lettuce, dipped in tart sauce. The Pesach feast in those days differed from ordinary banquets in only three things: no bread was eaten; dipping the salad green in spices was performed twice instead of once; and only roasted meat was served.[78]

The mode of life changed with the times, and it was, therefore, imperative that the questions asked at the Pesach feast by the youngest son should also change. When dipping the salad greens became obsolete, the third question was emphasized further, and became, not only a question as to why it was done twice, but also why it was done at all. Originally one of the questions dealt with the reason for the sacrificial animal, when the sacrifice was abolished this question was eliminated and a substitute was inserted, the reason for the reclining position, a question that would never have been asked in the old days. In the course of time the custom of reclining at feasts went out of fashion. There were rabbis even in the Middle Ages who wanted to eliminate the custom from the Seder ceremony, arguing that it was no longer a symbol of freedom, but rather a sign of illness and weakness, but the custom remained, and is observed to the present day.

A fourth question was added regarding the bitter herbs. On the whole, it is not a very important question, for other herbs besides the bitter ones are eaten on Pesach eve. But it was felt that there had to be four questions, since so many things about the Seder went in fours; four glasses of wine, four types of food (matsoh, lamb, bitter herbs and *charoses*), four types of sons who ask questions; so four questions were absolutely necessary. There was a symbolic, mystic quality about the number; it had always been a sacred number for Jews and many other eastern peoples.[79]

Elijah's Cup...One of the most interesting of the customs added during a later period to the Pesach eve ceremonial is related to the legendary figure of the prophet Elijah.

Even in very old times, following his death, there was a widespread belief that the prophet had not really died but had ascended to heaven in a fiery chariot, drawn by fiery horses. Later the belief arose that Elijah would return as the forerunner of the Messiah [80] and, therefore, the Elijah legend spread far and wide. It was because of this that the festival of redemption naturally became associated in the Jewish mind with the forerunner of the Messiah, whom the Jews awaited to bring the signal of the coming deliverance.

This, then, helps to explain the cup of wine that is poured for the prophet on Pesach eve. It was an old belief of the Jews that shortly before the coming of the Messiah, Elijah would solve all difficulties and doubts, and settle all confusions and differences of opinion. When a dispute arose and no decision could be made, it was customary to say, "It must be left for Elijah's decision." [81] The Talmudists could not decide whether four or five cups of wine were necessary for the Seder, so a fifth cup is poured and left for Elijah, as though to say, "He will decide whether this is necessary or not." [82]

As the years passed, the fifth cup of wine, standing on the table in Elijah's name, was associated in folk lore with the personal appearance of the prophet in Jewish homes. Far back in Talmudic days the belief arose and spread that the prophet often showed himself to people on earth. And it was natural to expect the forerunner of the Messiah to show himself on the eve of redemption and to drink from the cup that bore his name. In the course of time it became the custom to open the door on the Seder eve, which, people said, was done to facilitate Elijah's entry.

But the origin of the custom of opening the door remains obscure. It is obvious that the opening of the door had nothing to do with the Elijah legend. Originally, in fact, it was customary to open the door before the start of the Seder. The head of the household stepped out into the street and called out: "He that is hungry, come and eat; he that is needy, come and join our Pesach." But often Jews lived amongst non-Jews and were not in a position to call the poor of the street to their tables. This custom died and in its place grew up the custom of *mo-os chittim*, described earlier.[83] It is therefore possible that the opening of the door was transferred from the beginning to the end of the Seder. The custom is also explained as a demonstration that Pesach eve is a "night of watching unto the Lord" and one need have no fear of evil spirits that night.

But it seems that all these interpretations were thought of in later times, when the original meaning of the open door had been forgotten. We know that the doors of the Temple were opened the second part of Pesach eve,[84] and it is possible that the present custom remains from those days, since the doors of homes are also opened during the second part of the evening, after the Seder. But the real reason has vanished and today there lives only the folk-fancy that it is tied up with the coming of Elijah.

The Afikomon and "Kittel"...An important part in the Seder ceremonial is taken by the *afikomon*.

Various customs and beliefs are bound up with the *afikomon*. Other Jews, besides those of Morocco, take along a piece of the *afikomon* as a charm against misfortune when they travel. It was the custom to bore a hole in the *afikomon* and to hang it up as a charm in the synagogue or home. The Jews of Palestine were accustomed to present (some, perhaps, still do) dramatic scenes, such as are acted out in Morocco and the Caucasus, each participant placing the *afikomon*, wrapped in a napkin, on his shoulder and reciting from the Pentateuch the passage: "Their kneading-troughs being bound up in their clothes upon their shoulders." The master of the house traverses four yards and he is asked, "From whence comest thou?"; to which he replies, "From Egypt." Then he is asked, "And where goest thou?"; to which he replies, "To Jerusalem." At which all assembled shout, "May we celebrate next year in Jerusalem." [85]

What the ceremony of first hiding the *afikomon* and then eating it really is, is not entirely clear, but there is a clue in the meaning of the word. The famous Hebrew grammarian of the sixteenth century, Elijah Levita, was the first to rediscover the Greek origin of the word. The Greek word described the joyous revelry and entertainment after a banquet, the song, dance, and games that naturally followed a feast. It is, therefore, probable that in the days of the second Temple feasting was followed by joyous entertainment, in the Greek manner. It is also probable that the word took on, for the Jews, the meaning of the sweet desserts that were eaten after a feast. But after the Pesach feast no song or dance was allowed, nor was it permitted to eat sweets after the eating of the sacrifice.[86] In later times, when a sacrifice was no longer served, it became the custom to finish the meal with a bit of matsoh, instead of a bit of the sacrificial animal. This piece of matsoh inherited the name originally used for dessert, *afikomon*. The original meaning of the word had, by that time, been long forgotten.[87]

The custom of trying to steal the *afikomon* was no doubt instituted in order to keep the children awake during the long service. The custom of hiding the *afikomon* under a pillow can be somehow explained by the precept, "And ye shall guard the matsos," a quotation which the Jews in the Middle Ages took literally.[88]

The custom of conducting the Seder while dressed in a *kittel*, a long, white robe, shows how people forget the original meaning of certain rituals and ceremonials and how erroneously they re-interpret them later. It is declared that the *kittel* is worn as a reminder of the white shroud of the grave. It would be very curious for mementos of the grave to be introduced into the spring festival. In actuality it is a vestige of the days when the festive clothing of Jews was always white; it has nothing to do with burial robes or death.[89]

The Haggadah...It is impossible to picture the Seder night and all its ceremonies without the *Haggadah*. This book has a long history behind it, dating back almost two thousand years. The latter parts, the old folk songs, are no more than four or five hundred years old, it is true; but there are parts that the Jews recited in the days when the second Temple still stood in Jerusalem.

The four questions are among the oldest parts of the *Hag-gadah*, though, as we learned before, they differ from the original text. To the oldest parts of the *Haggadah* belong also: the passage beginning with the words, "a wandering Aramean was my father"; the explanation for the Paschal lamb, the matsoh, and the bitter herbs; the passages beginning with the words, "In every generation," and "So it is our duty"; the Psalms of praise, and the final benediction. All these passages are to be found in the Mishnah. Other passages were added from the *Aggadic* parts of the Talmud and the Midrash. To the Midrash we owe the discourse on the four types of sons, a very important part of the *Haggadah*.[90] These four sons became a source of many homilies, witticisms, *bon mots*, and illustrations that greatly enriched the book. In latter years these four sons have also been dramatized.

For a long time the *Haggadah* was a part of the book of common prayer. It was not till late in the Middle Ages that it became a separate book.

Many commentaries have been written on the *Haggadah*, by such noted figures as Rabbi Isaac Abrabanel, Rabbi Loew of Prague (the legendary creator of the Golem), the Gaon of Vilna, and a host of other more or less famous scholars. But the commentary of Rabbi Jacob Krantz of Dubno became the most popular and beloved. He was a popular preacher who lived in the time of the Gaon of Vilna and Moses Mendelssohn. He had a remarkable gift for interpreting passages in the Bible and in the *Haggadah* through the use of homely parables.

The *Haggadah* is a book that has been tied up with Jewish life for ages. And such a book, which is bound up with so many reminiscences of Jewish life of days gone by, can be best appraised, not by its content, but by the history through which it lived. The great poet Heine, in his novel, *The Rabbi of Bacharach*, has this to say about the *Haggadah*:

"The master of the house sits at the table and reads from a queer book called *Haggadah*. Its content is a marvelous mixture of age-old legends, miracles of the Exodus, curious discussions, prayers, and festive songs. The master reads this book with an old, traditional chant; again and again the others at the table join him in chorus. The tune of the chant is a fearfully hearty one; it lulls and soothes, and at the same time it rouses and calls, so that even those Jews who long since turned from the faith of their fathers and seek strange joys and foreign honors are touched when the well-remembered chants of Pesach happen to reach their ears."

Heine was right. It is not the content of the *Haggadah* that stirs one, as much as the chant with which it is sung, the ceremonies with which it is bound up, and the images the ceremonies evoke. One is also moved by the interpretations and *bon mots*, the stories and parables, the anecdotes and witticisms which the folk gathered about the *Haggadah* in the course of centuries.

In addition, the *Haggadah* played a great role in the development of Jewish art. Illustrations were made for the book at a time when art in its various forms was unusual among Jews. We also have the *Haggadah* to thank for saving us two old Jewish folk songs, "Who Knows One," and "A Kid, A Kid." There were, apparently, many such folk songs that, in time, were forgotten. All that is left to us of these are the above two songs, and for that the *Haggadah* is responsible.[91]

X. THE FESTIVAL OF $\mathfrak{Shovuos}$

Introduction...Shovuos, the Festival of Weeks (Pentecost), comes on the sixth day of the Jewish month Sivan. It is observed for two days by Orthodox and Conservative Jews. In Palestine and among Reform Jews one day is observed, as originally ordained. It is the festival when home and synagogue are decked in green, and all the world is fragrant with plants and flowers, for it occurs in the most beautiful and balmiest season of the year.

In the past Shovuos was an unpretentious holiday and made few special demands for its observance. In our day this holiday has assumed a new importance in Reform and in Conservative congregations, owing to the Confirmation ceremony which was introduced in the past century and which has become one of the outstanding characteristics of Shovuos.

The Wheat Harvest Festival...The word *Shovuos* means weeks, and was therefore used to designate the festival that ended the weeks of the grain harvest. We have already learned that the holiday originally had a more precise and apt name, *Chag ha-Kotsir*, the feast of harvest. The grain harvest started with the reaping of the barley and after seven weeks ended with the cutting of the wheat, an occasion for a festive holiday. It is understandable, therefore, that such a festival, bound up as it is with the agricultural seasons, sprang up among Jews only after they had settled in Palestine and had become tillers of the soil.

The beginning of the grain harvest was marked by the

sacrifice, at the sanctuary, of the *omer*, the first sheaf of the newly cut barley; fifty days later, at the close of the harvest period, two loaves of bread, baked from the wheat of the new crop, were offered as a sacrifice. This bread-offering was called "the first-fruits of wheat harvest," and the festival was therefore also called *Yom ha-Bikkurim*, the day of offering the first loaves of the new crop to God.[92]

In the early days of the Jewish kingdom this sacrifice was offered and the festival observed in the local sanctuary, the *Bomoh*, or "high place." [93] But later, when the "high places" were abolished, the sacrifice was made only in the Temple in Jerusalem. Even then, Shovuos played a minor role in comparison with the other two harvest festivals; it was considered no more than a continuation of and an epilogue to the Festival of Unleavened Bread.[94] There was no effort made, even in later biblical times, to tie up the festival with a historic event; it remained, through all that time, an agricultural holiday, the festival of the completion of the grain harvest. In none of the books of the Bible is there any trace or mention of Shovuos in connection with the giving of the Torah.

Without Fixed Date...Shovuos is the only Jewish festival for which there is no fixed date, and it was therefore a matter of great discussion in the period of the second Temple. The Pentateuch does not state on what day of the month Shovuos is to be observed. It says only that it is to be celebrated fifty days after the offering of the *omer*, the first sheaf of the barley harvest, which was to be offered on "the morrow after the Sabbath." [95] Thus, the Sadducees, the party of conservative priests, interpreted this as meaning that the *omer* was to be offered the first Sunday of Pesach, and that Shovuos, therefore, would always fall on the seventh Sunday after Pesach.

However, the Pharisees, who sought to interpret the Torah in accordance with the conditions of the day, interpreted the word Sabbath, in that case, as meaning not Saturday, but the day of rest, the first day of the festival. According to the Pharisees, therefore, it was necessary to offer the *omer* on the sixteenth day of Nisan; Shovuos, therefore, coming on the sixth day of Sivan.[96]

The Pharisaic tendency became standardized as the procedure for Orthodox Judaism, and to this very day Orthodox Jews begin "counting" *S'firoh*, on the second day of Pesach. The *S'firoh* is a form of benediction in connection with which the fifty days between the supposed offering of the *omer* and the observance of Shovuos are counted. Daily, after the evening prayers, the days and weeks are counted off and the fiftieth day is Shovuos. Among the Samaritans and the Karaites the time for the observance as recommended by the Sadducees is followed, and Shovuos is always observed on a Sunday.

The Falashas, the black Jews of Abyssinia, have still a third date for Shovuos. They observe it on the twelfth day of Sivan, six days after our observance.[97] In ancient days there was still a fourth date for the observance of the festival. "The Book of Jubilees," a product of the days of the second Temple, orders the observance of Shovuos in the middle of Sivan, that is, the fifteenth day of the month.[98]

The Giving of the Torah...Shovuos retained its character as a nature festival longer than any other of the Jewish holidays, but it could not remain so forever. It took on, in time, a new, historic significance and a new spiritual content.

It appears that as far back as the days of the second Temple, Shovuos was a twofold festival. It was the festival of the wheat harvest, when a sacrifice was offered from the new wheat crop; it was also considered the observance of the pact entered into between God and mankind. At least, that is the interpretation presented in the previously mentioned "Book of Jubilees." The festival is celebrated, according to this book, as a symbol that the pact God made with Noah, in which he promised no further general flood, is renewed each year.[99]

How widespread this interpretation of Shovuos was in the days of the second Temple we do not know, for we cannot tell if the above book presents the thoughts of the masses of the folk or of just a small group. But the book does show us that in the days of the second Temple there was already a demand for a new interpretation of Shovuos on an historical basis.

At any rate, Shovuos did not play a great role in the Jewish life of those days. It was obviously a festival observed only in the Temple, and not to any noticeable extent outside of Jerusalem. The holiday first attained importance when it became the festival of the giving of the Torah, of God revealing Himself on Mount Sinai.[100]

Through this association with the giving of the Torah, Shovuos attained a great importance and became an exalted, spiritual festival; a festival no longer associated with agriculture and nature, but symbolic of the spiritual treasure and culture that the Jewish people possess.

In the nineteenth century Shovuos was given new significance by Reform Jews, as a day of confirmation. Till the beginning of the nineteenth century (and amongst Orthodox Jews to this very day) only boys went through the *Bar Mitsvoh* ceremony, individually, on the Sabbath nearest to their thirteenth birthday. This was mainly a private family celebration. Reform Jews, when they modified the synagogue worship, also changed *Bar Mitsvoh* to Confirmation. They included girls in the ceremony, set aside a definite day of the year for it, and made it a community festival.

The early leaders of Reform Judaism selected Shovuos as the day of confirmation, because it is the holiday of the confirmation of the Jewish people in their faith by Moses. It is also the day on which the Book of Ruth is read in the synagogue, telling of Ruth's acceptance into the fold of Israel. This innovation was accepted in all progressive communities and gave new vitality and life to this old festival.

In Eastern Europe...Shovuos does not give Jewish children as many days of freedom as does Pesach, but the Hebrew school is open only half days from the beginning of the month of Sivan. *Rosh Chodesh*, the first day of the Jewish month, was always considered a semi-holiday in Jewish schools; since there are only four days after that till the coming of the festival itself, these are also made minor holidays. The three days before Shovuos are marked off as the days during which the Jews were forbidden to approach close to Mount Sinai.[101] The one day that remains, the day after the New Moon, also becomes a semi-holiday, and is called *Yom ha-M'yuchos*, the "choice day." Its exclusiveness, it is claimed, lies in the fact that on that same day of the week Yom Kippur is bound to fall. But what do children care for the importance ascribed to those days? They are satisfied that they are free and attend school for only half the day.

The weather is mild. The sun pours oceans of light and warmth upon the town. The trees are green with leaves and the fields are gay with flowers. The grass is fragrant and makes the heart feel light and summery. All await the beauteous festival, when Jewish homes are decked in green, when dairy dishes grace every Jewish table, and when the words of *Akdomus*, that beautiful Aramaic ode composed by the Chazan of Worms in the eleventh century, are chanted in the synagogue.

Even in school the instruction is festive and breathes the spirit of the holiday. The children are taught the Book of Ruth. So clear is the imagery thereof that they are carried back to the days of old, when Jews reaped the harvest of the fields of their own land.

The older children sit around a long table with the teacher and study the Book of Ruth. But their thoughts are not on their studies; they are thinking of Bethlehem, the town where David was born and spent his childhood. They imagine they are standing at harvest time in the fields that surround the town. Gentle breezes blow from the hills of Judah. The fields are filled with the freshly cut sheaves. They hear the whir of the reaping scythe, and the song of the workers in the fields. And everywhere is the pleasing aroma of the newly-fallen gleanings which Ruth is gathering in the field.

Their thoughts are carried still farther afield when the teacher recites, or rather sings, as he interprets *Akdomus*. King David descended from Ruth and Boaz, and from David's seed, it is believed, will come the Messiah. In *Akdomus* is presented vividly a picture of the day when the Messiah will have arrived, the time of eternal bliss on earth.

They see the golden thrones, approached by seven stairs; seated on the thrones are the saints, gleaming and shining like the stars of heaven. Above them are spread canopies of light, and below ripple streams of fragrant balsam. There is no end to the joy and happiness of the saints. They dance in Paradise, arm-in-arm with God himself; He entertains them with a mammoth spectacle, arranged especially for them, the combat between the Leviathan and the Behemoth.[102]

So enthusiastic does the teacher become at this point that his imagination expands and grows, and he paints a picture of the two fantastic creatures that is so clear, one would think he had seen them himself. The Leviathan, he says, encircles the sea that surrounds the world. He lies coiled up, with his tail in his mouth; should he, for one moment, release his tail, then the doom of the world would come. Just as great and fearful is the Behemoth. He eats, in one day, the pasturage on a thousand hills; and when he is thirsty, all the water that flows from the Jordan into the sea makes just one gulp for him.

The teacher tells of the feast which God will prepare after the coming of the Messiah, and his imagination makes it more vivid and colorful even than its description in *Akdomus*. He pictures the saints seated around a table made of precious stones, eating the flesh of the Leviathan and the Behemoth. But the feasting does not interest the listening children. Their thoughts recur to the combat between the two monsters; they see the monster of the deep giving mighty blows with his powerful fins, while the Behemoth again and again gores his rival with his gigantic horns.

Shovuos Eve...After feasting the congregation goes to the *Bes ha-Midrosh*, the House of Study, to spend the entire night reading *Tikkun*.[103] The children, alas, must go to bed. They are extremely envious of their older brothers and their parents who stay awake all night in the synagogue and pray at the earliest service in the morning.

At every festival it is customary to promenade about the town, but at no festival is there as much promenading as at

Shovuos. It seems as if this particular holiday was made for promenading. The streets of the town and the roads about the town are filled with Jews, walking after the midday meal, all dressed in their festival clothes. From every house comes the aroma of fried *blintzes*, cheese rolled in dough. It is just as much of a tradition to eat dairy dishes on Shovuos as it is to decorate the house with green plants.

The Second Evening...Only half of the second evening of Shovuos is spent in the synagogue. But this time the congregation recites, not *Tikkun*, but the Psalms of David. The practice of staying awake in the synagogue on this night is not bound up with the giving of the Torah, as is the first night, but with a tradition that King David died on Shovuos.

On the long table in the House of Study burns a great memorial candle. Around the table sit pious Jews, dressed in their holiday best, holding copies of the Psalms in their hands. The flame of the candle, large enough to last twenty-four hours, flickers above them as they read and chant the Psalms, the songs of David, king of Israel, and in this manner observe the anniversary of his death.

Shovuos in Custom and Ceremony...A whole series of customs and traditions are bound up with the observance of Shovuos, and these are so ancient that it is impossible for us to be certain of their origin. The interpretations given them are either later deductions or uncertain theories.

The custom of counting *S'firoh*, that is, counting the days from the offering of the *omer* (the first sheaf of grain) to the offering of the two loaves of new bread forty-nine days later, is very ancient; it is prescribed in the Pentateuch. Ancient, also, is the custom that no feasts or joyous events are to be held during those days, except on *Lag Bo-Omer*, the thirty-third day in the counting of the *omer*. Equally old is the custom of carrying bows into the woods on *Lag Bo-Omer*. These are all customs that come from ancient days and primitive conceptions.[104]

These and other Shovuos customs were later interpreted in various ways. The custom of decorating the homes and synagogues with green plants, for instance, is variously explained. One theory is that the day is marked in heaven as the day of judgment for the fruit of the trees.[105] A second explanation says that it is a reminder of the grass that grew on Mount Sinai at the giving of the Torah. The people who originated this latter explanation forgot, apparently, that on such a mountain as Sinai, that spouted fire, there was very little likelihood of grass growing. Most logical is the theory that it is bound up with the former meaning of the holiday, when it was the festival of the wheat harvest.

Even the custom of eating dairy dishes during the festival goes back to olden times. The people gave to this custom, also, their own interpretation. According to this explanation, when the Jews returned to their tents after receiving the Torah, they were so tired and hungry that they could not wait until the women prepared a meal of meat, so they rushed to eat whatever dairy products were about.

According to the interpretations given by popular lore, the custom of staying awake all of Shovuos eve is explained as follows: it is said that God made himself manifest on Mount Sinai at noon. It happened that the Jews were still asleep at the time and Moses had to go to their quarters to wake them. Therefore, Jews keep awake all of Shovuos eve to show that at present there would be no need to wake them to receive the Torah.

A strange and unexplainable custom is current among the Jews of Morocco, where all, young and old, pour water upon each other on Shovuos, paying no attention to the fact that holiday clothes are being worn. Pitcher upon pitcher of water is thus poured, especially in the late afternoon.[106]

Shovuos, therefore, is an ancient festival, with customs that are so old that it is impossible at this date to trace their origin with any certainty. It is not as old a festival as Pesach. It does not carry us back to desert days, but the holiday is as old as the settling of the Jews in Palestine and harks back to the period when Jews began to live off the fruit of the earth and to observe the agricultural seasons of the year.

XI. THE FAST OF Tishoh B'Ov

Why Mourn?...Tishoh B'Ov (the ninth day of the Jewish month Ov) is a day of mourning, during which Jews fast and bewail the destruction of the Temple and Jerusalem.

On this day pious Jews sit on the ground, with heads bowed low, and recite with a tearful, heartbreaking chant the mournful odes of "Lamentations," those cries of woe re-echoed in every Jewish poem of sorrow ever written.

It is accepted now by all modern biblical scholars that "Lamentations" was not written by Jeremiah, as traditionally believed, but was composed by various Jewish poets after the first destruction of Jerusalem and the Temple in the year 586 B.C.E. Nebuchadnezzar, the king of Babylon, destroyed Jerusalem in that year, burned Solomon's Temple, and abolished the Jewish kingdom in Palestine. About six hundred and fifty years later, in the year 70 C.E., the destruction was duplicated by the Roman legions under the command of Titus. They burnt the second Temple and barely left enough trace of Jerusalem to make one believe that a city once stood there.

These two great national catastrophes in the history of the Jews, now called the first destruction and the second destruction, did not really happen on the ninth day of Ov, the day on which they are observed. According to one statement in the Book of Kings, the first Temple was destroyed on the seventh day of Ov, while elsewhere we are told that it happened on the tenth of the month.[107] The second Temple was also destroyed on the tenth day of Ov.[108]

Despite this, the day of mourning was set for the ninth day, because that day, according to Talmudic tradition, is bound up with sorrowful events in Jewish life shortly after the second destruction, in the time of Bar Kochba's rebellion. Bar Kochba's last fortress, Bether, fell on that day and exactly a year later the site of Jerusalem was plowed under. Upon the orders of Hadrian, the Roman emperor, a new city was then erected on the site, filled with heathen temples and with statues of the Greco-Roman gods.[109]

Thus Jerusalem was captured and destroyed once by the Chaldeans, and twice by the Romans: the first time by Titus, and the second time, sixty-three to sixty-five years later, by Hadrian. For, under Bar Kochba's leadership, Jews had not only recaptured Jerusalem, but, it appears, had also started the erection of a third Temple.

In this way the ninth of Ov was declared the day of mourning for the great national calamities that happened not only on that day, but also a day earlier or later. The Talmud states that God decreed that particular day as a day of woe and misfortune in the very beginning of Jewish history. According to this interpretation, the ninth of Ov was the day when the Jews, in the desert of Sinai, bewailed their lot when the spies brought back bad tidings from Canaan. So God declared: "You cried without cause; I will, therefore, make this an eternal day of mourning for you." And it was then that the decree was ordered for the destruction of the Temple, and the scattering of the Jews amongst the peoples of the earth.[110]

It is not surprising, then, that every woe that befell Jews on that particular day was tied up, in the Jewish mind, with the general woe and misfortune that came with the day. The expulsion of the Jews from Spain happened to come on

Tishoh B'Ov. Even in our own day a great catastrophe is bound up with Tishoh B'Ov. It was on that day, in 1914, that Russia ordered the mobilization of her armies and the World War started; a year later there was an evacuation of all Jews from the border provinces of Russia. It marked the beginning of a great catastrophe for Jewish life in East Europe and Jews of that region still remember that their misfortunes began on Tishoh B'Ov.

Fasting in Ancient Times...Fasting is an old institution among Jews. Even in the days of the Jewish kindgdom in Palestine, it was customary to proclaim a fast day in a time of distress. If, for instance, there was a drought and consequently a fear of famine, or if locusts damaged the young fruit and crops, if plague broke out or an enemy threatened the peace of the land, it was customary for the priest to blow the trumpet and declare a fast day. Old and young would then join in a wailing procession to the sanctuary, dressed in sackcloth and covered with ashes; they would prostrate themselves before the altar and cry and moan while they prayed to God to deal lightly with His people 2nd to help them in their woe.[111]

These were impromptu penitential fasts, decreed for this or that special occasion. It is not stated anywhere that there were, in the days before the destruction of the first Temple, regularly ordained fast days that were observed year after year. Beginning with the Babylonian exile, however, there were certain days in the year which were ordained as national days of mourning for all Jews. One such fast day was known as the "Fast of the Fifth Month," as a memorial of the destruction of the Temple and of Jerusalem.

In addition to the fast of the fifth month, the month of Ov, three other fast days were established at that time; the fast day of the fourth month, of the seventh month, and of the tenth month. These were all days of mourning connected with events at the time of the destruction. On the tenth day of the tenth month, Teves, the siege of Jerusalem began, and to this day it is observed as a fast day. The walls of Jerusalem fell on the ninth day of the fourth month, Tammuz, and on that day the Chaldeans entered the city. After the destruction of the second Temple, this fast was transferred to the seventeenth day of the month; for on that day, due to the shortage of supplies, the daily sacrifices were discontinued at the Temple, during the Roman siege of Jerusalem. The fast day of the seventh month was in memory of the death of Gedaliah, ruler of Judah under the Babylonians after the first destruction.[112]

These fast days of the Babylonian exile became a problem in the time of the Restoration in the Persian Period. There was a new Temple, it was true, but the Jewish kingdom had not been re-established. A Persian governor sat in Jerusalem and the Jews of the country were under heavy pressure. In addition, the new Temple was small and quite poor in comparison with the Temple of Solomon destroyed by the Chaldeans. So Jews pondered whether or not to continue the fasts in memory of the destruction of Jerusalem.

The question arose while the second Temple was still in course of construction. It is told in the Book of Zechariah that in the fourth year of the Persian king, Darius (518 B.C.E.), a delegation came to the Temple of Jerusalem to ask the priests and the prophets whether it was still necessary to observe the fast of the fifth month. Zechariah's answer to this was that fasting had nothing to do with God, that men neither eat nor fast for the sake of God; both are done in answer to human needs. There is, therefore, no answer to be given in the name of God, since God demands neither feasting nor fasting of men. He only asks that they practise justice and mercy, goodness and compassion, and that they oppress not the lowly and the weak. Zechariah further told them that the time of fasting in general would soon pass and the fast days of the fourth, fifth, seventh, and tenth months would become days of joy.[113]

It seems, however, that the fasts were still observed in very pious circles. Otherwise such days of sorrow as the fast of Gedaliah, and the tenth of Teves, which are bound up with the events of the first destruction, would have been forgotten in the course of the six hundred years during which the second Temple stood.

The fast of Gedaliah and the Tenth of Teves remained as memorials of the first destruction only. But the fasts of the months of Tammuz and Ov assumed added importance as fast days through their association with events during and after the second destruction of Jerusalem.

It is told, however, that Rabbi Judah the Patriarch, the compiler of the Mishnah, at one time wanted to abolish Tishoh B'Ov. This patriarch, who lived a generation after Bar Kochba's revolt, was anxious to institute good will and tolerance between Jews and Romans. He, therefore, tried to institute a reform under which there would be no mourning on the ninth of Ov, because such mourning evoked hatred toward the Roman government. It happened, one year, that Tishoh B'Ov fell on a Saturday, a day on which all fasting is forbidden; so, the rabbi declared, since the fast could not be held on the exact date that year, let Jews cease observing it at all. But he failed to win his point, for all his colleagues were opposed to him. The people refused to let political considerations interfere with their observance of the memorial of the destruction of Jerusalem.[114]

It is remarkable that long afterwards, practically in the last few centuries, the rigor of mourning over the destruction of the second Temple increased rather than decreased. Confined originally to certain restricted circles of very pious Jews, the strict observance of mourning in the weeks preceding Tishoh B'Ov became the rule for all. In very recent years, however, the mourning of Tishoh B'Ov is definitely on the decline, even amongst professing Orthodox Jews. Reform Jews do not observe Tishoh B'Ov as a fast day.

The "Three Weeks" in Eastern Europe...Less than two months have passed since the period of *S'firoh;* and once more a season of mourning is at hand, a season lasting three weeks, from the seventeenth of Tammuz to the ninth of Ov.

During the *S'firoh* period no occasions of joy are celebrated except on *Lag Bo-Omer* and the New Moon; but there is no special sadness connected with it. The "Three Weeks," however, are melancholy for all, and the oppressive mood becomes even stronger during the nine days from the beginning of the month to Tishoh B'Ov.

Beginning with the Fast of the Seventeenth of Tammuz, all evidences of joy disappear from the town. All celebrations are forbidden; one is not allowed to cut his hair or don new clothing for the first time, and even the blessing of thanksgiving for the new fruits of the season is outlawed. Every face is clouded and it seems as if the chant of "Lamentations" is heard in every noise and whisper.

During the nine days between the New Moon and Tishoh B'Ov, the restrictions are so severe that all bathing is forbidden and no meat may be eaten. The lack of meat is not a great hardship on the Jews of the town; nobody eats much meat during the hot summer months. But the ban on bathing causes real hardship, for these are the hottest days of the year. But no matter what the heat, nor how strongly the sun burns, nobody goes to the river. Who would dream of bathing during the "Nine Days," when Jews mourn over the destruction of the Temple?

*In Cheder...*The school children also feel the spirit of general mourning and share in it. The main lesson for the period is the reading and translation of "Lamentations," and they chant the odes in low, almost tearful voices, the moisture gathering in their eyes. As if the sorrowful words and the despairing chant were not sufficient, the *m'lammed* (Hebrew teacher) punctuates the proceedings with deep sighs, straight from the heart, as deep as if he himself had lived through both destructions of Jerusalem.

The teacher is not content just to drill the children in the Book of Lamentations. He tells them those stories of the destruction of the Temple that come from the legends of the Talmud and Midrash, and the children stand open-mouthed and wide-eyed as they listen to him.

And as they listen to the legends and tales, everything becomes so real to them that they almost imagine that they are living in those woeful yet heroic times. In their minds the various events and the different epochs become one fearful drama, each scene of which is more moving and dreadful than the other.

They see Jeremiah, bent and broken, going to the Cave of Machpelah to ask the Patriarchs of Israel to pray to God and beg Him to have mercy on their children and not to allow the destruction. The scene changes quickly, and they see Nebuzaradan, the great general, mighty of build, a naked sword in his hand, slaughtering thousands of Jews, men and women, old and young, in order to still the seething blood of Zechariah, the priest and prophet that was slain by the Jews centuries before in the Temple. But the children's anger is soon allayed, for they are told by the teacher that later in life Nebuzaradan was converted and became a Jew.

The Emperor Nero appears on the scene. The story they are told makes them feel kindly and well-disposed to him. He was a fine and gentle individual who, the teacher states, abandoned his army near Jerusalem, escaped, and became a convert to Judaism. Not only that, but the great teacher, Rabbi Meir, was a descendant of his.

Most of the children's animosity is visited on Titus. Not only did that arch-villain destroy Jerusalem and burn the Temple, but he entered the Holy of Holies, blasphemed God, and pierced the holy drape with his sword. And they feel avenged when the teacher tells them about the gnat that entered his nostrils and kept boring into his head.

But most gratifying and heartening are the glorious tales about the great Bar Kochba. What daring heroes served in his army and what a picture they made, riding their huge steeds and plucking cedars from Lebanon by their roots! If a man were not strong enough to accomplish this uproot-ing, he was rejected by Bar Kochba; unless, and the children shudder at this, the man was brave enough to chop a finger off his own hand. They do not dwell on this; it is pleasanter to meditate upon the picture of the mighty riders tearing cedars out of Mount Lebanon.

They become enthusiastic and lively in their contempla-tion of Bar Kochba's heroes, but sadness descends on them again. For the teacher tells of Bar Kochba's death and how his head was brought to the Emperor Hadrian; that the current of the river of blood from the Jewish heroes who fell at Bether was so strong that it moved boulders out of its path.

The Eve of Tishoh B'Ov...It is the final meal before the fast. Many Jews dine on hard rolls shaped like doughnuts (beigel) and eggs, sprinkling the egg with ashes, the dish partaken after funerals. Directly after the meal the Jews make their way to the synagogue, copies of *Kinos*, a book containing odes of mourning for this occasion, under their arms.[115] Rubbers, or wooden-soled slippers cover their feet. The light in the synagogue is dim and ghostly. Occasional candles burn with a lack-lustre glow. The curtain has been removed from the Ark of the Torah. Book-rests are turned over on the floor and many sit on them; others sit on low benches or boxes that they brought to the synagogue. The worshipers sit like mourners with bowed heads. The official reader chants "Lamentations" to the traditional, mournful melody. The synagogue resounds with the ancient song of woe; in each heart burns a pain: pain at the destruction of Jerusalem, a city full of people that became as a widow; pain at the exile of Judah, who wanders amongst the peoples and finds no rest; pain for the daughter of Zion, whom He covered with a cloud.

The Morning...The services start very early and last until very late; the worshipers sit on the ground a long time and recite *Kinos*. There is something unusual about the entire proceeding. Generally, prayer robes and phylacteries are worn at morning services. On Tishoh B'Ov they are not used in the morning, but are donned for the afternoon services, when they are not ordinarily worn.

The children of the town are also impressed with the sadness of the day, but still, they find opportunity to indulge in a form of play. They throw the seed-burrs of plants at each other in the synagogue and after reciting *Kinos* they march, together with their elders, around the cemetery, with wooden swords, prepared weeks before, bound to their loins. Some children leave these swords sticking in the mounds of the graves.

Customs of Tishoh B'Ov...The customs that are bound up with Tishoh B'Ov are apparently very old. But it is only comparatively recently, in the last few centuries, that the people in general practiced the mourning customs in all their strictness. It was not so long ago that meat and wine were forbidden only at the last meal preceding the fast. Only in very pious circles was this prohibition observed for the nine days preceding the fast.

Not all of the mourning customs were adopted universally. The custom of sleeping on Tishoh B'Ov night with a stone for a pillow [116] and the custom of fasting till noon on the day after Tishoh B'Ov were observed only by certain highly pious Jews. A strange and remarkable custom is current amongst the Jewish women of the Orient. They anoint themselves with fragrant oils after midday of the fast, for it is believed to be the day of the birth of the Messiah.

The custom of going to the cemetery on Tishoh B'Ov is very old. It may have nothing to do with the destruction of the Temple, but is associated with Tishoh B'Ov as a fast day since in ancient days it was the custom to go to the cemetery on every fast day. However, the custom practiced by the children of carrying swords to be left in the mounds of the graves, is neither old nor generally observed.

xii. Sabbath Nachamu

Sabbaths Chazon and Nachamu...The Saturday before Tishoh B'Ov is called *Sabbath Chazon* and the following Saturday is known as *Sabbath Nachamu*. Both are so called because of the portion of the prophets (*Haftoroh*) that is recited in the synagogue on each of these Sabbaths. On the first of these Sabbaths the reader chants from the first chapter of Isaiah, which begins with the Hebrew word *Chazon* (vision, prophecy). The chapter starts, "The vision of Isaiah, the son of Amoz—," and predicts destruction and doom. The terrible predictions of the prophet are chanted to the melody of "Lamentations" and fearful foreboding is felt by all in the synagogue.

But a people cannot live only on memories of the woes of the past. It must also have hopes for a brighter and happier future. It is for this reason that the belief became current amongst Jews that the Messiah was born on the day of the destruction of the Temple. The month of Ov is therefore called *Menachem Ov*, for the meaning of *menachem* is "comforter." *Menachem* is also the name of the Messiah, according to one homiletical interpretation of "Lamentations." [117] The mourning over the destruction of Jerusalem was, therefore, always bound up in Jewish thought with the hope of deliverance, and for this reason it is natural that after Tishoh B'Ov should come *Sabbath Nachamu*, the Sabbath of Comfort. On that day the fortieth chapter of Isaiah is recited in the synagogue, the chapter beginning with, *Nachamu, Nachamu Ammi* (Comfort ye, comfort ye My people).

Sabbath Nachamu was always a joyous occasion in the small Jewish towns of Eastern Europe. It was, and still is, the Sabbath for festivities, especially for weddings which began usually on Friday and were continued for several days. It was rare that a *Sabbath Nachamu* should come and go without wedding festivities. The days succeeding Tishoh B'Ov are appropriate for weddings, for all feel more at ease; the sorrow has passed by, and a time of renewed hope and comfort has come.

The Prophet of Comfort...Sabbath Nachamu is named after one of the most uplifting poems and prophecies we have in the Books of the Prophets. The great prophets were all brilliant poets, in whom the poetic inspiration was fused with a boundless religious ecstasy. But none of them created such melodic odes as the great prophet and poet of "Comfort ye, comfort ye My people."

It is now universally accepted by all biblical scholars that the Book of Isaiah, from the fortieth chapter on, is not by the prophet Isaiah, but by an anonymous prophet who came later. For some reason the visions and predictions of this great prophet were not gathered into a book of their own, but were made a part of the Book of Isaiah, the son of Amoz. This unknown writer of the second part of Isaiah is therefore called "the great anonymous prophet." Where this anonymous prophet lived is not known, but most students of the Bible assume that he lived in Babylonia. The time, however, can safely be placed in the last years of the Babylonian Exile, when the Babylonian world dominion was about to fall.

Many Jews rejoiced then at the impending fall of Babylon.[118] But no great movement or exalted hopes arose among the exiled Jews in Babylonia because of the victories of

Cyrus. In the fifty years that had passed since their exile they had grown inured to their new life, and the longing for the old home had been considerably lessened. In addition, there was not much to be hoped for, in the opinion of very many Jews, from the fall of Babylon and the victory of a foreign king. The deliverance, they believed, would come only through a ruler of the House of David, who would re-establish the Jewish kingdom that David had founded, the free Jewish kingdom in Jerusalem.

It was in answer to such theories and in an effort to overcome the hopeless attitude adopted by many Jews that the great anonymous prophet of the exile arose. He neither admonished nor predicted doom, as had most of the great prophets who lived during the time of the Jewish kingdom. He was a comforter exclusively and predicted a new and happier era.

THE END OF EXILE HAS COME!

Comfort ye, comfort ye My people,
Saith your God.
Bid Jerusalem take heart,
And proclaim unto her,
That her time of service is accomplished,
That her guilt is paid off;
That she hath received of the Lord's hand
Double for all her sins.

Hark! one calleth:
"Clear ye in the wilderness the way of the Lord,
Make plain in the desert
A highway for our God."

O thou that tellest good tidings to Zion,
Get thee up into the high mountain;

O thou that tellest good tidings to Jerusalem,
Lift up thy voice with strength;
Lift it up, be not afraid;
Say unto the cities of Judah:
"Behold your God!"

THE DELIVERANCE IS AT HAND!

Remember ye not the former things,
Neither consider the things of old.
Behold, I will do a new thing;
Now shall it spring forth; shall ye not know it?
I will even make a way in the wilderness,
And rivers in the desert.

CYRUS IS THE MESSIAH, A TOOL IN GOD'S HAND

Thus saith the Lord to his anointed,
To Cyrus, whose right hand I have holden,
To subdue nations before him,
And to loose the loins of kings;
To open the doors before him,
And that the gates may not be shut:
I will go before thee,
And make the crooked places straight;
I will break in pieces the doors of brass,
And cut in sunder the bars of iron.

For the sake of Jacob My servant,
And Israel Mine elect,
I have called thee by thy name,
I have surnamed thee, though thou hast not
    known me.

JEWS RETURN HOME FROM EXILE

Say to the prisoners: "Go forth";
To them that are in darkness: "Show yourselves";
They shall feed in the ways,

And in the high hills shall be their pasture;
They shall not hunger nor thirst,
Neither shall the heat nor sun smite them;
For He that hath compassion on them will lead them,
Even by the springs of water will He guide them.

Sing, O heavens, and be joyful, O earth,
And break forth into singing, O mountains;
For the Lord hath comforted His people,
And hath compassion upon His afflicted.

GOD BEFORE HIS PEOPLE IN THE NEW ZION

Awake, awake,
Put on thy strength, O Zion;
Put on thy beautiful garments,
O Jerusalem, the holy city.

Hark, thy watchmen! they lift up the voice,
Together do they sing;
For they shall see, eye to eye,
The Lord returning to Zion.

Break forth into joy, sing together,
Ye waste places of Jerusalem;
For the Lord hath comforted His people,
He hath redeemed Jerusalem.

These hopes of the great and comforting prophet were not
realized, despite the capture of Babylon by Cyrus. The valleys
were not lifted up, nor were the mountains and hills made
low; no highways were made in the wilderness, nor did the
desert become a pool of water. The Persian government, it
is true, allowed the exiled Jews to return to their old home,
but only a small portion of them took advantage of this opportunity. It is true that a second Temple was erected, and,

somewhat later, Jerusalem rebuilt; but the Jewish community in Judah was small and poor, without any trace of the grandeur and hopefulness that the prophet of "Comfort ye" expected to come from the rule of the Persians.

The hopes of the great prophet were not fulfilled, but they never ceased to flicker in Jewish hearts. To this very day Jews observe the Saturday after Tishoh B'Ov as *Sabbath Nachamu,* the Sabbath of Comfort.

xiii. Rosh Hashonoh

The Days of Awe (Yomim Noroim)...Rosh Hashonoh (New Year) is the Jewish New Year, celebrated by Orthodox Jews everywhere, Palestine included, on the first two days of the Jewish month, Tishri. Among Reform Jews it is observed one day only, on the first day of Tishri.

Yom Kippur, the Day of Atonement, comes on the tenth day of Tishri, and is observed everywhere as a fast day, as the Great Day of the year.

Both Rosh Hashonoh and Yom Kippur are different, in atmosphere, from other Jewish festivals and are therefore known as the "Days of Awe." In all other festivals the spirit is one of exalted joyfulness. The exaltation of Rosh Hashonoh and Yom Kippur, however, has no traces of joy, for these are profoundly serious days, with a feeling of the heavy moral responsibility which life puts on all.

They are also different from other Jewish festivals in that they bear no relation to nature nor to any historic event in the Jewish past. They are concerned only with the life of the individual, with his religious feelings and innermost probings. Rosh Hashonoh is the Jewish New Year but, in contrast with the New Year of other peoples, it is greeted not with noise and joy, but with a serious and contrite heart.

The New Year of the Jews...The theme of the New Year of the Jews is a complex one. It is impossible to present it in clear and straightforward terms, in a minimum of words. There are many phases to discuss, and all are complicated.

The first thing to be explained is the fact that in the Pentateuch, in which Jews are told to observe the first day of Tishri as a holiday, that day is not labeled Rosh Hashonoh, the New Year; it is designated as the first day of the seventh month. Throughout the entire Bible there is no reference to that day as Rosh Hashonoh.[119] It is clear, therefore, that in biblical days there was no holiday by that name. It is curious, too, that according to the Pentateuch the New Year begins in the seventh month. How is such a thing possible?

To these and to similar questions there can be but one answer: Jews, in the days of old, before the Babylonian Exile, observed neither Rosh Hashonoh nor Yom Kippur. In those days they observed only one festival at that time of the year, the Festival of the Ingathering of the fruits and grapes. That festival had many rites that are now associated with Rosh Hashonoh, Yom Kippur, and Sukkos. It was only later, after the Babylonian Exile, that the autumn festival was divided into three separate holidays. For this reason Jews observe, in one season of the year, three festivals which are all actually New Year festivals. We shall discuss later, in the chapters on Yom Kippur and Sukkos, the type of holiday the original autumn festival must have been, and why it was divided into three parts.

We shall consider now the question of why the first day in Tishri is called, in the Pentateuch, the first day of the seventh month, and why Yom Kippur comes exactly on the tenth day of that month. However, we must first acquaint ourselves with the Jewish calendar and the conditions under which the Jews of old reckoned the year and the month.

The Jewish Calendar... The calendar in common use throughout the western world is based on the sun. Neither the year nor the months have anything to do with the phases of the moon. The Mohammedans, on the other hand, reckon both the year and the month according to the phases of the moon. Their year is therefore shorter than the general year by about eleven days. A moon-year has 354 days, and the sun-year 365 days. The Jewish calendar is based on a compromise between the two, and is reckoned according to both the sun and the moon. The months are figured according to the moon (twelve months of 29½ days each), and the year according to the sun. In order to take up the extra eleven days, a whole month is added to the calendar in leap years. Every second or third year there is a thirteenth month, a second Adar.[120]

The Jewish calendar is a very old one. It has been established a long time and every point and detail has been ironed out.[121] But the history of the calendar, how it evolved and how, in time, it came to be an established fact, is very obscure.

It is to be presumed that in pre-historic times, when Jews were still nomadic shepherd tribes in the wilderness, they reckoned time entirely by the moon, as did all nomadic peoples. But it seems that after they settled in Palestine and began to observe the agriculture seasons, they also began to reckon according to the position of the sun. How the Jews of the period equalized the sun-year and the moon-year we do not know. It is possible that at one time they just added a number of days at the end of each year. In time, however, the method of making every second or third year a leap year was apparently established.[122]

It appears that in the old days Jews figured their calendar —the month, the year, and the festivals—entirely by observation, by the testimony offered that the moon had appeared

and had been seen. Later, astronomic calculation was instituted in connection with the calendar, but the Jews were
not certain of its exactness and still had recourse to witnesses.
The authority to hear this testimony and through it to establish the beginning of the month, the intercalation of the
calendar, and the dates of the festivals was vested in the
Sanhedrin.

When they accepted the report of the witnesses, the New
Moon was announced through the lighting of fires on the
hill-tops. Later, this method was not considered safe enough,
and messengers were sent out to proclaim the date. However, it took time for the messengers of the Sanhedrin in
Palestine to reach the further lands inhabited by Jews and
proclaim there the arrival of the New Moon. It was, therefore, decreed that outside of Palestine, in the lands of the
Diaspora, festivals were to be observed for two days instead
of one. This added second day was called "the second holiday of the Diaspora." An exception was made in the case
of Yom Kippur which, because of the hardship of fasting,
could not be prolonged. Rosh Hashonoh was also an exception in that it was observed for two days even in Palestine,
for Rosh Hashonoh was also the New Moon, the first day
of Tishri. Even in Palestine it could not always be ascertained
on the preceding day whether the particular day was the
first day of Tishri or the last day of Ellul.

In later times the astronomical calculation of the calendar
became so precise that the practice of hearing witnesses was
discarded. The Jewish calendar was established in every
detail. Despite this, the observance of the second day of
festivals is still retained in the Diaspora, for people are conservative when it comes to religious affairs, and they are not
willing to change long established customs.[123]

To this day Orthodox and Conservative Jews in all lands, outside of Palestine, observe Pesach for eight days, Shovuos for two days, and Sukkos for nine days. In Palestine, only seven days of Pesach are observed (the first and seventh days as holidays, the intervening five days as semi-festivals); Shovuos is celebrated only one day, and Sukkos for eight days (the first day a full festival, five days as semi-festivals, Hoshano Rabboh, and finally Sh'mini Atseres, which is observed also as Simchas Torah). Reform Judaism, recognizing the present stability of the Jewish calendar, has discarded the "second holiday of the Diaspora."

The History of the New Year . . . As we have learned, various peoples have various ways of reckoning their calendar. There is a long history behind the Jewish calendar. The same statements may be made regarding the New Year.

Various peoples observe the New Year at different seasons of the year. The Babylonians and the Persians, for instance, began their year in the spring. The ancient Egyptians began theirs in the summer, when the waters of the Nile begin to rise; the Romans celebrated the new year in the winter, the present secular New Year; and the inhabitants of Palestine began their year in the fall.

Under what conditions the Jews of old observed the New Year is a matter that is somewhat obscure and complicated. The Bible calls for the observance, in autumn, of the "feast of ingathering, *at the end of the year.*"[124] From that we learn that the Jews started the year in the fall, when all the work of the year was completed and all the produce of field and orchard were gathered in barn and bin; when the earth was seared with heat and the rains were awaited to bring forth new growth and life.

But another passage of the Bible tells us that the first month of the year is Nisan,[125] and the months were numbered beginning with the spring, making Pesach the first festival.[126] The usual explanation given by critics of the Bible is that, in older times, Jews began the year in the fall, but that they were later influenced by the practices of the Babylonians, who observed the New Year in the spring. The Jews, therefore, arranged their calendar to begin at that time. The religious ceremonies in honor of the New Year, however, they continued to observe in the fall. It was in this way that the observance of the New Year occurred in the seventh month of the calendar.[127]

The Jews of old, then, began the year in the fall, but there was no special New Year festival, no holiday by the name of Rosh Hashonoh. Such a festival originated among Jews quite late, a long time after the Babylonian Exile. The Pentateuch states only that "in the seventh month, in the first day of the month, shall be a solemn rest unto you, a memorial proclaimed with the blast of horns, a holy convocation." But the first of every month was an occasion for the blowing of trumpets, as a memorial before God. The only difference was that short blasts were blown at the New Moons of other months, while long alarm blasts were sounded on the New Moon of the seventh month.[128]

We cannot, then, be certain what kind of festival the first of Tishri was in ancient times. It is possible that it was already a form of New Year, the beginning of the year, according to the moon. But it is also possible that it was nothing more than an exalted New Moon observance, the holiest one of the year, the New Moon of the holy seventh month. For exactly as the seventh day and the seventh year were holy, so, undoubtedly, was the seventh month.[129]

It is worthy of note that the Bible does not refer to the day as the New Year; neither do any Jewish books written in the period of the second Temple.[130] We must, however, take it for granted that about the time of the destruction of the second Temple the day was observed as the New Year. For in the literature of the Tannaim,[131] which dates to the years shortly after the destruction, the first of Tishri is called Rosh Hashonoh. In those days the belief was already popular that Rosh Hashonoh marked the day on which mankind was judged in heaven and man's fate settled.[132]

At any rate, a generation or two after the destruction of the second Temple, Rosh Hashonoh had all the outstanding characteristics associated with it today. The Shofar was blown in the synagogue and various interpretations had been read into the custom. The festival was observed, as today, mainly in the synagogue. The services were longer and already included the prayers of *Malchiyos, Zichronos, Shoforos*,[133] and the use of different leaders of prayer for the morning and *Musaf* (additional) services. Later, other prayers were added, and still later the *Piyut*, the liturgical poetry of the Middle Ages, making the Rosh Hashonoh services still richer and more impressive.[134]

Of all the prayers and the poetical insertions that were added to the Rosh Hashonoh services none became as popular as the prayer, *Un'saneh Tokef*.[135] This poetic prayer gives the most vivid picture of Rosh Hashonoh as the day of God's judgment of the world. The moment when *Un'saneh Tokef* is recited is the most earnest and awesome in the entire service of Rosh Hashonoh.

xiv. Yom Kippur - IN OLDEN DAYS

Old and New Earnestness... We have already mentioned that in olden times, before the Babylonian Exile, neither Rosh Hashonoh nor Yom Kippur were distinct holidays, separate from the autumn festival, Sukkos. These two serious holidays are very different in character from the three joyous festivals (Pesach, Shovuos, and Sukkos), and are obviously a product of a later epoch, carrying that epoch's imprint.

In each era of ancient Jewish history festivals were created which were bound up with the ideas, the emotions, and the conceptions of the Jews of that particular era. It was not necessary to create new holidays. The old festivals were altered and re-created; a new spiritual content was poured into them and they became new institutions.

In very ancient times, when Jews were still shepherds in the wilderness, they observed festivals that were in keeping with the life of nomadic shepherd tribes. They observed, for instance, Pesach, the New Moon, and the shearing of the sheep, as festival days.[136] Later, when they settled in Palestine and became peasants, rooted in the soil of the land, they began the observance of the three nature festivals that were bound up with tilling the soil and the seasons.[137]

But as the Jews traveled further on their own path of higher spiritual culture, they sought more and more to separate their festivals from nature, from the seasons of the year, and surround them with a new religious content. This process began in the time of the Jewish kingdom, and attained bold and far-reaching results after the Babylonian Exile.

Jewish life had changed considerably after the exile. Jewish religious ideas and feelings had become purer and more earnest. Their life as a people had changed, too, for Jews were, in that time, spread over many near and distant lands. The three great festivals of the Jewish peasants of the older days were no longer suited to the conditions and the spirit of the newer day. Jews had no longer the desire to observe nature festivals, which consisted of eating, drinking, and rejoicing before God,[138] especially since that type of festival, which was closely bound up with the village life of the peasants, no longer fitted the conditions under which Jews lived in scattered communities in various countries.

So the three great, yearly festivals took on, with time, a new character. From village revels they evolved into national observances. They lost their connection with the seasons of the year and made of the entire people one festive community. Some of the customs still pointed to the agricultural origin of the festivals, as, for instance, the first sheaf of barley offered at Pesach, and the two loaves of bread offered at Shovuos.[139] But the agricultural season was no longer the reason for the festival, and the entire observance was no longer planned as an expression of rejoicing before God, but was a means by which the celebrants sought to approach nearer to God. The festival of the day was no longer a folk revel but a "holy convocation" in the Temple or synagogue, a day of rest, of earnestness, and of spiritual uplift.[140] Such festivals could be observed not only in the Temple in Jerusalem, but everywhere, in all the lands to which the Jews of that day were already scattered.

The only festival which still retained forms of the old village revels was Sukkos; and it was for that very reason, apparently, that Yom Kippur was instituted in those days as

a distinct holiday, so that five days earlier, before the beginning of the revels, there should come a great and sanctified
day, a day of fasting and reflection on one's sins.

The Development of a Holy Day...Later we shall treat the
Sukkos festival as it was celebrated in ancient days. Suffice
it to say that this festival had the character of a wild revel,
which the Jews took over from the peoples about them. It
displeased the spiritual leaders, the religious teachers of the
day, that Jews should open the year with revelry just as did
their heathen neighbors. It was, therefore, arranged that the
joyous festival be observed several days later, and that the
New Year be started with a great fast. Revelry was not to be
practiced when an old year ended and a new year of life
began; instead fasting would be the order of the day, reciting
confessional prayers, and a "reckoning of the soul" to renew
one's inner life for the coming new year. After the fast,
when sins were forgiven and one felt himself a new man
again, would be the time for revelry and joy.

In this way, in the course of time, it was arranged that the
tenth day of Tishri, the day on which the new year officially
started,[141] was to be a day of ridding one's self of sin; and
the joyous autumn festival, parallel with the festival of spring,
was to begin on the fifteenth day of the month, at the full
of the moon.[142]

Speculation arises as to why the beginning of the year, in
ancient days, came on the tenth of the month instead of the
first.[143] The only logical explanation for this is that it stems
from a time when there was no leap year in the Jewish
calendar, no thirteenth month to equalize the sun-year and
moon-year. In order to accomplish this equalization, ten days
or so were added to the end of the previous year before

reckoning the new year. It is possible, then, that in the practical life of the period the new year began on the first of the month; but officially the year began on the tenth of the month, thus meeting the sun-year. These ten intervening days were declared days of penitence.

When it is said, however, that Yom Kippur is a product of the epoch after the Babylonian exile, it is not meant that it was entirely a new institution. Yom Kippur became, in that time, a new holiday only in that it was entirely separated from Sukkos and assumed a new character and a new significance, but the core of Yom Kippur was not new. We must assume that even in the time of Solomon's Temple a definite day, or perhaps days were established to cleanse the sanctuary of its profanations; but we do not know exactly what the day was and what ceremonies attended it.[144] We must also take for granted that the joyous autumn festival, even far back in history, began with a day of serious mien and fasting and ended in revelry, or else that it began as a revel and ended as a fast. But we do not know what motive or character was attributed to this day that preceded or succeeded the revelry.[145] Later, as has been explained, the fast day was entirely separated from the autumn festival and became a distinct and genuine Jewish festival. It was remembered however that the day before the last day of the festival, the day on which the revelry reached its height, was one of seriousness; and *Hoshano Rabboh*, the seventh day of Sukkos, the day before *Sh'mini Atseres*, remained, therefore, through all time a minor Yom Kippur.

We cannot be certain when all these changes and reforms in the Jewish calendar took place. For all this happened in a period of Jewish history, regarding which there is little documentation—the four hundred years between the first destruction of Jerusalem and the rise of the Hasmoneans. In these four hundred years there evolved a practically new Jewish spiritual life with new forms and institutions. How and under what conditions these new forms and institutions arose we cannot know. It is, therefore, not surprising that we know so little of the greatest holiday that arose in that period: Yom Kippur.

We can be certain, however, that Yom Kippur did not assume its importance as the greatest fast day of the year and the great day for all Jews all at once; it went through a long period of evolution. Nor is its ritual uniform; it is made up of various customs and ceremonies, some very ancient and some that were added in later years.

It appears that for a certain length of time the tenth day of Tishri was both the beginning of the year and a day of atonement. It was the latter in the Temple, but outside of the Temple it still carried the traits of a festival. Jewish maidens went to the vineyards on that day in a joyous dance procession.[146] The day still had a double character and this hindered its importance as a day of penitence. For this reason a separation was made: the first day of Tishri was made Rosh Hashonoh, the official New Year, and the tenth day of the month became almost entirely a day of confession and penitence. But the separation never had the full effect it was supposed to produce. Rosh Hashonoh and Yom Kippur intermingle in their roles. Yom Kippur never actually became entirely a day of sorrow, a day which casts shadow on all. Despite the fast, the confession, and the wailing, it remains a festival with an undercurrent of joy. One must not eat, but still, one wears festive clothes.

The Jews of that period felt the need of a genuine Jewish holiday in which they could express their deepest religious feelings, and the tenth of Tishri became that day. It is not surprising that the Jews realized the great importance of Yom Kippur, and the day became and remained the greatest and holiest day in the Jewish year.

xv. Yom Kippur = IN TEMPLE DAYS

The Great Day...During the latter period of the second Temple Yom Kippur was already the holiest day of the year for all Jews. It was called "The Great Day" or, more simply, "The Day." Jews in all lands fasted on that day and spent it entirely in the synagogue, earnestly praying. Even those Jews who were comparatively unobservant the rest of the year became very pious on that day, according to Philo, the Jewish philosopher who lived in Alexandria a generation before the destruction of the second Temple.[147]

But, while praying in their synagogues, Jews everywhere turned their eyes and their hearts to one spot, to the Temple, where the High Priest conducted the sacred and mystic ceremonies of the day. For that was the only day of the year on which the High Priest entered the Holy of Holies. Not in the golden ceremonial robes of the High Priest did he present himself before God, but in the linen robes of an ordinary priest.

The High Priest did not ordinarily perform the rites of the Temple. He showed himself to the people, dressed in his gold robes, only on Sabbaths, festivals, and New Moons.[148] On Yom Kippur, however, he became the priest of the sanctuary, and he, himself, conducted the entire service and confessed to God for his own sins, for the sins of the other priests, and for the sins of the entire people of Israel.

Seven days before Yom Kippur the High Priest moved from his home to his chamber in the Temple. During this week he alone conducted the service, offered the daily sacrifices, sprinkled the blood, burned the incense, and tended the lighting of the Menorah. He did this for seven successive days in order to become well versed in the details, so that he would make no mistake on Yom Kippur. In addition, he had to study to read the Torah before the public; he had to read two portions of the Pentateuch from the Torah-scroll on Yom Kippur, and recite one portion by heart. In the last century before the destruction of the Temple the High Priest was more often a noted politician than a learned man. Therefore, learned members of the Sanhedrin would tutor him during the week before Yom Kippur, teaching him what was necessary.

But before continuing with the proceedings of the Yom Kippur service, let us spend some time on a tour of the Temple.

A Tour of the Temple...A new, a third Temple, was constructed during the time of which we speak. The second Temple, the one that was erected under the leadership of Zerubbabel in the beginning of the Persian world dominion, was small and poorly constructed of ordinary wood and stone. It **stood for about five** hundred years, until Herod demolished it and erected a larger and grander structure on the site. Due to the fact that no enemy destroyed Zerubbabel's Temple, that it was removed only to make way for a much more beautiful building, the new Temple was also referred to as the second Temple.

Decades after Herod's Temple was finished the work of beautifying it went on. More than eighty years passed before it was entirely completed, with all its adornments, a comparatively few years before the destruction of Jerusalem by the Romans. The completed Temple, therefore, stood only a little while before it was burned down by the Roman army under Titus. This Temple of Herod is the one we are to observe.

The Temple glistens in the distance and makes a clear impression, for it is built of the finest of white marble, snow-like in its purity. It is covered with thick golden plates. When the sun shines on these a fiery glow comes forth, and the Temple looks like a mountain of snow, from which issue golden flames.

We approach the Mount of the Temple now. This holy mount rises on a series of broad terraces, flat mounds that rise regularly above each other. On the topmost terrace stands the altar, and above it rises the House of God. Only priests are allowed in the front room of the House of God, and then only in the performance of the services; beyond is the rear room, the "Holy of Holies," where only the High Priest may enter, and only one day of the year, Yom Kippur.

The entire structure is encircled by a very broad wall and is quite similar to a fortress. The wall is studded with high points and staunch towers. On all four sides of the wall there are gates leading into the Temple. We enter one of these gates and approach a colonnade, four rows of marble pillars, surmounted with cedar. There are many colonnades in the Temple but the one under which we now stand is the largest and loveliest. It is called the Regal Colonnade and has one hundred and sixty-two marble pillars.

We enter a second colonnade and see souvenirs of vic-tories: swords, armor, and flags that Jewish armies once brought back from battlefields as mementoes of victory. We lift our eyes, however, and are deterred from all thoughts of war and victory; over the main gate hangs a golden Roman eagle as a symbol of the sovereignty of Rome over Jerusa-lem. No matter where we look, the reflection of that eagle shines from the white marble of the walls and from the polished stones of the floor. Amongst these colonnades are rooms for the Levites and rooms for the sages, where those with great knowledge of God's Torah sit and study with their pupils.

From the covered colonnades we step into the great, open outer court, plastered with vari-colored stones. All may enter this court, even non-Jews. It is immense in size, larger than any of the other courts.

We pass through the outer court and come to a stone fence. This is the boundary line beyond which non-Jews may not pass. Stone tablets surmount this fence, telling us, in Latin and in Greek, that no outsider may go further, under penalty of death.

Beyond this fence we climb fourteen stairs and come to a flat terrace, about ten yards wide. We then mount more steps and come to the gate leading to the inner court. There are many gates to this inner court on the north and south; but we enter through the great double gate in the east. The other gates are covered with gold plates, but the great eastern gate has no covering, for it is made of costly bronze, that shines even brighter than gold. It is called "Nicanor's Gate," after a rich Egyptian Jew who presented it to the Temple as a gift. The golden plates on the other gates are also a gift, from a rich Alexandrian Jew.

Nicanor's Gate is so large that when it is shut every evening twenty men are needed to push together the heavy doors and to shove the bolts and bars into the stone threshold. In all, two hundred men are employed in the daily opening and shutting of the gates of the Temple.

We pass through Nicanor's Gate into the inner court, the Court of the Women, which is a square area of over two hundred feet square. Men may enter the Court of the Women, but women may not enter the Court of the Men, which is further on in the Temple. High balconies, however, are provided for the women, and from these they can observe the ceremonies in the inner courts. There are four rooms in the corners of the Court of the Women, open to the skies. One is for the use of *Nazarites*, men under oath not to touch wine, nor cut their hair. The second room is a storehouse for wood. Here sit those priests who are disqualified, because of physical defects, from service at the altar of the Temple. But they may do other work, and they sit examining the pieces of wood designed for the altar, discarding those with even the tiniest worm-hole, for only perfect wood may be used in the fire of the altar. The third room is reserved for lepers who have come to the Temple to become cleansed. In the fourth room wine and oil are stored.

We pass through the Court of the Women and come to a flight of fifteen steps, built in the form of an amphitheatre. Above these stairs is the wall that separates the women from the Court of the Men. We go through another gate and enter the Court of the Men, which encircles the Temple on three sides. The greatest and loveliest sight that a Jew can behold now appears before us: the great altar of uncut stones and behind it the House of God itself. The altar is quite large, and has four points that are like horns. An eternal fire burns there, a fire that must never be extinguished.

Only half of the Court of the Men is available for the use of laymen. A low fence runs through the center of the court and only the priests may venture beyond it. This area is known as the Court of the Priests.

On both sides of the Court of the Priests are the treasuries of the Temple. To the right of the altar is the slaughter area, with twenty-four rings to tether the sacrificial animals. Behind are eight small posts, with three rows of hooks on each one, to hang the slain animals, and eight marble tables on which the inners of the sacrifices are washed. In addition there are tables for the altar utensils and for the dismembered bodies of the animals. There is also a bronze wash-basin in which the priests bathe their hands and feet.

Along the walls of the Court of the Priests are built several halls: the hall in which the Sanhedrin meets; the hall in which the High Priest lives the week before Yom Kippur; the rooms in which the priests dress and bathe, and various other halls and rooms.

Through a very high opening, without doors, the priests go from their court to the *Ulam*, the porch of the House of God. Another door leads from the porch, which is beautifully decorated in gold, into the front room of the House of God. The door is open, but a heavy, colored curtain hangs over it. Over this door hangs a gigantic, golden grape-vine. It is supported by cedar balconies and spreads its branches under the cornices of the porch. Rich Jews coming from distant lands make contributions to this vine, a gold grape or a gold leaf or such, till it seems as if the vine will break beneath the mass of the golden fruit hanging from it.

Twice a day priests pass through the porch and into the sanctuary for the daily services. They pass into a long room, the walls of which are decked in gold, but which is dark and window-less. The only light comes from the golden Menorah, in which seven oil wicks burn. Opposite the Menorah stands the golden table bearing the twelve loaves of showbread. Between these two objects stands the golden altar on which incense is burned twice a day.

Beyond the Anteroom is the Holy of Holies, the greatest

sanctuary of all, separated from the rest of the Temple by two drapes. Only one day a year, on Yom Kippur, are these hangings removed for the entry of the High Priest. It is a pitch-black, empty room. The only object in the room is a stone, three fingers high, which is called the "Foundation-stone." [149]

The entrance of the High Priest into the Holy of Holies was the main event in the ceremonies and ritual of "the Great Day."

The High Priests...During the first three hundred and fifty years of the second Temple the high priesthood belonged to one family and descended by succession. This family based its superiority on the fact that it descended from Zadok, the first priest in the Temple of Jerusalem when it was built by Solomon. The line extended thus until the time of Antiochus Epiphanes.

When the Hasmoneans won over the Greek forces they became the rulers of the Jewish country. But it was not possible, in those days, to just set one's self up as ruler over the Jews. Rulership was vested in the High Priest. But since the Hasmoneans were of the priestly caste, they had no trouble on that score. They founded a new dynasty of High Priests and set on their own heads a double crown, that of the High Priest and that of the King.

After the fall of the Hasmonean kingdom, when Palestine became a province of Rome, the high priesthood became more of a political than a religious position. The Romans refused to permit the descent of the high priesthood from father to son, for they were unwilling to set up a dynasty of High Priests. For this reason a new High Priest was appointed at intervals. Not every priest could attain to this high position. There were, in Jerusalem, a few aristocratic priestly families, and members of these families were the regular candidates, securing the position through political influence or through bribery.[150] It obviously was worthwhile to become High Priest, for it was a position that brought power and riches. The High Priest of those days was officially the religious head of the Jewish people, the master of the Temple, and the leader of the Sanhedrin. As such he was the ruler of Jerusalem and of all Palestine, insofar as the Jews had autonomy under the Roman rule.

But despite the fact that the High Priests of those days were not spiritually great and the real spiritual leaders of the people were the scribes, the heads of the Pharisees, the observance of the service in the Temple was not weakened. On the contrary, the services were never carried out more precisely or with greater grandeur and impressiveness than in the period before the destruction of the Temple. And of all the services of the year there was none as richly mystical and impressive as the Yom Kippur service.

The Day before Yom Kippur...The High Priest stands at the eastern gate of the Temple in the morning. The various animals that he will offer are led before him for final examination before the service of sacrifice.

Jews prepare themselves for the Great Day. They beg forgiveness of each other and remind themselves of sins they committed in the course of the year; they are regretful and penitent. But one, the High Priest, makes greater preparations than all others. Religious awe fills his heart as he thinks of entering the Holy of Holies. He also fears that through some accident he may be disqualified. Should that happen, his understudy would have to conduct the services of "the Great

Day." The understudy is therefore also prepared and ready for the occasion.

Yom Kippur Eve...The sun is about to set. The daily Temple service is finished. A sanctified peace rests over the Mount of the Temple. Jews feast hugely in preparation for the coming fast. The High Priest, however, is not allowed much food, lest it make him sleepy. On this night he must not sleep. The learned sages of the Sanhedrin, who have been tutoring him all week in the order of the service, make him vow not to depart from it in any detail.[151] They turn him over to the elders of the priesthood and leave. These priests lead him to the room of the incense-makers, where he practices gathering incense into his palms, so that they be full, and yet not overflow.

Yom Kippur Night...Various means are used to keep the High Priest from falling asleep. Portions of the latter books of the Bible are read to him, or, if he can, he reads and gives interpretations. These books of the Bible are less known than others and are therefore calculated to arouse more interest and drive away the desire for sleep. Should the High Priest still drowse, a group of young priests stand about him, snapping their fingers, and he is made to stand with his bare feet on the cold stone. They also sing Psalms to him. In one way or another he is kept awake.

The respectable and pious Jews of Jerusalem also stay awake that night, as do many in the provinces outside of Jerusalem.[152]

Ordinarily, preparations for the Temple service begin at dawn, but for this occasion the preparations are started in the middle of the night. Long before the cock has crowed, the court of the Temple is filled with people. In the meantime priests, stationed on the roof of the Temple, look for the first light of dawn. When the light is sufficient for them to see Hebron between the hills to the southeast they call out, "The light of morning has reached Hebron." And the service begins.

Attiring the High Priest...First the High Priest is conducted to the bath house. The High Priest bathes himself five times on this day; in addition, he washes his hands and feet ten times. These bathings and washings are performed in a special room in the Temple, near the Court of the Priests. The first bath, however, the one in the morning, takes place outside of the innermost court, beyond the water tower.

Each time he bathes a curtain of byssus (costly linen) is spread between him and the people. He doffs his ordinary raiment, bathes, dons the golden vestments, washes his hands and feet in a golden basin, and starts the daily sacrifice. He performs it in his golden robes, and the congregation stands enthralled at the sight. From their point of observation, the High Priest is a glowing spectacle, with his golden diadem, the precious gems on his breast, and the golden bells which hang on the hem of his purple robe and which tinkle with every movement that he makes.

He then goes into the anteroom in order to burn the incense on the golden altar, and to put the lamps of the Menorah in order. This ends the regular daily service; now comes the special Yom Kippur service, for which the High Priest dons garments of white linen.

He is led to the bathhouse near the Court of the Priests. He washes his hands and feet, divests himself of his ceremonial golden robes, bathes himself, puts on the garments of white linen, and again washes his hands and feet.

The Temple Service...And now, when the High Priest enters the court in simple white, he makes an even stronger impression on the assemblage than when he appeared in gold. The young bull that is destined for the sacrifice stands ready between the porch and the altar. The High Priest lays his hands on the bull's head and recites the first confessional:

"I beseech Thee, O Lord! I have sinned, I have been iniquitous, I have transgressed against Thee, I and my household. I beseech Thee, O Lord, pardon the sins, iniquities and transgressions which I have committed against Thee, I and my household, as it is said: 'On this day shall atonement be made for you, to cleanse you; from all your sins shall ye be clean before the Lord.'"

Three times in this prayer does the High Priest expressly pronounce the mystic and ineffable name of God, *Yhwh*. In all, he pronounces God's explicit name ten times during the Yom Kippur service.[153] And as the ineffable name of God is pronounced by the High Priest the assembled priests and worshipers prostrate themselves and call out, "Blessed be the Name, the glory of His kingdom forever and ever."

The first part of the special Yom Kippur service is held in the area between the porch of the Temple and the altar. The second part, which starts now, is performed on the eastern side of the altar, nearer to the assembled congregation.

The Sacrificial Goats...East of the altar two goats stand ready, with their heads toward the sanctuary. Both are of equal size, the same appearance, and cost an equal sum of money. In an urn next to them are two golden tablets, identical in every detail, except that one is inscribed, "For *Yhwh*," and the other is inscribed, "For *Azazel*."[154]

The white-robed High Priest proceeds to the eastern side

of the altar escorted by two priests. The priest who acts as his understudy walks to his right and on his left is the representative of the subdivision of priests appointed for the service on this day.[155] The High Priest shuffles the tablets in the urn, withdraws them, and places one on the head of each goat. He calls out, "A sin offering for *Yhwh*," and the congregation answers, "Blessed be the Name, the glory of His kingdom forever and ever."

It is a good omen if the tablet marked "For God" comes up in the High Priest's right hand. But in this period, year after year, the tablet marked "For *Azazel*," has come up in the right hand. Fear grips the heart of the people. And when the Jews learn of it they pray to the Almighty to help the Temple and the holy city.

When the lot is decided the High Priest ties a red sash on the horns of the *Azazel* goat, the scapegoat for the people. The other goat will be sacrificed to God. The scapegoat faces the assembled congregation who stare at him and await the ritual by which the sins of the people will be loaded upon him and he will be driven out, deep into the wilderness.

This ends the second part of the Yom Kippur service and now begins the third and most awesome service of the day, when the High Priest enters the Holy of Holies.

In the Holy of Holies . . . The High Priest goes back to the area between the porch and the altar, where the young bull is tethered, places his hands on the animal and once more confesses, reciting the same prayer as before. But now he also confesses the sins of the priests, and when he says, "I and my household," he adds "and the sons of Aaron, thy holy tribe."

Again the assembly prostrates itself and calls out, "Blessed be the Name, the glory of His kingdom forever and ever."

After this second confessional the High Priest slaughters the bull, gathering the blood in a basin which he hands to a waiting priest. It is the duty of this priest to keep stirring the blood, so that it does not coagulate.

The High Priest walks up the ramp leading to the altar and fills a golden fire-pan with burning coals; he then pours handfuls of incense into a golden ladle and, in this way, with the fire-pan in his right hand and the ladle in the left, he proceeds slowly into the Holy of Holies. He enters between the two drapes and, apart from everybody, he stands in the somber dimness of the Holy of Holies, barely illuminated by the burning coals in the fire-pan.

Filled with pious awe and fear, the High Priest places the fire-pan on the "Foundation-stone" and pours the incense upon it. The Holy of Holies is filled with smoke. The High Priest retires into the anteroom and there offers prayers for the coming year. The people in the court pray at the same time, quietly, but with great fervor.

Finally, the High Priest emerges from the House of God and enters the court. Great relief is felt by all present, for it is a fearful thing, all believe, to be so near to God, in His holy dwelling.

There is no rest for the High Priest. He takes the basin of blood from the priest who is still stirring it, goes back into the Holy of Holies, and sprinkles the blood upon the drape, once above and seven times below, counting as he sprinkles: "One, one and one, one and two, one and three, one and four, one and five, one and six, one and seven." He counts the sprinkling he made above with every one he makes below. He then returns to the anteroom and places the basin on a golden stand.

The goat destined as a sacrifice for God is now brought to

him. He slaughters it, gathers the blood in a basin, enters the Holy of Holies for the third time, sprinkles the blood and goes back into the anteroom, where he places the basin on another golden stand. He then sprinkles the drape from the outside, first with the blood of the bull, and then with the blood of the goat. He then mixes the blood of the two animals and sprinkles it on the golden incense-altar in the anteroom; what is left he pours on the cornerstone of the great altar outside.

The Scapegoat . . . The ceremonial for forgiveness of sins committed against the sanctuary is thus completed, and the symbolic ceremony of transferring the sins of the entire people to the *Azazel* is now begun. This ceremony is not as awesome as the preceding ritual. There is, in fact, an undercurrent of joy, and the congregation is alive with interest.

The scapegoat has been standing all this time in the same place, and one would think he himself was waiting for the burden of sin to be placed upon him. The High Priest now approaches the goat and lays his hands upon him. As the representative of the Jewish people he now makes the third confessional, similar to the other two. But this time, instead of pronouncing, "I and my household and the sons of Aaron, Thy holy tribe," he says, "Thy people, the House of Israel." The High Priest faces the sanctuary throughout the three confessionals. But, as he pronounces the concluding words, "before the Lord ye shall be clean," he turns and faces the people as he recites, "Ye shall be clean."

Again the worshipers prostrate themselves and call out, "Blessed be the Name, the glory of His kingdom forever and ever."

Now comes a lively and interesting scene. Priests lead the

scapegoat through a gate of the Temple and hand him over to a priest or Levite who had previously been selected. A great crowd forms about them shouting, "Hurry and go, hurry and go."

The goat is led to a specified spot about ten miles beyond the city, where a precipitious cliff overhangs a ravine. Prior to Yom Kippur ten booths were erected as stations along the way. Food and drink is available in each booth for the escorter of the scapegoat, for he may break his fast if the journey weakens him. But he never does break his fast. A group of Jews escort him from the Temple to the first booth, and in each booth there is somebody to meet him and escort him to the next booth. He is not escorted, however, all the way to the cliff, his escort stopping and watching from afar.

When man and goat come to the cliff the red sash is removed from the goat's horns and divided in two. One part is attached to the cliff and the other half tied to the horns of the goat, which is then pushed over the cliff, life passing out of him as he falls into the ravine.[156]

The news that the scapegoat is in the wilderness is quickly brought to the High Priest. Meanwhile he has sacrificed the young bull and the second goat on the altar; he now begins the reading of the Torah.

The Torah Reading...The Yom Kippur service is almost, but not quite, completed. There are various items the High Priest must still attend to. First he chants with great pomp those portions of the Pentateuch that deal with Yom Kippur. This takes place in the synagogue which is in the Temple.[157]

The sexton[158] of the synagogue presents the Torah-scroll to the head of the synagogue; he presents it to the High Priest's understudy who, in turn, presents it to the High

Priest. The High Priest reads two portions of Leviticus from the scroll. He reads and the congregation listens attentively reflecting on how fine the words sound as they are chanted by the High Priest.

He rolls the scroll together and, holding it to his heart, he says to the congregation, "Much more than this, that I have read to you, is inscribed here." He then recites the portion of the Book of Numbers that he learned by heart, says eight benedictions, and the ceremony of the reading of the Torah is completed.

The Service Ends...The High Priest then washes his hands and feet, doffs the white linen garments, bathes himself, dons the golden robes, again washes his hands and feet, and offers the *Musaf* (the additional) sacrifice for Yom Kippur. Again he washes his hands and feet, removes his golden robes, bathes himself, puts on the white robes, washes his hands and feet again, and enters the Holy of Holies for the last time to remove the fire-pan and the ladle.

This concludes the special Yom Kippur service. But the High Priest has further duties. He now performs the regular service which is performed daily in the Temple, toward sunset. For this he again goes through the washing and bathing process, changing back to the gold robes, washes his hands and feet again and enters the anteroom, where he burns the incense on the golden altar and lights the lamps of the Menorah.

Now the High Priest's work is really ended for the day. For the last time he washes, changes his golden robes for his everyday clothing, and sets out for his home. But not alone. A crowd of people escort him, pushing and shoving for the honor of walking close to him.

Towards Evening...All is lively and joyous on the streets of Jerusalem. People go about, light of heart after the fast, and prepare themselves for the joyous holiday of Sukkos. Every household is festive. But the greatest festivity takes place at the home of the High Priest. A group of priests of the higher caste and the aristocrats of the city have come to greet him. The house is full, and all partake of a luxurious feast, and frolic till late in the night.

After the Destruction...The destruction of the second Temple brought an end to the Yom Kippur service as practiced in the Temple, with its symbolic rituals of forgiveness. But Yom Kippur did not lose its importance in Jewish life. Even before the Temple was destroyed Yom Kippur no longer depended entirely on the High Priest and the special service that he conducted in the sanctuary.

Had Yom Kippur remained a holiday on which the High Priest alone begged forgiveness for the sins of the people, it would never have survived the destruction of the Temple. But Yom Kippur had already gone through a long period of evolution; the people continually took an ever greater part in the observance of the day. Thus its importance grew outside of the Temple.

It has already been stated that while the Temple still stood, in the last period before its destruction, Yom Kippur had become the Great Day for Jews of the entire world, a day of fasting and prayer in the synagogues. The day continued this character after the destruction of the Temple. There was no longer the special Temple service nor a High Priest to act as intermediary between man and God. But Jews continued to observe the day, without any intermediary, addressing themselves directly to God through prayers and confessions.

Characteristic of the attitude of the Jews in Palestine to Yom Kippur after the destruction of the Temple is the following tale from the Talmud:

Rabban Jochanan ben Zakkai, together with his pupil, Rabbi Joshua, once stood gazing at the ruins of the Temple. And Rabbi Joshua said, "Woe to us, that the place where Jews were forgiven for their sins is destroyed." To which Rabban Jochanan answered, "My son, regret it not. We have another medium, just as good, for the forgiveness of sin. It is: Do good to mankind. For it is written: 'I desire mercy and not sacrifice.' " [159]

In this way Jews at the time of the second destruction of Jerusalem were prepared, through their religious ideals, and with the religious ceremonies they had evolved for their homes and the synagogue, to carry on without the Temple service.

But Jews did not forget the Yom Kippur ritual of the Temple and the remembrance of it forms the most interesting part of the Yom Kippur services. The order of the Temple ceremonial is recited, and made dramatic and vivid in its rendition by the cantor and the congregation. The three confessionals of the High Priest are recited, the sprinkling of the blood is counted, the congregation prostrates itself and, in its thoughts, relives the ceremonial of Yom Kippur in the Temple.

The religious content of the day became so profound, and the synagogue ritual became so rich, that Yom Kippur has remained till this very day the greatest day in the Jewish year.

xvi. Days of Awe = IN EASTERN EUROPE

Elul Approaches...The Days of Awe do not arrive suddenly and unexpectedly; people start preparing for them a long time in advance. The attitude during the entire month of Elul is already an earnest and sober one, and all feel that soon the solemn days, the days of penitence will begin.

But undercurrents of the coming holidays are felt even earlier, are felt on the Sabbath at which the blessing for the coming New Moon, that of Elul, is recited. Every Sabbath before a New Moon is a special Sabbath in the synagogue. But the Sabbath before Elul is exalted above all the other pre-New Moon Sabbaths. One knows that very soon, in just a few days, the call of the Shofar will be heard and when the cantor, holding the Torah-scroll, calls out "Rosh Chodesh Elul," the ring of his voice is far different from the tone he uses on other Sabbaths on which he announces Rosh Chodesh.

The first real sign that the Days of Awe are nearing appears on the day before the New Moon of Elul. The day before each New Moon is called a minor Day of Atonement. There are no more than three or four very pious old Jews in town who observe all these minor days of atonement. But the day before Elul is different. Many Jews fast on that day, and there is a big congregation present for the afternoon prayers, to recite *S'lichos*, prayers of supplication and confessions; it really feels like Yom Kippur.

On the second day of Rosh Chodesh, the first of Elul, at the end of the morning services the blowing of the shofar begins, after which Psalm xxvII is recited. The shofar call is a signal that the time for penitence is approaching, and sober earnestness descends on all.

The Days of Elul... The life of the town goes on as ordinarily. But it is easy to see that the Jews are deliberately more pious. Certain petty sins, common the year round, are now guarded against. People pray more carefully and with greater fervor, and those with ample time remain in the *Bes ha-Midrosh*, the House of Study, to recite Psalms, to study a chapter of Mishnah, or other religious and devotional books. For these are days, it is said, when the very fish in the stream shiver with foreboding.

The solemnity of the month of Elul is more in evidence in the cemetery than anywhere else, for these are the days on which one visits the graves of his ancestors. Women, for the most part, come and weep and bare their hearts to those who were once near and dear to them, and who now lie between the markers of stone and wood. Some stand at the headstones and weep silently; others, however, moan and howl hysterically and are heard far afield. There is a special book of prayers written for this occasion, but most of the women lack the education to pick out the appropriate ones. There are, however, a couple of learned women in town, and they recite these prayers at the cemetery with the mourning women. It is understood that they are to be paid for their trouble. Some of the women are not content just to mourn at the cemetery. They "measure the field." That is, they pace about the cemetery with a spool of cotton which they unroll, and with which they span the ground. This cotton is then taken to the candle-maker, who uses it as wicks for candles, which the women donate to the synagogue.

For the children it is, in many ways, a very pleasant period.

For the days from the middle of Elul till after Sukkos are vacation days between the summer and fall semesters, and school is open only half-days. But they do not get much satisfaction from their freedom. The sober air of penitence that rules over the adults has its influence on them. Their conscience forbids them to frolic and joy. The children also know that life hangs in the balance now, and the time is coming when the fate of every man will be judged and inscribed in heaven.

S'lichos...The awesome atmosphere becomes even more pronounced, and still more circumspect becomes the attitude of the townspeople during the week of *S'lichos* (supplications) which begins on the Sunday before Rosh Hashonoh. On that day all rise very early, while it is still pitch dark outside. Since the hour of arising is much earlier than usual, the beadle goes about the town with a lantern in his hand, knocking on windows with a wooden mallet, waking the Jews for *S'lichos*. There are some pious people in town, women as well as men, who fast on this day.

Even the school-boys, the older ones, rise early to attend the *S'lichos* services in the House of Study. They attend only on the first day's services and not on the succeeding days with the exception of the day before Rosh Hashonoh.

The Day before New Year...Old and young alike rise early on the day before Rosh Hashonoh to attend the special *S'lichos* services of that day, even earlier in the morning than they did for the first *S'lichos*. Some take a glass of tea and a cracker before going to the synagogue; that is allowed because it is still night. Afterwards eating is forbidden, for on this day all fast till noon. Afternoon services are held at one o'clock, and after that all go home for a light lunch.

Many Jews go to the public bath, even before breaking their fast. It is also customary to go to the bath on the day preceding other festivals. There are even certain Jews who go to the bath every Friday, provided it is heated. Bathing, however, on the day before Rosh Hashonoh, and also on the day before Yom Kippur, is a religious precept. It is especially creditable to immerse oneself in the ritual bath on those days.

Rosh Hashonoh Eve...In the synagogue the atmosphere is festive for the evening services, but the prayers are chanted with the intonation associated with the Days of Awe, which induces a highly religious attitude. After the services all wish one another "A Festive Holiday," and add, in Hebrew, "May you be inscribed and sealed for a good year"; but everyone does not know Hebrew well and the words are difficult to pronounce, so many content themselves with just saying simply, "A good year."

The table is festively arrayed when the worshipers arrive home from the synagogue. On the table is a small jar filled with honey, an omen for a sweet year; this is spread on the first slice of bread eaten. In many homes some new fruit of the season is served. This fruit is generally grapes, for all other fruits have been tasted in the course of the summer. But grapes come from distant, warm countries and are expensive, so not all can afford to partake of this luxury. Pious Jews, therefore, deny themselves one certain fruit all summer long, in order to be able to make the special blessing over it at the Rosh Hashonoh table on the second evening.[160]

In the Synagogue...Rosh Hashonoh is not a home festival. Meals are eaten in the home, but the entire observance and ceremonial is in the synagogue. For this reason the cantor plays the chief role in the festival, and the better his voice, the more involved his trills and arpeggios, the greater is the satisfaction one receives from the festival.

Services start very early in the morning and do not end till after midday. All the prayers are recited and chanted with pious fervor. But there are, in addition, certain exalted moments when the spirit that fills all hearts on the Days of Awe expands and religious feelings are raised to the highest pitch. Such an exalted moment comes at the blowing of the shofar. Psalm XLVII is recited seven times; then all quiets down. The hearts of the worshipers beat fast; and when the trumpeter calls out "Blessed be," the beginning of the benediction, a tremor of awe and fear passes through the congregation.

The Most Exalted Moment... The greatest and most exalted moment of the services comes when the Ark of the Torah is opened and the chant of *Un'saneh Tokef* begins. An unnatural fear grips the hearts of the worshipers. They pull their prayer shawls over their heads and recite the words in a loud voice, with tears and sobs. The sobbing and weeping is much louder in the women's section. The women weep oceans of tears as they read the simple, yet expressive words that tell how God judges the world on that fearful and solemn day:

"We will declare the greatness and the holiness of this Day, for thereon Thy kingdom is exalted, Thy throne established in mercy, and Thou judgest in truth. It is true that Thou art the judge; Thou reprovest; Thou knowest all; Thou bearest witness, recordest and sealest: Thou also rememberest all things that seem to be forgotten; and all that enter the world must pass before Thee, even as the shepherd causes his sheep to pass under his rod. Thou numberest and countest, and visitest every living soul, appointest the limitations of all Thy creatures, and recordest the sentence of their judgment:

"How many are to pass away, and how many are to come into existence; who are to live and who are to die; who are to accomplish the full number of their days, and who are not to accomplish them; who are to perish by water and who by fire; who by the sword and who by hunger; who by earthquake and who by plagues; who shall have repose and who shall be troubled; who shall be tranquil and who shall be disturbed; who shall be prosperous and who shall be afflicted; who shall become poor and who shall become rich; who shall be cast down and who shall be exalted."

The moans die down and the congregation calms itself somewhat at the words: "But Repentance, Prayer and Charity avert the evil decree."

However, the prayer does not end with this. There still comes a sharp reminder of the shortness and impotence of man's life:

"How weak is man! He comes from the dust and returns to the dust; must toil for his sustenance; passes away like withered grass, a vanishing shadow, a fleeting dream.

"But Thou, O God, art eternal; Thou art King everlasting."

Tashlich...There is no sleeping or promenading after the midday meal. As soon as dinner is finished, the worshipers return to the synagogue to recite Psalms and conduct the afternoon services. And after that comes the *Tashlich* custom. The entire town, young and old, dressed in festive array, goes out to a near by stream, men and women at different points on the river, and recite the *Tashlich* prayers, so named from the passage in Micah read there which begins with the word, *v'sashlich* (and Thou wilt cast [all their sins into the depths of the sea]).

There is a slight respite after this ceremony, during which

tea is served, and a festive feeling rules. But then people rush back to the synagogue and chant Psalms again, until it is time for evening prayers.

With the exception of the *Tashlich* ceremony, the entire ritual of the day is repeated on the morrow.

The Days of Penitence... The day after Rosh Hashonoh is a fast day, the Fast of Gedaliah, in memory of the death of Gedaliah, son of Ahikam.[161] But people do not care about the historical origin of the day; it is for them just one of the many fasts between the first day of *S'lichos* and Yom Kippur.

The first ten days of Tishri, which include both Rosh Hashonoh and Yom Kippur, are known as the "The Ten Days of Penitence." The days between the two holidays are already colored by the solemnity of Yom Kippur. The very pious fast till midday every day of this period, with the exception of the Sabbath and the day before Yom Kippur, days on which it is forbidden to fast.

The Saturday between the two holidays is called *Sabbath Shuvoh,* from the first word of the portion of the Prophets which is read on that day.[162] This Sabbath is observed much more strictly than are ordinary Sabbaths, and the rabbi delivers a long sermon before the afternoon prayers, in which he endeavors to arouse the congregation to whole-hearted penitence.

Kaporos... The second day before Yom Kippur has special significance in that it is the day of *Kaporos* (see p. 164). There is no specified time for this ceremony; some observe it in the afternoon, some early in the evening, some late at night and others the following morning. The men use roosters for the ceremony and the women hens. When the family is large it is rather expensive to supply a fowl for each member of the family, so money is used instead. Those who use money for the ceremony generally perform it the morning before Yom Kippur.

The homes are unusually noisy. The fowls, their legs tied, cluck and crow at the tops of their voices. It generally happens, too, that a rooster gets excited and begins to run and fly all over the house, despite his bound feet, and there follows a long struggle to subdue him.

First the fowl, or the money, is held in the hand and everyone reads selections from certain Psalms, beginning with the words, "Sons of Adam." Then the fowl is circled about the head nine times, the following being recited at the same time: "This is instead of me, this is an offering on my account, this is in expiation for me; this rooster, or hen, shall go to his, or her, death (or, this money shall go to charity), and may I enter a long and healthy life."

The greatest ado is in the yard of the *shochet*, the ritual slaughterer, where the *Kaporos* are taken to be slaughtered after the above ceremony has taken place. Only the poorer Jews carry their *Kaporos* to the *shochet*, however. The well-to-do have the *shochet* call at their homes and dispatch the fowls there, for there should be no time lost between the *Kaporos* ceremony and the slaughtering of the fowl. This can be done only when the *shochet* is present at the ceremony. The ritual is delayed in the well-to-do homes until the *shochet* arrives, sometimes late in the night. This has its compensations, however, for at that hour the fowls are asleep and easy to take off the roost.

The *Kaporos* ceremony is so universal in its appeal that it has crept into the language of the people. When one stares at a thing unknowingly, it is said of him that he looks like a rooster at the words "Sons of Adam." Should there be a great fuss and ado somewhere in town it is said that the stir is as great as at the *Kaporos* ceremony.

The Day before Yom Kippur...The day before Yom Kippur has a double character. It is the day on which Jews prepare for Yom Kippur, and it is also a holiday in its own right. Exactly as it is a religious commandment to fast on Yom Kippur, so is it a religious requirement to eat heartily the day before.

The Jewish population is busy all day. Immediately after the morning services the ceremony for the release from vows is observed. Any personal vow, affecting only the vower himself, that he regrets, can be declared void by one ordained teacher or by three laymen. Some have already attended to the release the day before Rosh Hashonoh, but many wait for this day. The ceremony is performed in groups, for, as said before, a court of at least three must be present. The pleader stands and recites the text relating to the release from vows, and the other three sit and listen, answering him according to the text. When he is through he sits down and becomes one of the court, another rising and reciting from the text, and so on, till the entire group is finished.

Some Jews perform the *Kaporos* ceremony on the morning of this day. There are also some who make it an occasion for visiting the cemetery. The pious go to the bath-house to bathe in the ritual pool, some even making a confessional in the water. The holiday feast is eaten about eleven or twelve o'clock; it consists of soup, *kreplech* (a three-cornered pastry filled with meat), and carrot-pudding. The meal is served early, to allow time for the next meal, the final one before the fast.

The Afternoon...At about two in the afternoon people begin to go to the synagogue for *minchoh*, afternoon services. Not all pray together. When a group of ten assembles a service begins. This occurs several times during the afternoon.

The older and more pious Jews of the town go through *Malkus*, the symbolic ceremony of being flogged for sins committed. There is one flogger for the entire town, a certain poor man who does it regularly, year after year; he gets coins from each one he flogs and this augments his yearly income. It is said that in former days there were more pious people so that many Jews acted as floggers on the day before Yom Kippur and barely had time to finish their work.

The flogger appears in the synagogue at the beginning of the afternoon services, a leather lash in his hand. He spreads some hay on the floor near the door. The elders, wearing their overcoats, stretch out on the hay face down and make a confessional, while the flogger strikes the coat lightly with his lash, reciting a prescribed sentence three times (Psalm LXXVIII, 38). The sentence consists of thirteen words which, repeated three times, makes thirty-nine, the number of lashes inflicted upon sentenced criminals in olden days. The flogger races through his ritual so fast that the pious Jew receiving the lashes barely has time to finish his confessional.

Long tables are set up in the corridor of the synagogue, bearing alms-plates for the various institutions and charities of the community. Each member of the community pays his congregational dues after the afternoon services and distributes coins in the various plates. At the door are many paupers, townspeople, and strangers, and all who pass give them alms.

Yom Kippur Eve...The sun falls lower and lower in the heavens. It is time for the evening meal, the last one before the fast, at which the rooster of the *Kaporos* ceremony and soup made from it is eaten. After the meal the blessing is repeated accompanied by tears and sighs. Then wishes for the coming year are expressed, and all rush off to the synagogue, the men in prayer-shawls and white robes, the women in white dresses.

All is quiet and peaceful in the town. Not a living soul is visible in the streets. All are in the synagogue. Only the older girls and younger children have been left at home. The older girls stand with prayer books in their hands and beat their breasts in prayer, and watch the huge, twenty-four hour candle burning on the table. Each family has at least two of them, one for the dead, which is taken to the synagogue, and one for the living, which burns at home.

The synagogue is crowded. Candles glow everywhere, wherever there is room to put one. Lamps and pendant candelabra gleam overhead, casting additional light on the crowded congregation, which stands praying and shaking in white robes and white *talesim* (prayer-shawls); the worshipers beat their breasts and weep, shouting their prayers over the sobs and screams which come from the women's section.

The most solemn and exalted moment of the Yom Kippur Eve services comes when the cantor sings *Kol Nidre*. As soon as he begins the well-known chant, an air of solemn and exalted absorption falls on the congregation. A deep sadness pervades the melody, but it imparts, at the same time, warmth and tenderness, and arouses all the hidden religious feelings and longings of man.

The Temple Service...A second tense moment in the Yom Kippur service comes in the prayers of the next day when the order of the Temple Service is recited and sung; through poetic descriptions and beautiful melodies, sung by the cantor and congregation in unison, the Temple Service is dramatically relived.

There is life and stir in the synagogue when the time comes for this prayer. The cantor sings, but not alone; the worshipers join him in a wordless, exalted melody. And when he mentions the prostration in the court of the Temple, all throw themselves to the ground and bury their faces, exactly as did their ancestors in the Temple in Jerusalem when they heard the High Priest call out the ineffable Name of God.

Afternoon and Evening...A third exalted moment comes at the *N'iloh* or concluding prayers of Yom Kippur. The word means closing, and it originally meant the closing of the gates of the Temple. But it was interpreted to mean the closing of the gates of heaven, when one has the final opportunity to do penance whole-heartedly and to plead for a successful year.

It is an extraordinary moment. The sun is already setting, and shadows begin to fall. The great Yom Kippur candles are almost burned down. The congregation stands, weakened from the long fast and arduous prayers. This is the end. In a moment, a man's fate will be sealed.

Pale stars begin to appear in the sky. The shofar is blown, one long, resounding *t'kioh*. And the trumpet call is answered with the cry and hope that next year will find them all in Jerusalem. With lightened spirits they recite the evening prayers. Yom Kippur is over. If it is a clear evening, the people do not rush home to eat. First they recite the appropriate blessing for the appearance of the New Moon.

Pious Jews partake of the barest amount of food necessary and then begin preparations for the building of the *Sukkoh*, the booth for the *Sukkos* holiday. Only after they have observed this religious precept do they really sit down to the feast that breaks their fast.

Worshipers arise earlier than usual on the morning after Yom Kippur. They do this so that Satan will have no cause to argue before God that, once Yom Kippur is over, Jews become lax and are too lazy to get up for the morning services.

New Year Greetings...One of the main observances of the Jewish New Year is the expression of the wish that one's fate be inscribed and sealed in heaven for a successful and happy year. This wish is expressed both personally and through cards, which bear the inscription, *L'shonoh Tovoh Tikosevu V'sechosemu* (may you be inscribed and sealed for a good year). These cards are called, for short, *L'shonoh Tovohs*. Since the Jewish New Year stretches from Rosh Hashonoh till Hoshano Rabboh, the cards are sent throughout the period.

The text of this Jewish greeting for the New Year comes from the belief that God judges the entire world on Rosh Hashonoh and decrees the fate of all. This belief is first recorded in the literature of the *Tannaim*, a product of the second century. "All are judged on Rosh Hashonoh and their fate is sealed on Yom Kippur," are the words attributed to Rabbi Meir. This is amplified as follows:

"Three books are opened on Rosh Hashonoh. One is for the out-and-out wicked; a second for the truly righteous; and a third for those in between. The righteous are at once inscribed and sealed for life; the wicked for death; judgment on the middle group is suspended till Yom Kippur. Should one of that group attain merit during those days then he is inscribed for life; otherwise for death." [163]

It must not be thought, however, that this belief was created then, in the *Tannaitic* period.[164] The Babylonians held such a belief long before the very beginning of Jewish history. We must accept the fact, then, that this belief came to the

Jews from the Babylonians in olden days, even before the Babylonian Exile.[165] It is also true, however, that it took a long time before this belief was accepted by all Jews.

The ancient Babylonians believed that the fate of the world is decided anew in heaven every year. According to the religion of the Babylonians it was done not by one god, but at a meeting of all the gods, held yearly in a room in heaven called, "The Room of Fate." According to this belief, Marduk, chief of the gods, led this meeting and Nabu, god of wisdom and literature, and the messenger of the gods, acted as secretary, and recorded all things on tablets. It was he who carried with him the tablets of fate, on which the judgment for all was inscribed at the New Year.

We have here, in a Babylonian version, the Jewish idea of Rosh Hashonoh as a day of judgment. Various other Jewish observances were found amongst the Babylonians. For instance, in the New Year services in the Temple of Marduk, the god was declared king and creator of the world, and the High Priest of the temple recited the account of the creation of the world in front of an image of Marduk.

But, despite the fact that in this or that detail Jews were influenced by the Babylonians, Rosh Hashonoh has an entirely different content from the Babylonian New Year. When we compare the two New Years we first see clearly the unique and original road traveled by the Jews in their spiritual life. To do this we must first study the New Year festival of the Babylonians.

The Babylonians observed their New Year not in the fall, as did the Jews, but in spring, in the first days of Nisan, and the observance lasted about two weeks. This was the festival during which they celebrated the resurrection of Marduk and his wedding to the goddess, Sarpanitu. Marduk represented in himself the sun, or rather the eternal forces of nature through which the world is resurrected every spring after the slumber of the winter. Since Marduk did not represent spirituality, as did the Jewish God, but nature, which grows and multiplies, it is natural that the Babylonians celebrated on the New Year his marriage to a goddess. Not only Marduk, but the gods of all other peoples, with the exception of the Jews, had goddesses by their side.

The Babylonians began their New Year ceremonies with a dramatic presentation on earth of that which transpires in the heavens. They brought the images of all their gods to one room in Marduk's temple, a room which they designated as the "Room of Fate." The most important ceremony of their New Year was the religious procession in which they carried Marduk in his holy chariot through a certain street, a street which was lately uncovered in the excavations in Babylon.[166]

We can see, then, that Rosh Hashonoh has very little relationship to the Babylonian New Year. A much closer relationship exists between the Babylonian New Year and the Christian Easter, during which the resurrection of a demigod is celebrated.

Table Delicacies As Omens...It is an old Jewish custom to set sweets on the Rosh Hashonoh table and to avoid eating sour.[167] This presages the sweetness of the coming year, and no Jewish table lacks a dish of honey or syrup on Rosh Hashonoh, the day before Yom Kippur, and Sukkos. The sweet is spread on the first slice of bread with which the meal is started.

This custom is based on an ancient magical belief that every activity calls forth its counterpart. For instance, if one brings bread into a new dwelling, bread will never be lacking there; if one pours water at the beginning of the year, especially on an altar, there will be ample rain the coming year; and if one eats sweet dishes at the beginning of the year, sweetness will abide for the entire year. This is an old primitive belief, widespread amongst all peoples. A similar custom, based on the same principle, is to eat the head of some animal on Rosh Hashonoh, for a head represents greatness and leadership.[168]

The Shofar...There is no ceremony so characteristic of the Rosh Hashonoh festival as the blowing of the shofar. Even before the day was known as Rosh Hashonoh it was called, *Yom T'ruoh*, the day of the blowing of the shofar.

It has already been noted that not only on Rosh Hashonoh, the first day of Tishri, but on the first of every month, trumpets were blown. These trumpets were called *chatsotsros*, and were evidently artists' instruments, made of silver. The shofar, however, is a natural wind instrument, one of the oldest known to the world.[169]

In the old days the shofar was used as a musical instrument by Jews at various religious ceremonies, but, its most important use was to intimidate the enemy, to declare war, and, in general, to make proclamations to the people.[170]

The origin of the custom of blowing the shofar on the first of every month, and especially loudly and alarmingly on the first day of the seventh month, is not entirely clear. We have to take for granted that this custom once was connected with the New Moon ceremonies and was bound up with various other ancient conceptions and beliefs. Later new ideas and meanings were read into it.

The oldest reason for blowing the shofar is presented in the Pentateuch. There it is mentioned as a means of asking God to remember man.[171] This is a later interpretation of an old custom, the ancient meaning of which had been forgotten.

In still later times further symbolic thoughts were read into the custom of blowing the shofar. It had double importance for Philo, the Greco-Jewish philosopher, from both the national and universal viewpoints. In the first place, he said, the shofar was a reminder of the giving of the Torah. Secondly, he pointed out, the shofar was the signal given on the battlefield to advance and retire. Blowing the shofar is, therefore, a call of thanks to God, who halts the war between the nations and the struggle among the elements of nature, thus bringing peace and harmony to the world.[172]

The Talmud states that the shofar is blown in order to confuse Satan, so that he will not bring his charges against Jews before God on the day of judgment. Hearing so much shofar blowing, Satan believes that the Messiah has arrived and the end of his power on earth has come.[173]

Even later, in the Middle Ages, various interpretations and meanings continued to be given regarding the shofar. A historic reason for the blowing of the shofar on the first day of Elul was even figured out. It was declared that on the first day of Elul, Moses ascended Mount Sinai for the second time, and he blew the shofar as a reminder to Jews not to err a second time, and not to make another golden calf.[174] Originally, apparently, the shofar was blown only on the first day of Elul, as a signal of the approach of the month that precedes the days of penitence. It was only later that the custom of blowing it during the entire month of Elul was instituted.

Tashlich...The custom of going to a body of water on the first day of Rosh Hashonoh (or on the second day when the first day is Saturday) is usually explained on the basis of casting the sins into the depths of the water, expressed in the passage of Micah read there.[175] It is obvious that the custom did not grow out of the citation, but the passage was quoted because of the custom. How the custom originated was no longer known, nor was there any desire to know the origin. So a new meaning was sought for it, a meaning that would be in keeping with the Jewish spirit and Jewish belief. Such a meaning was found in a certain passage in Micah.

But this interpretation did not please all. It did not seem sensible, to some Jews, to go to a stream on Rosh Hashonoh because of a biblical phrase. They, therefore, evolved another interpretation, one even less tenable. According to this second interpretation, the reason for going to a stream on Rosh Hashonoh was explained as a reminder of Abraham's attempted sacrifice of Isaac.

In the Bible story of the sacrifice of Isaac there is no mention of a stream. The stream enters the story in the tales of the Midrash. The homiletical expounders of the Bible altered the tale considerably, and made of it a form of drama, based on a wager between God and Satan, such a wager as is found in the Book of Job.

According to this tale Satan wagered that Abraham would not stand the test made of him to offer his only son as a sacrifice; he therefore tried to hinder Abraham in every way. When he saw that Abraham was intent upon making the sacrifice he turned himself into a deep stream, over which Abraham could not pass. On seeing this, God reproved the stream and it dried up.

For this reason, said the Gaon of Vilna and, centuries before him, the famous Rabbi Jacob ben Moses Halevi, known by his abbreviated name, Maharil, Jews go to a stream on Rosh Hashonoh, to remind God of the merits of Abraham and Isaac.

The Maharil was the greatest German rabbi at the end of the fourteenth and the beginning of the fifteenth centuries. He died at Worms in 1427. In the famous Book of Customs which carries his name, *Tashlich* is mentioned and strict orders are given that no crumbs of bread should be thrown to the fish when Jews go to the stream on Rosh Hashonoh.

We learn two things from this. First, that in that time, in the fourteenth century, it was already a German-Jewish custom to go to *Tashlich;* second, we see that an important part of the ceremony was the casting of crumbs into the water. Some Jews shake their pockets into the stream to this day at *Tashlich,* but it is not the customary usage. It is apparent, however, that in olden days all did it, and the shaking of the crumbs out of one's pocket was of paramount importance to the ceremony.

We see now that in the custom of *Tashlich* lies the ancient and primitive conception of giving the devil a gift, so that he will do no harm. It was the old belief that evil spirits dwell in streams, in wells and springs, and the best way to placate them is to offer them gifts.

That each stream is the home of a spirit who is lord of the stream is an old superstition that is still widespread. It is said of every stream that it demands a human victim each year, not the stream actually, but the evil spirit that dwells in it. Bread was, therefore, cast upon the water each year, in an effort to placate the evil spirit.

In addition to this idea of casting bread to the evil spirit, there is also the primitive idea behind *Tashlich* that a certain object or living thing could carry off with it, to the depths of the sea or to the furthest reaches of the wilderness, all sins and woes that beset man. In the *Tashlich* ceremony it is apparently the fish who are to accomplish this.

These two primitive conceptions were already inherent in the "scapegoat" idea, the goat sent to the *Azazel*, and they both appear in the *Tashlich* ceremony. Jews cast their bread on the waters and also shook their sins into the stream. This latter custom we learn from Rabbi Isaiah Hurwitz, who lived toward the end of the sixteenth century. This famed Rabbi and Kabbalist mentions in his book, *The Two Tablets of the Covenant*, that Jews practice the custom of shaking their pockets into the stream, thinking that they can thus shake off their sins. He protests violently against the custom, declaring that it is a desecration. His own interpretation of the *Tashlich* ceremony is that Jews go to a fish-bearing stream as a reminder that man himself is like a fish, and just as likely to be ensnared and trapped.

When the *Tashlich* custom originated amongst Jews is not certain. It is first discussed in the fourteenth century in the book of the aforementioned Maharil. But one is not to judge that the custom therefore arose in the fourteenth century. It is more likely that it was practiced earlier by certain Jews and that in the fourteenth century, it was first adopted by the mass of Jews. In fact, a form of *Tashlich*, which was combined with a form of *Kaporos*, was practiced by the Babylonian Jews in the time of the *G'onim*.

It was then the custom for Jews to weave baskets out of palm leaves and fill them with soil and earth, and to plant beans or peas in them fifteen or twenty-two days before Rosh Hashonoh. On the day before Rosh Hashonoh the basket was waved about the head seven times, the pronouncement being made that this was to serve as a substitute for the man, and the basket was then thrown into the river.[176]

Similar customs and habits have been found among other peoples. It is a custom in certain sections of India to cram all sins into a pot and throw it into the river. In Borneo and Siam it is the yearly custom to load everybody's sins and woes into a boat and to send it far out into the sea.[177]

In time, as was pointed out, *Tashlich* lost its ancient significance for Jews. New ideas and thoughts were attached to the custom and it became merely a symbolic ceremony.

Kaporos...Much older than the *Tashlich* ceremony is the ceremony of *Kaporos*, practiced with a fowl before Yom Kippur. It was already a widespread custom amongst the Jews of Babylonia in the tenth century. In that period richer Jews performed the ceremony with a ram, as a reminder of the ram of Isaac, but the rooster prevailed over the ram and was generally used.[178]

The *Kaporos* ceremony is to be found not only among Jews, but among many peoples, for an old belief, a primitive conception that was common to most peoples, forms the basis of the custom. The belief is that it is possible to transfer illness, pain, or sin to a living thing or to a lifeless object, as, for instance, a stone or stick. The belief still persists among primitive and semi-civilized people.

The primitive man does not differentiate between the spiritual and the physical. The primitive man, therefore, believes that just as it is possible to transfer a stone or a piece of wood from one man's back to another's, so can sin and pain be transferred. Prehistoric man understood nothing about the world around him, and attributed everything to the spirits which he believed resided everywhere. The stone and the tree, the stream and the swamp were all living things to him. In each resided a spirit, good or evil. He believed that by magical means he could influence the spirit, triumph over the manifestations of nature, and perform all kinds of miracles.

One of the magical procedures that primitive people used was to disturb the evil spirit, to get him to move to another place, no matter where, thus releasing the person to whom he had attached himself. In addition the primitive man thought out an endless number of rituals and enchantments to forestall ill fortune, sin, and woe by transferring them to a proxy, who would suffer in his stead.

The belief that inert objects can become the agent of man and absorb woe and misfortune is found also among Jews. When a costly dish breaks, people often comfort themselves by saying, "It doesn't matter. May it be a *Kaporoh* for all of us." It is believed that were some accident fated to happen to a member of the household the dish becomes the proxy of man, takes over the misfortune, and is thus broken.

Woe and misfortune and evil are much more easily transferred to living creatures than to inert objects, especially fowls; and of all fowls the rooster and the hen always played the greatest role in the superstitious beliefs of people the world over. A hen or rooster, when sacrificed, it was believed, would not only placate the evil spirits, but would also frighten them. Evil spirits shun the light, and it is the rooster who scares them away when he crows in the morning and announces the first light of day, according to popular belief. According to the ancient Persians the rooster was created for the purpose of driving the devils away.

There was another reason for ascribing a magical nature to the rooster—his big, red comb. The color red, in the superstition of many peoples, keeps the devils away. The devil, by the way, in Jewish lore, had the feet of a rooster.[179] And, as the rooster had magical powers, some of the same power was transferred to the hen.

The hen and the rooster to which man transfers his sins,

are therefore a sacrifice which is offered to the devil. They are also, at the same time, a means of frightening and chasing away the evil spirits. There are various conceptions regarding the color of the *Kaporos* fowl. The devil, as all know, is black. Many people believe that the magic used against the devil must be of the same color as the devil, and many others believe just the opposite. Jews, for instance, prefer to perform the ceremony with a white fowl. They, of course, interpreted the use of a white fowl, as a symbol of the release from sin. This is, however, a later interpretation; originally the whiteness of the fowl was obviously a means of frightening the black devil.

The custom of swinging the fowl about the head is part of this same primitive attempt to frighten the devil.[180]

The *Kaporos* ceremony, it seems, arose first among the Jews of Babylonia and from them it spread to the Jews of other lands. Many great rabbis warned the people against the practice of the custom. Rabbi Solomon ben Adrath, for instance, who lived in Spain in the thirteenth century, absolutely forbade the practice of the custom in his community, Barcelona. Nachmanides, too, branded the custom as one of idol-worshipers. Rabbi Solomon ben Adrath admitted, however, that, according to what he had heard, all the rabbis of Germany practiced the custom. Rabbi Joseph Caro, author of the *Shulchan Aruch*, the code of laws accepted by Orthodox Jews, branded *Kaporos* as a stupid custom. On the other hand, Rabbi Moses Iserles, in his "Remarks" to Joseph Caro's book, approved of the custom, which was, by that time (the sixteenth century), already strongly entrenched amongst the German and Polish Jews.

It seems that, before the widespread acceptance of *Tashlich*, *Kaporos* was not confined solely to the day preceding Yom

Kippur; in some places it was also performed the day before Rosh Hashonoh. Some pious Jews observed the ceremony twice, before Rosh Hashonoh and Yom Kippur.[181] It was only later that it was decided that *Tashlich* was to be performed before Rosh Hashonoh, and *Kaporos* before Yom Kippur. The Jews of Morocco, however, observe *Tashlich* on Yom Kippur.[182]

Jews sought to make every custom that they borrowed from other peoples distinctively Jewish and, bit by bit, they made *Kaporos* a distinctly Jewish custom. They sought to imbue it with a Jewish spirit, with a spirit of social morality. Among the heathen the *Kaporoh* fowl is always destined for the devil; among Jews, however, it is not thrown into a stream or driven into the wilderness but donated to the poor. Only a specified portion, the entrails, are cast on the roof to be carried off into the woods by the birds. Even into this custom, a moral interpretation was introduced. The hen, it was said, is a robber, eating and pecking at everybody's food. The fruits of this robbery, contained in the entrails, is what the birds carry off.[183]

Kol Nidre . . . The custom of having one's self flogged on the day before Yom Kippur is an ancient one. It was already practiced in the time of Rashi (died 1105).[184] The custom of seeking remission of vows on the day before Rosh Hashonoh or Yom Kippur is, on the other hand, of later origin.[185]

The reciting of Kol Nidre on Yom Kippur eve originated in the time of the *G'onim*.[186] It is not yet certain how it originated, nor why the Yom Kippur service should begin not with prayer, but with a plea for the remission of vows. We do know, however, the following facts about Kol Nidre: Kol Nidre is first mentioned in the ninth century. It was not recited in the Talmudic academies of Babylonia, because the *G'onim* were against it, labeling it a foolish custom. It was not whole-heartedly adopted in Spain either.[187] Originally it was available in two languages, Hebrew for the learned, and Aramaic for the masses. At first the text called for the remission of vows committed during the past year; and only later was the text changed to read: from this Yom Kippur to the next one.[188]

We do not know, with any certainty, in what time, in what country, or under what conditions Kol Nidre first appeared. But two things are certain: that it arose in oriental countries in the time of the *G'onim;* and that it had nothing to do, originally, with the secret Jews, with Jews upon whom baptism was forced, as was at one time presumed.[189]

In actuality, Kol Nidre plays a very small role in the Yom Kippur ceremonial. Not the words, but the melody of Kol Nidre is important. This wonderful and stirring melody has made such an imprint on the observance of Yom Kippur eve, that the evening is often referred to as "The Eve of Kol Nidre." The tune of Kol Nidre originated in a far different land and at a far later period than did the words. The melody first appeared among the Jews of southern Germany some time between the middle of the fifteenth and the middle of the sixteenth centuries.[190] The S'fardim and the Jews of the Orient do not use the melody of the Ashkenazic Jews, but recite it to the chant of *S'lichos* (Supplications).

For a number of centuries Kol Nidre dominated the Yom Kippur eve services. Only in the nineteenth century did the Reform Jews of Western Europe and America revolt against it. In some Reform communities a new prayer has been written to replace Kol Nidre, and in others the Yom Kippur eve services are begun with the reading of Psalm cxxx. This is not a new custom, however, but a reversion to an old custom. For, before Kol Nidre appeared, the Jews of Palestine used to start the Yom Kippur services with a reading from Psalms CIII and CXXX.

xviii. Sukkos = THROUGH THE AGES

Introduction...Sukkos, the Feast of Tabernacles, is the Jewish autumn festival. It begins on the eve of the fifteenth day of the Jewish month Tishri and is observed by Orthodox and Conservative Jews for nine days, of which the first two and last two are full holidays, the intervening five days being semi-holidays. In Palestine and amongst Reform Jews it is observed for only eight days. The first and eighth days are full holidays, with cessation from work, as originally prescribed.

It is the most joyous and the longest of the Jewish festivals, and was at one time considered the greatest Jewish festival. The seventh day of the holiday is known as *Hoshano Rabboh*, the eighth as *Sh'mini Atseres*, and the ninth as *Simchas Torah*. Each of these three days has its own special observance.

In Ancient Days...Sukkos is the joyous festival that the Jews of old observed in the Palestinian autumn, when they had finished the agricultural toil of the year.

When we observe Sukkos we go back to ancient days, when the Jews were peasants in their own land. At the autumn season after they had finished gathering all their crops from the fields and orchards, especially the grapes from the vineyards, they observed a great festival and were joyous before God. They thanked Him and praised Him for the abundance stored in barn and bin and offered prayers to Him that He send new rains for the coming year. For Sukkos, as stated before, was the festival of the beginning of the year in those days.[191]

This festival had, at one time, many names and titles. It was called *Chag ho-Osif*, the Festival of the Ingathering; also *Chag ha-Sukkos*, the Festival of the Booths. Its name was shortened, too, to *He-chog*, the Festival, and it was even called *Chag Adonoy*, God's Festival.[192] We can thus see that though Sukkos, officially, had the same status as Pesach and Shovuos, it played a much greater role in the life of the people than did the other two agricultural festivals; and when people said, "The Festival," without any other specifications, the great autumn festival, Sukkos, was meant.

In the older books of the Bible which tell of the life of the people in the time of the independent Jewish kingdom, the only festival given considerable attention is Sukkos.[193] Sukkos, then, was apparently the main festival of the Jews of those times.

We learn, from these old biblical books, that this festival was celebrated by the Canaanites, the older inhabitants of Palestine. We are told in the Book of Judges that the Canaanites of the town of Shechem observed a joyous festival after they had gathered the grapes from their vineyards, and that they ate, drank, and reveled in the temple of their god, Baal.[194]

When the Jews were settled in Palestine and lived on the fruits of the earth they also began the observance of this autumn festival. But, of course, they observed it in honor of their God, the God of Israel.

We do not know the exact day of the month and with what rites the Jews of very old times observed this autumn festival.[195] We do know, however, that it was the merriest time of the year, and that there was song and rejoicing throughout the land.

The Jews of that time were, on the whole, a joyous and festive people, and were very fond of wine and song. But at no season of the year did they drink and sing as much as they did during the autumn festival.[196] Along the trails of Palestine resounded the songs of the festive pilgrims who, together with all their household, entire caravans of Jewish peasants, wended their way to a sanctuary to observe the great festival and to rejoice before God. One led an ox, a second a sheep, and a third a goat to offer to God at the sanctuary, where they would recite prayers and sing hymns and dance in religious processions about the altar. If the peasant were poor, and could afford neither an ox nor a sheep, he presented a jar of flour as a meal-offering, or a bottle of wine for a libation on the altar.

According to the prescribed regulation, every male had to make the pilgrimage to a great sanctuary at all three great festivals. It was difficult for the Jewish peasant to leave his village at Pesach and Shovuos, since they were the seasons for cutting and threshing the grain. He was able to leave only at the autumn festival, when the crops had been gathered from field and orchard. He could then travel with an easy conscience to rejoice before God at a great sanctuary.[197]

In the days of the Jewish kingdom it was not necessary to go to Jerusalem when one wanted to make a pilgrimage to a great sanctuary. In many other cities temples were erected, perhaps not as gorgeous but much older than the Temple in Jerusalem, and the autumn festival was observed with grandeur at all of these temples.

In the very old days, before the founding of the Jewish kingdom, the most noted sanctuary was at Shiloh on Mount Ephraim, and we are told in the Book of Judges that the daughters of Shiloh would hold a dance procession in the vineyards in honor of the Festival of God. In another part of the Bible we are told of pilgrims from the hills of Ephraim who came to the sanctuary at Shiloh with their wives and children to observe the festival. They would slaughter their sacrificial animals there, and, in families, would dine on the meat of the sacrifices, and drink and revel. Elkanah, the father of Samuel, is presented to us as such a pilgrim, who made the journey to Shiloh yearly with all his household.[198]

When the Temple of Solomon was erected in Jerusalem Sukkos was the first festival observed there. The Bible tells us that all the heads of the tribes and the elders of Israel came to Jerusalem for the dedication of the Temple, and they came at "The Festival," the holiday of the fall. The observance of the festival is further mentioned in the time of the prophet Isaiah, about two hundred years after the reign of Solomon. On the eve of the holiday a great, festive crowd marched in a sacred procession. They sang hymns and played on pipes; with gay hearts they ascended the Mount of the Temple, to God, the Rock of Israel.[199]

It seems that both in the Temple in Jerusalem and in the other temples throughout the country those participating in the celebration often went beyond the limits in revelry and drink, and the festival often became a tumultuous, wild bacchanalia. The more serious-minded amongst the Jews protested against this character of the festival. The prophet Amos visited the temple at Beth-El during the autumn festival, and the revelry that he saw made such an unfavorable impression upon him that he condemned the sanctuary and the entire ritual of the festival. Hosea, who appeared as a prophet in the Kingdom of Israel a short time after Amos, also protested against the bacchanalia of the autumn festival. The same festivities doubtless took place in the Kingdom of Judah, for Isaiah, who was a prophet in Jerusalem, tells us that all, even priests and prophets, were drunk in the sanctuary.[200]

We can well believe that not only the above-mentioned prophets, but all other spiritual leaders of the Jews, looked upon the unbridled revelry of the autumn festival as something un-Jewish and distinctly heathen. The people, however, paid little attention to their spiritual leaders and teachers, and continued to drink and revel at "The Festival."

After the Babylonian Exile... The movement against Baal, against the "high places," and against the nature-worship which the Jews had taken over from the Canaanites, the older inhabitants of Palestine, agitated Jewish life in the time of the divided kingdom; it made of the Jews an entirely different people and, in time, changed the character of all the Jewish festivals. They were separated further and further from the soil, from nature and the agricultural seasons of the year, and instead of village revels they were promoted to exalted national religious observances.[201]

This happened to all the festivals, including Sukkos. The very fact that the provincial sanctuaries, the "high places," were abolished during Josiah's reign, and the Temple in Jerusalem was declared the only sanctuary for Jews, changed the character of Sukkos. The very appearance of the festival must have been different from the old days, now that all Jews made the pilgrimage to the one sanctuary in Jerusalem. The fact that all Jews were united in one place added a new national significance to the festival.

Even a greater influence toward modifying the revelry of the festival was the Babylonian exile, and the circumstances in which Jews found themselves after the exile. The primary objective at that time was to find some means of ridding the festival of its connection with nature and of giving it a historical and national aspect. It was, therefore, bound up with the great events of ancient days, at the beginning of Jewish history, when the Jews were still wandering shepherds and dwelt in tents. It was declared, that for this reason Jews sit in booths during this festival.[202]

However, this bond between Sukkos and the memory of the life in the desert could not be stretched too far. It was impossible to make of it a second festival of the Exodus, and the nomadic life in the wilderness did not accord very well with the joyous autumn festival and its customs and ceremonials. In many details, therefore, Sukkos remained the revel of the old days. It was no longer the greatest festival of the year, since that role in the days of the second Temple was taken over by Pesach, but it still remained the merriest Jewish holiday.[203]

Since we know much more about Jewish life in the later days of the second Temple, let us pause and see how Sukkos was observed in the Jerusalem of that period.

*A Pilgrim Festival...*Twice each year Jerusalem opened its gates wide to welcome countless thousands of Jews. At Pesach and again at Sukkos pilgrims flocked into the city from all parts of Palestine, from every foreign land known to the Roman world, from every place that harbored a Jewish community. One could feel in Jerusalem during those days the pulse of the entire Jewish people; one could meet in the streets every type of Jew from every corner of the earth and one could learn, at first hand, the lot of these dispersed Jews, how they lived, what they believed, and what they hoped.

Shovuos at that time did not play a significant role in Jewish life.[204] The two great festivals of the year were Pesach and Sukkos. Pesach brought a greater number of pilgrims to Jerusalem; but it was far more interesting and joyous to make the pilgrimage at Sukkos, that holiday being much richer in parades and ceremonials. Besides, one felt more free at Sukkos. The festival had a joyous outlook and invited to revelry. Especially joyous and unrestrained were the Jewish peasants, who had by then finished the year's agricultural toil; they had gathered the fruits of the fields and orchards and were waiting for God to send the winter rains, to create again a world of green on the now barren, brown earth.

Those Jews who lived in lands far from Jerusalem were gratified if fate gave them the opportunity to make the pilgrimage once in a lifetime. Jews who lived closer to the holy city made the pilgrimage at least once a year, but those who lived fairly close to Jerusalem came three times a year, for all three great festivals, especially for Pesach and Sukkos. It is reported that the town of Ludd was entirely deserted at Sukkos, every man, woman, and child, having gone off to Jerusalem; no doubt this also occurred at Pesach.[205]

When a Jew from afar wanted to make the pilgrimage to Jerusalem he had to find a group to go with him. Traveling alone was dangerous, as many robbers infested the countryside despite the fact that the Roman government policed the roads.[206] Pilgrims never went to the holy city alone; from every direction they made their way in caravans.

Even during the dry season, in which Sukkos fell, the roads were in bad condition. Difficulties always arose, here a stream to ford, there a cleft in the earth to cross, in a third place a swamp to wade through. A few of the roads were good, especially the one that connected Babylonia with Palestine. There were, here and there, stretches of road built by the Romans, who are famous to this day for their road building. But one had to pay toll on these roads, and the people would have preferred to do without both the roads and the tax.[207]

The Babylonian Jews came in great masses to Jerusalem, thousands of them for each festival. They would meet at two cities, Nahardea and Nisibis, leaving in huge caravans, carrying with them the head tax for the Temple sent by those Mesopotamian Jews who were unable to make the pilgrimage themselves.[208]

The trip from Babylonia to Jerusalem usually took two weeks, and Babylonia was close to Palestine compared to some of the countries from which pilgrims came.[209] Many traveled from the western edges of the Mediterranean Sea, making the pilgrimage by boat. There were some rich Jews who drove in chariots; others rode to the holy city on donkeys and camels, especially those who brought merchandise to sell in Jerusalem. Most of the pilgrims came on foot, for it was considered more meritorious to make the pilgrimage that way. It is told that the famous Hillel made the pilgrimage from Babylonia to Palestine entirely on foot.[210]

On to Jerusalem...It is the period before Sukkos. In many towns and cities, near to and far from Jerusalem, pious Jews gather to make the pilgrimage to the holy city. As they prepare for the journey, they are filled with pious longings and can hardly wait for the day when they will really find themselves in God's city, marching in festive parade to the Temple, dancing and singing hymns of praise to God.[211] Especially eager and impatient are those who are making the pilgrimage for the first time; they have heard so much about the beauty of Jerusalem, of its scholars and sages, of the wonderful ceremonials in Herod's Temple; they are filled with a longing to walk the streets, to enter the gates, to dine in the taverns, and to be a part of the throbbing life of this great city.

The pilgrims start at last for the main city of the region,

which is the starting point of the pilgrimage. They carry staffs in their hands; sandals cover their feet; their shoulders bear waterskins and food containers. Many carry money for the second tithe; others carry baskets of belated "first-fruits" to offer up to God in the Temple.[212]

They gather before the gates of the city. One man is elected leader. He stands before the caravan and calls out, "Arise ye, and let us go up to Zion, to the House of our God." [213] He sets out and the caravans follow. The people are in an exalted mood. They are on their way to the gates of Zion, which "God loves more than all the dwellings of Jacob." [214] Their hearts are full and they express the intensity of their feeling by singing Psalms:

> "How lovely are Thy tabernacles, O Lord
>   of Hosts!
> My soul yearneth, yea, even pineth, for the
>   courts of the Lord:
> My heart and my flesh sing for joy unto the
>   living God."

It grows warm; the way is hard and full of obstacles; the pious travelers are exhausted; yet they pay no heed to their aching muscles. For they travel to the House of God; and "it is better to spend one day in God's courts than a thousand days elsewhere." [215]

The roads of Palestine resound with pious song. More and more groups of pilgrims join forces and greater and greater becomes the enthusiasm of the travelers. They meet peasants from the countryside around Jerusalem, driving oxen to be sacrificed in the Temple, the horns of the cattle bedecked with flowers. They are almost there! Pipers lead the procession and the pilgrims march to music.

Entering the City...The pilgrims approach the holy city. From the hilltops the towers and roofs of Jerusalem are visible. They look upon the city and sing:

> "As the mountains are round about Jerusalem,
> So the Lord is round about His people
> From this time forth and forever."

Arriving finally at the gates of Jerusalem, again they sing:

> "I rejoiced when they said unto me:
> Let us go unto the House of the Lord.
> Our feet are standing
> Within thy gates, O Jerusalem,
> Jerusalem that art builded
> As a city that is compact together;
> Whither the tribes went up, even the
>   tribes of the Lord,
> As a testimony unto Israel,
> To give thanks unto the name of the Lord.
> For there were set thrones for judgment,
> The thrones of the House of David.
> Pray for the peace of Jerusalem:
> May they prosper that love thee.
> Peace be within thy walls,
> And prosperity within thy palaces.
> For my brethren and companions' sakes
> I will now say, 'Peace be within thee.'
> For the sake of the House of the Lord our God
> I will seek thy good." [216]

The Temple is now clearly visible to the pilgrims. The golden plates with which it is covered glisten in the sun and the white marble dazzles their eyes; they are hypnotized into silence as they view the House of God, the goal of their travels.

Representatives of the holy city are present at the gate to

welcome the countless number of pilgrims. They come from many lands, and they speak various languages and dialects, but they are all brethren, children of the same folk, and Jerusalem is, for all of them, the holy city.

In Jerusalem... The weather is balmy and since there is no fear of rain, very few pilgrims make their way to the taverns of the city. Why be confined to a house? An open booth is enough. Wherever there is a bit of room, in the courtyards, in the squares, in empty lots, even on the roofs of houses, booths are hastily constructed of green branches with leaves intertwined.

All Jerusalem seems covered with green branches and fruit. Wherever one turns one sees palm leaves, olive branches, odorous myrtle, fragrant willow, and other leafy twigs and branches, from which hang citrous fruits. Even the streets are adorned with fruit. And through the adorned streets and squares of the holy city move thousands of people, each man carrying with him a *lulov*, a ceremonial branch of palm leaves. No man is seen during this festival without a *lulov* grasped firmly in his hand. The more wealthy and aristocratic Jew has his *lulov* tied with a golden ribbon.[217]

All are happy; every face bears a smile. In the open places groups gather, singing and dancing. To some, however, the festival is an occasion for reflection. Among the pilgrims there are many proselytes. The serious Jew, seeing their whole-hearted adoption of Jewish ways, wonders whether the time is not at hand for the fulfillment of the words of the prophet, who said that a time would come when "every one that is left of all the nations . . . shall go up from year to year to worship the King, the Lord of hosts, and to keep the feast of tabernacles (Sukkos)." [218]

The pilgrims are occupied every moment of the time. He that wishes to observe all the ceremonies and services of the festival has not time to close an eye; there is barely time to eat. The very first thing in the morning the ceremony of pouring the libation of water upon the altar is held, and the last ceremony at night, the torch dance, continues almost till dawn. Sleep must be put off for a time. But who comes to Jerusalem to sleep?

Libation of Water...At last, it is the morning of the first day of Sukkos. Every day, after the burning of the daily sacrifice, a libation of wine is poured on the altar. But during Sukkos there is also a libation of water, with special ceremonies that all wish to see.[219]

A merry throng gathers for the procession from the Mount of the Temple down to the spring of Shiloah. Leading the procession is a priest bearing a large golden ewer, in which he draws the water to be poured on the altar. He returns to the Temple and comes to the Water Gate which leads to the inner court. A great crowd awaits him there and greets him with joy. Priests carrying silver trumpets blow the ceremonial calls, *t'ki-oh, t'ru-oh, t'ki-oh,* and other priests chant the words of the Prophet, "With joy shall ye draw water out of the wells of salvation." [220]

At the same time another group of priests goes to Moza, a place near the city, to gather long willow branches which they place alongside the altar, with their points inward. The priest bearing the golden ewer of water marches into the inner court of the Temple, followed by the crowd, which joins the even greater assembly already in the court. The morning sacrifice has already been burned. The priest with the ewer proceeds to the altar, above which stand two containers made of silver, one for water and one for wine. Each of these containers has a narrow spout which is trained on the altar. The priest holds the ewer of water above the container and is about to pour. Many of the assembled multitude call out, asking him to raise his hand still higher, so that they can see that he is really pouring the water upon the altar, and not upon the ground.[221]

After the libation the priests with the trumpets again blow three calls, *t'ki-oh*, *t'ru-oh*, *t'ki-oh*, and the ceremonial procession begins. Around the altar circles the long line of priests, bearing the willow branches. The Levites stand in choir formation and sing the Psalms of Praise. When they come to the words, "We beseech Thee, O Lord, save now! We beseech Thee, O Lord, make us now to prosper!" the entire congregation gathered in the inner court raises the palm branches and twirls them in the air, joining the Levites and reciting in a great chorus: "We beseech Thee, O Lord, save now! We beseech Thee, O Lord, make us now to prosper!" Were one looking down from above it would seem that not men but a forest of palm trees is shaking in the wind and asking the aid of God.

Afternoon in the Temple...When this ceremony is finished it is time for the *Musaf* sacrifice which is added on festivals. Later in the afternoon comes the regular second daily sacrifice. In addition to these standard sacrificial ceremonies countless special sacrifices are offered all day long by the pilgrims, either free will offerings or according to vows made. So throughout the day, there is great ado and bustle on the Mount of the Temple and the priests in charge know no rest. So great is the demand made upon them that during the festival every priest in the country is stationed in Jerusalem.

The sacrificial ceremonies, however, are not the only things these pilgrims, who made the long trip to Jerusalem, came to see. They wander, singly and in groups, through the colonnades of the Temple. They stop to listen to a caustic debate between a group of Pharisees and a group of Sadducees, or they pause to hear expositions of the Torah as propounded by the great sages, the disciples of Hillel and Shammai. They find Jews belonging to various sects, observing ceremonies that differ from those of other Jews, but these sectarians also consider Jerusalem the holy city and come to serve God in the Temple. It is interesting to hear and see all these things and the pilgrims barely take time to eat hasty meals outside, so eager are they to rush back to the Temple.

The Torch Dance...The most interesting and joyous ceremonial of the festival is still to come, the fire-observance with its torch dance, which takes place at night in the Court of the Women.[222] This ceremony is called *Simchas Bes Hashoevoh*, the festivity of the water-drawing, and it is said that he who has not witnessed it has not seen what real festivity is.[223]

Evening has come. The great Court of the Women is crowded with people, ready for the celebration. Above, on the roof of the colonnades that encircle the court, galleries have been built for the women; below them are the men. In the center of the court burn great golden menorahs, set on bases that are fifty yards high. Each menorah has four branches, which terminate in huge cups into which oil is poured. Four ladders are placed against each menorah and four young priests mount them and pour oil into the cups to keep the wicks burning. (The wicks were made from the worn-out garments of the priests.) The light of these menorahs attains such intensity that all Jerusalem is lit up by them.

The lights flare up, higher and still higher; the sound of flutes is heard. Men gather in the spacious court, fine men, the choice men of Jerusalem. They bear torches in their hands and they dance, waving the torches, throwing them in the air and catching them again. And again and again! Others stand on tiptoe and bend their heads down to the ground, rising again without getting off their toes. These are dancers! And songs arise. One sings:

> "Blessed be our youth
> That hath not shamed our later years."

Another sings:

> "Blessed be our later years
> That atoned for our youth."

A third sings:

> "Blessed be he who hath not sinned;
> And he who sinned and repented,
> He is forgiven." [224]

It is late in the night. The dance goes on. On the fifteen steps that lead from the Court of the Women to the Court of the Laymen stand Levites, bearing harps, cymbals, flutes, trumpets, and other instruments; they play and as they play they sing the Psalms of Ascents.[225]

It is almost morning. The Levites have retired. The congregation chants Psalm after Psalm. At the top of the flight of stairs stand two priests, with silver trumpets in their hands. Suddenly a rooster crows. It is the signal for which the priests have been waiting. They blow the three calls, *t'ki-oh*, *t'ru-oh*, *t'ki-oh*. They march down ten steps and blow again, *t'ki-oh*, *t'ru-oh*, *t'ki-oh*. They march down all the way and, blowing a third time, they march across the court to the eastern gate.

They turn and, with their backs to the gate, recite, "Our fore-fathers stood on this spot with their backs to God's house and with their faces to the east and worshiped the sun—but we turn to God and our eyes always turn to God." [226]

And now, as the dawn of day appears, the gates of the Temple are opened and the assembled congregation goes home.

The Festival Ends... These ceremonies are repeated every day during the festival, and always before a great congregation. On the morning of the seventh day, however, the priests march around the altar seven times instead of just once. And on that day they beat the earth with their willow branches. This is the official end of Sukkos and the children seize and dismember the *lulovim* and eat the citrons.

The next day is *Sh'mini Atseres*, the eighth day of convocation, a special day for concluding the festivities of the holiday.[227] It is still Sukkos, but without the symbols of that festival, no sukkoh and no palms or willows.

The day is almost over and the pilgrims are preparing to leave. In the Temple the evening sacrifice is being offered. A host of Jews stand in the court, watching intently to see the direction in which the smoke from the sacrificial fire will blow. It is an omen for the coming year. Should the smoke blow to the north, then the poor are happy and the rich mournful, since this is an omen of a wet, rainy year; in such a year foodstuffs are cheap, and the poor people, the consumers, profit. If the smoke blows south, the poor are sad and the rich merchants happy, for a dry year means a rise in the cost of food, and the dealers will profit at the expense of the consumers. If the smoke blows to the east, then all are pleased. This is a sign of good for all. And if the smoke turns to the west, all are sad; this foretells a famine year, when there will be nothing to sell and nothing to eat.[228]

Sukkos in Later Times...Sukkos lost much of its brilliance after the destruction of the second Temple, but it remained the most joyous of Jewish festivals. The symbols of the festival have been preserved to this very day.

In the time of the second Temple, Sukkos was a great festival even outside of Jerusalem. In all the lands to which the Jews of that day had wandered Sukkos was a day for sitting in booths and holding feasts. And after the destruction of the Temple Jews continued to observe Sukkos with great ceremony in their synagogues and homes. The palm branch (*lulov*) and the citron (*esrog*) remained Jewish symbols, and to this day Jews shake the *lulov* in the synagogue while reciting certain passages from *Hallel*. The religious procession has also been retained, but instead of marching around an altar, the procession winds about a Torah-scroll, which is held on the *bimoh*, the center platform of the orthodox synagogue. Even the *Simchas Bes Hashoevoh* is observed, in one form or another, to this day.

The Jews continued to beat the earth with willow branches on the seventh day of Sukkos which became known later as *Yom Hoshano*, and still later it was given the title, *Hoshano Rabboh*, the great day of *Hoshanos*. This name is derived from the fact that, during the procession around the altar in the Temple, the words *Hoshioh No* (save now) were called out. The two words were contracted into one *Hoshano*, and the word became the designation for the willow branches carried in the hand during the procession, and also for the day in which the willow branches played an important role. The prayers which, later in the Middle Ages, were composed for the procession around the Torah-scroll were also called *Hoshanos* because they begin and end with the word, *Hoshano.*

During the Middle Ages *Hoshano Rabboh* took over more and more of the traits of the Days of Awe, till it became almost a second Yom Kippur, from the fourteenth century onward. This Yom Kippur character of the day is even stronger amongst the S'fardim (Spanish and Portuguese Jews) than amongst the Ashkenazim (German and Polish Jews).[229]

Centuries after the destruction of the Temple a ninth day was added to Sukkos. This was done in an effort to observe strictly the "second holiday of the Diaspora," [230] thus a second day was also decreed for *Sh'mini Atseres.* This extra day was later (about the tenth century) given the name *Simchas Torah,* rejoicing in the Torah, for, during that time it became the universal custom to finish the cycle of the reading of the Torah on that day.[231]

It also became customary to turn at once to the beginning of the Pentateuch, after finishing the last chapter, and to start reading the first chapter.

Through this custom the joyousness of Sukkos lost the last bond that had tied it to the life of nature and the seasons of the year. There was still revelry, as in olden times, but the joy and revelry took on a new meaning. Jews celebrated not because of the grapes and the other crops, but because of the Torah. The booth and the *lulov* were given new interpretations and became no more than religious symbols.

During the late Middle Ages the custom developed of taking all the Torah-scrolls out of the Ark for the procession around the *bimoh* (platform). Thus *Simchas Torah,* the added ninth day, became in the course of time the merriest day of Sukkos and the *Simchas Torah* procession became an interesting folk-observance in which all, men and women, both the aged and the young, take part.

In our own century, among Reform Jews, the observance of Sukkos as a harvest festival has been re-instituted, in a new and symbolic form. A small sukkoh is erected on the platform inside the synagogue and sukkoh, pulpit, and platform are decorated with fruits and flowers. On Sukkos a procession of children enters the synagogue, singing songs of praise. The leaders of the procession carry the four traditional Sukkos plants, citron, palm, myrtle, and willow. The other children are divided into classes and groups, each group carrying a specific fruit or vegetable. Thus, the old motif of Sukkos as a harvest festival has been added to the newer religious aspect.

XIX. Sukkos = IN EASTERN EUROPE

Building Booths...The Jews of the town suddenly become builders in the days between Yom Kippur and Sukkos. Jews draw poles, drag lumber, hammer nails. Even those old Jews who usually sit in the *Bes ha-Midrosh*, the House of Study, reading the Torah and chanting the Psalms, desire to observe the precept in person and help erect the sukkoh (the booth). Not that there is very much work connected with it. The erection of one wall is saved entirely, for the sukkoh is built against the house, either in the back yard or the front yard. About half of the second wall is taken up by the door, leaving only a little more than two walls to put up. These are thrown together with fence rails and odd pieces of lumber and poles. There is no need to make the sukkoh really strong; it will surely last till *Sh'mini Atseres*.

Sukkos are built individually, each man erecting one for his own household. Some neighbors, however, join forces and erect a great sukkoh, in which several families eat together and are assured a religious quorum of three and sometimes ten for the purpose of pronouncing the Benediction after the meal.

So Jews build sukkos and feel themselves fortunate in observing such an important religious precept. But the cheder children are the happiest and most fortunate of all. It is a great occasion for them when they sit in the sukkoh, and it is a still greater occasion for them to help build the structure. There is no school for them, so they drag planks and green branches and help erect the sukkoh. In addition, it is a promise that *Simchas Torah* is almost at hand, when they will march in the procession bearing flags and will mount the synagogue *bimoh* when the call comes for "all the lads."

Even the non-Jews of the neighboring region are interested in the sukkos that Jews build. They learn of the approach of the day on which Jews need a certain type of branches, and they ride into town with their wagons laden with pine branches for sale. The festival is quite profitable for them financially.

Lulov and Esrog... The sukkoh is complete in every detail; its roof is covered with pine branches, the floor is sprinkled with fine sand, and the walls are hung with white sheets and decorated with various fruits and flowers. The decoration is the work of the girls, eager to help even though they are not enjoined to use the sukkoh, entering it just to hear *Kiddush*, the sanctification before meals, and to recite the benediction over the *esrog* and *lulov*.

The *lulov* and the *esrog* are ready, too, but only in certain homes, for few are wealthy enough to buy an *esrog* for individual use. All others own *esrogim* in partnership, usually in groups of six. Services are held in three places, the synagogue, the *Bes ha-Midrosh*, and the *klaus*, the chapel, and they are not held simultaneously. While *Hallel* is being recited in the *klaus*, the worshipers have barely begun services in the *Bes ha-Midrosh*. So it is possible to recite *Hallel* and *Hoshanos* with the same *esrog* in all three places of worship. And in each place there are two of the partners, for there is no hurry. First one partner performs the ceremony with the *lulov* and *esrog*, and then the other one. For the procession when the *Hoshano* prayers are recited the two partners in each place of worship take the *esrog* on alternate days. On *Hoshano*

Rabboh there are seven processions around the platform and it is easy for the partners to arrange for participation.

In this way there are six partners for each *esrog* and the *esrogim* are continually being carried about, from early morning until midday. As soon as *Hallel* is finished in the *klaus*, the *esrogim* are taken to the synagogue. After the *Hallel* prayer in the synagogue the fruits are carried to the *Bes ha-Midrosh*. By the time *Hallel* is finished in the *Bes ha-Midrosh*, it is time for *Hoshanos* in the *klaus*, and so on, all morning long. The masses, the ordinary Jews, use the *klaus* and they hurry to finish the services as soon as possible. The worshipers in the synagogue are also not over-fond of prolonging the services. But in the *Bes ha-Midrosh* the rabbi himself attends the services, and with him are the learned class, the members of the Talmud study circle. These are Jews who have no desire to rush through the services, in order to eat sooner; on the contrary, the longer the services, the greater the satisfaction they get from them.

In addition to the fact that the *esrog* must be in the *klaus*, synagogue, and *Bes ha-Midrosh* twice each day, except Saturday, it must also be in six houses every morning before breakfast. For all, including women and children, must pronounce the benediction over the *esrog* before they eat. So there is a messenger for each *esrog*, a youth who carries it about until all the services are over, and until everyone has pronounced the benediction over it. Then the *esrog* is deposited in the home of one of the six partners, where it is carefully guarded. The messenger, of course, receives payment from each of those to whom he carries the *esrog*.

There are, in town, a mass of poor people, who cannot even afford a sixth of an *esrog*. There are, therefore, a few communal *esrogim* which are utilized by the poorer Jews.

The communal *esrog* passes through so many hands, and becomes so soiled and worn away that, by the time *Hoshano Rabboh* comes, it barely resembles the original *esrog*.

A couple of days before Sukkos the arrangements for all the partnerships have been completed. The *Shamosh* (sexton) who generally makes the arrangements, is not overworked, for, as a general rule, the same partners share the *esrog* year after year.

On coming home from the synagogue the master of the house goes directly to the sukkoh and, before sitting down, recites a prayer in Aramaic, in which he invites seven holy guests to come and sit with him in the sukkoh. These holy guests are Abraham, Isaac, Jacob, Joseph, Moses, Aaron, and David. A special invitation is tendered the first of these on the first evening of the festival, to the second on the second evening, and so on. It is customary to have at least one poor Jew as a guest in the sukkoh, for these holy ones would certainly reject an invitation to sit in a sukkoh where the poor and needy are not fed and entertained.

It is only after this invitation has been given that the *Kiddush*, the sanctification of the day, is chanted aloud, in the presence of the entire family, and in an atmosphere of tender warmth and pious fervor which pervades the *sukkoh*.

The Booths... Great satisfaction is derived from the sukkoh when the weather is fair. The pines and flowers and fruit that adorn the booth send forth a delicious fragrance, and fill the hearts of the occupants with festive joy. Jews eat the holiday meal in the sukkoh; they sing and pronounce the Benediction *bim'zumon* (in groups of three or more); their joy on this holiday is boundless.

Most of the sukkos are small and there is room for only the

males of the family. The women of the house enter the sukkoh just to light the candles and recite the benedictions over them, to hear the *Kiddush* (Sanctification), and to recite the benediction over the *esrog*. They go back into the house for their meals, for women are exempt from the precept to abide in the sukkoh. There are, however, some larger sukkos, in which the entire household eats.

It happens, sometimes, that rain comes down right in the midst of the meal, ruining the festivity of the occasion. If the rain is not too heavy, the occupants stubbornly refuse to leave the flimsy booth, and rush through the meal, even managing to pronounce the grace after the meal. But sometimes it rains so hard that the very soup is watered and the occupants hastily gather food and cloth and run into the house.

Libation Celebration...On the evening of the second day of the festival, the first evening of the half-holiday period, many lamps and candles are kindled in the *Bes ha-Midrosh*, and the ceremony of *Simchas Bes Hashoevoh* is celebrated by the pious Jews of the community.

The privilege of reciting the Psalms of Ascents is sold to the highest bidders, and the purchasers distribute the honor of chanting the verses to various members of the congregation. The money is used to buy apples and brandy; the participants in the ceremony partake of the food and drink, and they sing and revel in a continuation of the *Simchas Bes Hashoevoh* in the Temple of old.

Hoshano Rabboh...The day before *Hoshano Rabboh* the assistant-sexton of the synagogue, accompanied by a horde of youngsters, goes to a grove on the banks of the stream and cuts willow branches. These willow branches are sold the next day in the synagogue and the money is contributed to communal institutions.

Hoshano Rabboh Eve...The women are busy baking wheaten loaves, long loaves with braided ladders on top, such as are made and served the day before Yom Kippur. The women claim that these are ladders to heaven. They also roll dough which will be filled with meat for *kreplech*.

The men stay in the *Bes ha-Midrosh* most of the night, reciting *Tikkun*.[232] Some of them go to the bath-house during the night and immerse themselves in the ritual bath.

It is a strange night, filled with mysteries and curious beliefs. It is said that the heavens split on that night, and he who observes it and makes a wish at the same moment will have that wish granted. It is also believed that he who sees his own headless shadow on that night will die within the year.

Hoshano Rabboh Morning...The attitude in the synagogue is a varied one. It is still part of the semi-holiday period, yet the services are as rich and impressive as on a full holiday. In addition the day is a mixture of Yom Kippur and Sukkos; there are the *esrogim* and willow branches of Sukkos, together with the candles, the white robes and the chants of Yom Kippur.

The highest point in the ceremonial of *Hoshano Rabboh* is the procession around the *bimoh*. During the first six days of Sukkos the procession winds about the platform only once and there is but one Torah-scroll on the *bimoh*. On the seventh day, however, on *Hoshano Rabboh*, the procession makes seven circuits around the *bimoh*, on which every

Torah-scroll from the ark is held by members of the congregation. It differs from the *Simchas Torah* procession in that it is earnest and serious. The procession winds its way around and around, the men bearing the *lulovim* and *esrogim* in their hands and chanting their prayers earnestly and fervently.

After the procession the *lulov* and the *esrog* are laid aside and the willow branches taken up, five of them bound with a leaf of the *lulov*. At the close of the *Hoshano* prayers, the worshipers beat their willow branches on the ground and chant a ritual passage. According to the ritual law it is necessary to beat the branches only five times, but the mass of the congregation beats and beats, till all the leaves have been knocked off the twigs.

Everyone performs this ceremony, including the women in their section of the synagogue, but none enjoy it as much as do the youngsters. They keep beating their branches long after the others are through and continue till their elders brusquely tell them to cease.

Many Jews carry their bundle of branches home and save them for Pesach, to use in the yearly search for leaven.

After the services a feast is served in the sukkoh. There must be soup with *kreplech* served at this feast, exactly as at the meal on the day before Yom Kippur. But after the holiday services and the holiday feast the day becomes again a part of the semi-holiday period and all go about their regular tasks.

This is the happiest day of the Sukkos festival for the youths who have been serving as messengers with the *esrog* during the week; this is the day they are paid for their work. It is a gay day for the youngsters in general. They carry around the long palm leaves of the *lulov* and braid themselves rings and bracelets of it.

Sh'mini Atseres...It is raining, it is pouring outside. The streets of the town are filled with mud. Everyone hopes that the rain will cease soon, so that it will be possible to do business after the festival. In the synagogue there is a special benediction to be pronounced: in a pleading chant, accompanied by the congregation, the cantor offers up the prayers for rain!

It all seems so strange and foreign; and yet there is something heartwarming about it. As the song of prayer for rain rises the thoughts of the worshipers revert to ancient days. They are peasants in Palestine and they wait for the new seasonal rains and for an abundant crop in field and orchard.

The rain has ceased by midday, the sun shines once more, and Jews gather for the last time in their *sukkos*. They partake of food and offer a prayer that they may merit the privilege of sitting in the sukkoh that God will fashion from the skin of the Leviathan, when the Messiah comes.[233]

After the afternoon prayers young and old begin to revel. Each "brotherhood" assembles for its own joyous party. *The Chevroh Kadisho*, the burial-brotherhood, meets in the *Bes ha-Midrosh*. They sit at long tables, eat apples, drink beer and brandy, and sing and revel. They sing Yiddish folk songs, chants, and bits of the services and the Psalms. The feast in the *klaus* is conducted by the Bible study circle, and the one at the home of the rabbi is conducted by the exalted ones, the Talmud study circle.

Simchas Torah Eve...The congregation is lively and merry by evening. There are even those who obviously took a glass too much and sway as they move about the synagogue, but they manage to recite the evening prayers properly, nevertheless.

After the evening prayers the sexton auctions off the privilege of reciting certain passages from the Bible. But the auc-
tion is more fancied than real, for there is one certain Jew
who has gained the unchallenged right to it through many
years of purchase. He recites only one sentence, and appor-
tions the other sentences amongst relatives, friends, and es-
teemed householders. He whispers the name of his choice to
the sexton, who calls out the name of the next reader. The
reader recites his sentence which the congregation repeats.
He then thanks the purchaser for the honor.

After this comes the main ceremony of the evening, the
procession. Even women and girls are permitted to enter in
the main part of the synagogue on *Simchas Torah* and to kiss
the Torah-scrolls as they are carried around the *bimoh* seven
times. But only girls and young matrons avail themselves of
this privilege. The elder women look on at the ceremony
from the women's gallery above.

The youngsters play a great part in the procession, for
which they prepared themselves during the semi-holiday period. They bear flags mounted on sticks, and above are attached large apples or beets, hollowed out, a candle burning
inside. The flags bear the inscription, *Degel Machane Yehu-
doh*, "standard of the camp of Judah," some bearing
"Ephraim" instead of "Judah." Even tiny children mounted on
the shoulders of their fathers or older brothers take part in
the procession around the *bimoh*.

In this manner they parade about the *bimoh*, older Jews
bearing the Torah-scrolls, youngsters bearing illuminated
flags, all chanting alphabetically arranged songs of prayer.

Simchas Torah Morning...The morning prayers last till
afternoon. But right after the early part of the services the

worshipers begin to partake of food and drink. This is done in the synagogue, and also in private homes, while the last section of the Pentateuch is being read in the synagogue.

This reading of the Pentateuch drags on for hours and hours on this day. Again and again the last section is read, until every member of the congregation has been called to the *bimoh* to witness the reading and to recite the benediction. The service would never end if each member were called up individually, so two men mount the *bimoh* together. There are two benedictions to be repeated over each reading of the Torah, one before the reading and one after, and the two men called up share the benedictions.

After everyone in the synagogue, adult males and boys who have been confirmed, are disposed of in this way, the call goes forth for "all the lads." This is the ceremony in which all the boys under thirteen are called up to witness the reading of the Torah. Together with them an adult Jew, usually an elderly and very pious man, recites the benediction. This recitation, "together with all the children," is a great honor and, as a rule, a certain Jew has the privilege, gained through years of usage, and all know that it belongs to him.

The picture is wonderful to behold. The lads come forth from all sides and mount the *bimoh*, ranging themselves in front of the older man, who spreads his prayer shawl over their heads and pronounces the benediction. He recites it slowly, word by word, and the children repeat it after him, the entire congregation shouting "Amen" at the end, with great fervor. Who knows how many good and pious Jews, how many rabbis and scholars of the Torah will grow up from this group of children?

Revelry goes on all day long, in the synagogue and in the homes, dancing and singing in the very streets of the town.

Old, pious men, with long cloaks and gray beards, cavort about and sing, and act as if a sudden, wild joy had taken complete possession of them.

Still the Jews of the older generation claim that the joyous years of old, when Jews really celebrated on *Simchas Torah*, are gone. Nowadays, they say, nobody really indulges in revelry; in the old days they knew how.

So say these Jews, but, at the same time, they dance and sing joyously. But there is not, in all the revelry of *Simchas Torah*, a trace of looseness or licentiousness. They drink, but none becomes really drunk. Jews revel and pray; they drink and they read the Torah.

The finale of the festival comes at night, after the official close of the holiday. The holiday feast which is the greatest and finest of the nine-day period is served then.

This feast is not the end, however. The revelry continues on the next Sabbath, the Sabbath on which the first section of Genesis is read in the synagogue. It is only on the day after this Sabbath that one feels that the season of festivals is really over, and the cold and cloudy autumn settles on the town.

XX. Sukkos = IN CUSTOM AND CEREMONY

Origin of the Sukkoh...The *sukkoh* is the main feature of the Sukkos festival. It is from the *sukkoh* that the festival took its name. But the origin of the practise of living in booths during the festival is not certain.

The Pentateuch tells us that the *sukkoh* is a reminder of ancient days, when the Jews wandered in the desert and lived in tents. This is, however, a forced interpretation and was evolved in later times. If the *sukkoh* was really connected with the Exodus, then Pesach would be the time for dwelling in booths. Besides, the Jews resided in tents during their wanderings in the desert, and there is quite a difference between a tent and a booth. The tent of the desert Bedouin consists of a sheet of goatskin, hung over poles driven into the earth. The main feature of a *sukkoh* is the open roof, which is covered with branches and leaves.[234]

In addition to the reason for dwelling in booths as given in the Pentateuch, the Jewish philosopher of Alexandria, Philo, evolved a new meaning for the *sukkoh*. He said that it was erected to bring evidence of misfortune at a time of good fortune, and a reminder of poverty to those who were wealthy. Maimonides gave the same interpretation for the *sukkoh*.[235]

Still other thoughts and ideas were read into the *sukkoh*. It was said, for instance, that Jews abided in the *sukkoh* to show the temporary quality and the uncertainty of Jewish life in general. The *sukkoh*, the preachers said, reminds us that Jews live everywhere for only a little while, as in the booths;

they wander eternally from country to country.[236] But these thoughts that were later bound up with the *sukkoh* give us no clue to the scientific understanding of its origin and the connection it had in ancient times with the festival.

It is well first to review what we do know about the *sukkoh* in ancient days. In the older, historical books of the Bible no *sukkos* are mentioned in the passages which tell of the celebration of the joyous autumn festival. In those days the festival did not bear the name *Sukkos*.[237] The first time we hear mention of abiding in booths in the historical books of the Bible is in the Book of Nehemiah, which says that on the first day of the seventh month Ezra read from the Torah:

"And on the second day were gathered together the heads of fathers' houses of all the people, the priests, and the Levites, unto Ezra the scribe, even to give attention to the words of the Law. And they found written in the Law, how that the Lord had commanded by Moses, that the children of Israel should dwell in booths in the feast of the seventh month; and that they should publish and proclaim in all their cities, and in Jerusalem, saying: 'Go forth unto the mount, and fetch olive branches, and branches of wild olive, and myrtle branches, and palm branches, and branches of thick trees, to make booths, as it is written.' So the people went forth, and brought them, and made themselves booths, every one upon the roof of his house, and in their courts, and in the courts of the house of God, and in the broad place of the water gate, and in the broad place of the gate of Ephraim. And all the congregation of them that were come back out of the captivity made booths, and dwelt in the booths; for since the days of Joshua the son of Nun unto that day had not the children of Israel done so. And there was very great gladness. Also day by day from the first day unto the last day, he read in the book of the Law of God. And they kept the feast seven days; and on the eighth day was a solemn assembly, according unto the ordinance." [238]

Here it is stated that when Ezra came from Babylon, *sukkos* were built in Jerusalem, made of leaves and branches, and the Jews dwelt in them during the seven days of the autumn festival; we are also told that this was an innovation at the time. The question arises: In what way was it a novelty?

It is impossible for us to assume that we deal here with an entirely new thing, something never known before. New customs are not introduced; old customs are rather reformed and re-interpreted. There are three possibilities before us:

1. We can assume that the novelty spoken of was in the materials used in the making of the *sukkos;* in the old days, before the Babylonian exile, Jews lived, during the festival, in nomadic tents and, in Ezra's day, it became mandatory to use booths made of branches.

2. It can also be said that the novelty was in the fact that, till that time, only certain groups of Jews dwelt in booths. From the time of Ezra it became a religious precept for all Jews.

3. The third explanation is that in the olden days the custom of abiding in booths during the festival was practised only by the Jewish peasants, who erected the *sukkos* in fields and orchards. During Ezra's time the custom was also taken over by the Jews of the towns and cities, who erected their booths on the roofs of their houses and in the squares of the town.

The basic point, however, is that, in Ezra's time, it became mandatory to abide in a booth made of branches and leaves during the autumn festival, and that this law was based on an old custom. What this old custom was we do not know today. There are various theories and conjectures regarding this custom, but every one of them has some flaw, some point that remains unexplained.

According to one popular theory, the *sukkoh* originated from an ordinary shack that was erected in field and orchard during the time of harvesting the fruit. But this theory leaves two important questions unanswered. First, how did such an important Jewish law evolve from the natural practice of dwelling in booths? Secondly, building a shack and living in it during the harvest period was an ordinary occurrence; why, then, did it become a regulation to erect such a booth during the festival marking the completion of the harvest?

There is also a theory that the *sukkoh* originated from the booths that were erected by the pilgrims who came to Jerusalem to observe the autumn festival. In this theory there are also flaws. In the first place we do not know that the pilgrims of the olden days erected booths. It seems that they lived in tents during the time they stayed at the sanctuary.[239] Again, it seems hardly understandable that from a natural need there should arise a religious regulation.[240]

On the whole, we know nothing about the *sukkoh* in the olden days, before Ezra. We know only that, beginning with Ezra, the *sukkoh* became the main feature of the festival.

In more recent times a great change in the custom came about among the Jews who live in the great cities of Europe and America, where there is no place to erect *sukkos*. In these cities there are generally only congregational *sukkos*, erected by the synagogue, where, after services, *Kiddush* is pronounced over light food and drink.

The Four Species...We know as little about the *lulov* and the *esrog* (the branch of palm leaves and citron) of ancient days as we do about the *sukkoh*. In old days these were obviously used only as materials with which to build and decorate the *sukkoh*. This is apparent from the passages of

Nehemiah quoted above. We also know that the Samaritans and the Karaites always used these materials in that way. All that is told in the Pentateuch is that Jews are to take fruit from a "goodly" tree, leaves from the date-palm, branches from a tree, and willows from a stream, and rejoice with them before God.[241] But no instructions are given regarding them, as to whether they should be held in the hand or used to decorate the *sukkoh*.

Later, however,—we do not know when or through what circumstances—the passage began to be interpreted that, at Sukkos, Jews are to hold an *esrog* and a *lulov* in their hands, together with three sprigs of myrtle and two willow twigs, as a festival wreath, and to shake them and point them in all directions.[242]

This *Sukkos* bouquet is thus made up of four species, and Jews have read all sorts of meanings into them. The oldest explanation is that the four species are a talisman for rain. Jews show God that exactly as these four plants cannot exist without water, so the entire world cannot exist without rain.[243] Later, further meanings were attached to the *lulov* and *esrog;* for instance, that the four species represent the three patriarchs (Abraham, Isaac, and Jacob), and Joseph; or that they represent the four classes into which Jews are divided. The citron has both taste and aroma, and represents those Jews who have knowledge of the Torah and do good deeds; the palm, or rather the date that grows on it, has taste, but no aroma, and represents those Jews who know the Torah, but do not practice good deeds; the myrtle has aroma, but no taste, and represents those Jews who perform good deeds, but do not know the Torah; while the willow has neither taste nor aroma and represents that group of Jews who neither know the Torah nor do good deeds. There was also an interpretation that the *lulov* is the symbol for the backbone, the citron for the heart, the myrtle for the eye, and the willow for the mouth.[244]

Beating Willow Branches...Beating the ground with willow branches (*Hoshanos*) is an old custom that played a great role in the *Sukkos* ceremonial far back in the time of the second Temple. The Jews of the period were such staunch observers of the custom of beating the earth at the sides of the altar with willow branches that they did it even on the Sabbath. Later, however, when the Jewish calendar was reformed, it was arranged that the first day of Tishri was never to fall on Sunday, in order that *Hoshano Rabboh* would always come during the week-days and there would be no disturbance of the custom of *Hoshanos*.

The custom is not mentioned in the Pentateuch, and there is therefore a controversy in the Talmud about its origin.[245] But it seems that it is a very ancient custom that Jews observed even in the time of the first Temple. Like many other customs of this sort, it was not recognized officially as a part of the Jewish religion, and remained only a custom of the people, a part of the folk-belief which was not incorporated into the official law book, the Torah.

Pouring water on the altar was a related custom. These two customs had the same motive, both were originally talismans for an abundant crop in the coming year. Pouring water was a sign of rain, exactly as eating honey at New Year is an augury of a year of sweetness; and beating the earth with fresh willow branches was a talisman for making the earth fertile, because the willow grows only in moist places, and anything which grows in a damp place, and is very vigorous, is a symbol of growth and life to primitive man.

Only in the olden days, however, was this custom of beating the earth with reeds of the stream a talisman of fertility. In time it was incorporated into the Temple ceremonial and it became a religious ceremony. At that time the willows were beaten on the earth near the altar, and it was believed that the power to call forth fertility resided not in the willows, but in God's altar.[246]

Encirclings...The circling of an object in a religious procession is a popular Jewish custom. It is done on various occasions. Jews circle the groom under the wedding canopy; they circle the cemetery on certain occasions; and there are places where a procession is made around the coffin of a corpse at a funeral.

This custom of making a circular procession was interpreted in various ways in later days. The truth, however, is that it is a very old, primitive custom of ancient days that is found among all peoples of the earth. It arose from the belief shared by all peoples in the course of their spiritual development that the world is full of spirits, and that there are many magic means of overcoming them.

One of the best and surest means with which to fight the spirits, primitive men believed, was through the use of the circle, what was called and is still known as the "magic ring."

The closed circle played a great and important part in the beliefs of people since oldest times. As late as in the Middle Ages there was strong belief in the magical power of the closed circle. When a magician of the Middle Ages wanted to prove his magic, he first drew a circle about himself and sat in it. There, in the center of the magic ring, he sat as in a fortress, and was able to do as he pleased with the spirits, without their being able to reach him. Even the devil, people believed, feared a closed circle, for were he to enter within the ring he would become entirely helpless and would have to obey all orders given him.

From this practice, too, comes the belief in the "wishing-ring" which, when worn on the hand, brings fulfillment of every wish.

The custom of the circular procession, of making a circle around an object, has its origin, then, in this old, primitive belief which, however, survived, and remained in man's religious development. As it was originally believed that man could conquer the spirits with the use of a magic circle, so it was later believed that man could gain favor with God through the circling of an object. Man stood in a ring, a circle, and did not release God until He heard man's prayer and granted it. Such a tale is told in the Aggadah of the Talmud regarding Honi, the Circle-drawer, who lived in Jerusalem at the time of the war between the two Hasmonean brothers, Hyrcanus and Aristobulus. He was nicknamed "the circle-drawer" from his habit of making a circle about himself and then telling God that he would not move from the spot until his prayer was granted.[247]

Not only Jews believed that they could have their way with God through the use of circles, but also the Hindus, the Persians, the Greeks, and the Romans shared this idea. With all these peoples it was a popular custom to make processions about the temples, the altars, and the statues of their gods. One of the most vital ceremonies of the Arabs consists of circling their sanctuary.

What happened to all customs happened also to that of the circular procession. People forgot its original meaning. New meanings were woven into it and it became a symbolic ceremony, an important part of the ritual of Sukkos.[248]

xxi. 𝕮hanukkoh ⹀ ITS ORIGINS

Introduction...Chanukkoh is observed for eight days, beginning with the twenty-fifth day of the month of Kislev.

It is not one of the great Jewish festivals, and bears no aura of sanctity. No special ceremonials have been built around it. There is no cessation of work, except briefly for the women of the household, who cease their labors during the short time each evening when the Chanukkoh lights burn.

A Dated Festival...Chanukkoh differs from all other Jewish festivals in one important respect; its origin is not lost in the dimness of antiquity; it stands clear and bold in the light of history. It is a dated festival, a festival that commemorates great events in the history of the Jewish people—the revolt and victory of the Hasmoneans.

These events left their imprint on the entire future course of Jewish history and, to a great measure, of world history. We must, therefore, examine the Jewish life of that period in order to learn what led to those events, to the great crisis under Antiochus Epiphanes and the revolt of the Hasmoneans.

Under Persia...From the time of the Babylonian exile to the Maccabean uprising, the Jews had no independent kingdom in Palestine, but lived under the rule of foreign empires, to whom they were subject.

Jews lived about two hundred years (539 to 333 B.C.E.) under Persian rule. The Persians at that time ruled over an empire that stretched from India to the southern boundary of

Egypt. Both Syria to the north of Palestine and Egypt to the south belonged to the same world-empire, Persia.

Since all the lands about Palestine belonged to one kingdom, Jews had no reason or opportunity to play politics and did not come into conflict with the ruling power. They, therefore, lived quietly and peacefully in the weak little commonwealth of Judah and, separated from the peoples about them, they practiced and developed their own spiritual life, which was based mainly on two fundamentals, the Torah and the Temple.

The Persian government did not interfere with the inner life of the Jews, who had full religious autonomy. A Persian governor dwelt in Jerusalem, and he collected the taxes and kept order in the land. The representative of the Jews was the High Priest. Any communication between the governor and the Jews went through the High Priest, their representative and chief.

Under Greece... This state of affairs lasted a considerable time, till the end of the fourth century, B.C.E., when Alexander of Macedonia conquered the Persians. The Greeks then became the rulers of the world, and Palestine, too, became a part of the Grecian world empire.

The period after Alexander's conquests is called the Hellenistic Period in world history. All of the Near East—western Asia and northern Africa—was Hellenized, and not only fell under the rule of the Greeks, but also came under the influence of the Greek spirit, of the Hellenistic culture. In the towns of western Asia and Egypt people began to speak Greek and to take on the outward appearance of Greeks.

Alexander's world empire lasted only a decade or so. After his sudden death his empire broke up into many kingdoms, in each of which there were Grecian rulers. Palestine was now wedged in between two separate kingdoms. To the north was the Grecian kingdom of Syria, under the dynasty of the Seleucids, and to the south the Grecian kingdom of Egypt, under the Ptolemies. These two were continually at war, and the Jews of Palestine were again, as in the days of the Babylonians and Assyrians, pinioned between the hammer and anvil.

In the first century of Greek world rule (the third century B.C.E.) Palestine belonged to the Greco-Egyptian kingdom. Jews, at that time, suffered economically from the wars between Egypt and Syria, but they had greater political freedom than under the Persians. The Grecian monarchs of Egypt gave them a greater measure of self-rule. No longer did a foreign governor reside in Jerusalem, as formerly under the Persians; the High Priest was also the political leader and the crown's representative in Judah.

From this time onward High Priest and governor were one and the same. The word *Archaereus* (Greek for high priest) was used to designate the Jewish chief, the king's representative in the province of Judah, as well as the religious leader of the Jews, the High Priest of the Temple.

*Under Syria and Egypt...*By the end of the third century, B.C.E., after Palestine had been under the rule of the Ptolemies for one hundred years, it was conquered by the Seleucids. For decades a state of war had existed between Egypt and Syria, and often the Jews of Palestine were unable to tell to which kingdom the country belonged. Jewish parties arose at that time, an Egyptian party and a Syrian party; one section of Jews was in favor of Egypt, the other in favor of Syria.

This political division into an Egyptian and a Syrian party went hand in hand with a division in the spiritual life of the Jews. The Egyptian and Syrian kingdoms were entirely different from each other. The Egyptian kingdom was self-contained and exclusively Egyptian, and had no fear of disintegration. There were two classes in the population, the native Egyptians, who had no voice in the rule of the land, and the ruling class of Macedonians and Greeks. The ruling class kept itself apart from the inferior native inhabitants, and there was no talk of a melting-pot for the nation, or of forcing upon the lower classes the new Hellenistic world culture.

While Palestine was under the rule of Egypt it is possible that Jews absorbed a certain amount of cultural influence from the Greeks, but this Hellenizing had no political importance. The Egyptian government had no interest in the Hellenizing process, and it was impossible to use it as a political weapon in Jerusalem.

The Grecian kingdom of Asia had an entirely different character. It was a state formed of various nationalities, the type of state that Austria was before the World War. It was made up of various peoples and countries and could not, therefore, arrive at strength and unity. So the Seleucids strove to hold and weld the various elements in their kingdom through the universal Hellenistic culture. Hellenism, in the kingdom of the Seleucids, was, therefore, a part of the political policy of the government, and stood for loyalty to the kingdom.

The conservative Jewish circles of Judah were, therefore, in favor of Egypt, because of their religious interests. On the other hand, those who were in favor of Syria had to be, in accordance with its political trend, Hellenists. The introduction of Hellenistic ways into Palestine had to be part of their political program. In addition, Hellenism was to their economic interest. The East, at that time, was experiencing a boom in trade and manufacture; it was a time of wealth and riches. Many Jews, therefore, strove to take leave of their religious separateness and to participate in the rich life of the world in which they lived.

There arose, then, a Jewish aristocracy that was in favor of Syria and that strove to introduce Hellenistic ways into Judah. This Hellenistic-aristocratic party was the governing party in Jerusalem under Syrian rule. It was only on this group that the Syrian government could rely.

This situation, this division into separate parties, carried with it great complications and dangers for the Jews, especially the danger of collision with a foreign power. This conflict arose when Antiochus Epiphanes ascended the Syrian throne.

The Struggle in Judah...Antiochus Epiphanes was a restless and energetic person, greatly self-opinionated, and without any inner balance. He could not stand being contradicted and, with his undisciplined and capricious nature, he was always in danger of becoming entangled in the mesh of one error after another.

When Antiochus became king of Syria, there was a great upheaval in the local political situation of the Jews in Palestine. The conservative party could not take charge of Jewish self-rule, for its sympathies lay with Egypt; because of its antagonistic attitude to Hellenism it was considered unpatriotic and against the interests of the Syrian kingdom. The position of High Priest, that is, of governor, was won, therefore, by a Hellenized priest by the name of Jason, an aristocratic priest, a brother of the High Priest Onias. (He altered his Hebrew name, Joshua, to Jason.)

Jason belonged to the moderate Hellenists. He was apparently a compromise candidate on whom both parties had united. He won the king to his side with his promise to Hellenize Jerusalem, thus proving his political soundness, his willingness to work for the interests of the Syrian kingdom.

Jason was not an extreme Hellenist and did not disturb the fundamentals of Jewish religious life. He only desired that Jerusalem should attain the appearance of the Hellenistic cities of the region, and that Jews should take on those Grecian manners which would give them the ability to deal with their non-Jewish neighbors. For this purpose he erected a gymnasium in Jerusalem, and introduced Greek games.

Jews began to change their names to Grecian ones, and to clothe themselves as the Greeks. There was no real danger to Judaism in Jason's middle-of-the-road Hellenism. However, he set a bad precedent in openly playing politics with Hellenism in Jerusalem. He showed Antiochus a strategy which the king, perhaps, would never have seen by himself.

Jason retained his position as governor of the province of Judah for three years of Antiochus' reign. But a moderate Hellenist could represent the king only in a time of peace. Soon the war between Syria and Egypt broke out again and, in connection with it, a war broke out between the rival political leaders in Jerusalem.

The Syrian party now had the opportunity to depose Jason, the compromise candidate, and to obtain complete rule. It was not difficult to persuade Antiochus that Jason was not a trustworthy person in time of war, that he sympathized, in his heart, with the conservative Egyptian party. Antiochus deposed Jason and put in his place Menelaus

(Menachem), the leader of the extreme Greco-Syrian party.

We must remember that Menelaus, like his predecessor, Jason, was not the religious head of the Jews.[249] Menelaus was no more than a Jewish aristocrat, a political leader in Jerusalem, who placed the political interests of his party above the national and religious interests of his people.

Menelaus' strict Hellenistic regime in Jerusalem evoked bitter resentment in the masses, and revived and strengthened the sympathy for Egypt. When a rumor spread through Jerusalem that Antiochus had been slain on the battlefield, Jason, with a battalion of a thousand men, besieged the city and forced Menelaus to seek refuge in the citadel.

But Antiochus at once marched with his great army on Jerusalem, and put the city in the hands of his soldiers, ordering them to slay every adherent of the Egyptian party. The soldiers, naturally, did not discriminate and a dreadful slaughter took place in Jerusalem. In addition, Antiochus plundered the Temple and removed the treasure and all the golden and silver utensils. Jerusalem was left mourning, in sackcloth and ashes. But this did not upset Menelaus, as long as his party had won and he remained in office.

A year later Antiochus led a second expedition against Egypt. Because of his earlier successes, he now expected to attain the rulership over all of Egypt. But he was approached by a messenger empowered by the Roman Senate to order him to withdraw his forces at once. Antiochus, alas, had to obey, and gave up his plans for the conquest of Egypt.

Judaism in Danger...Antiochus now betook himself to convert his realm of diverse nationalities into a powerful, homogeneous kingdom, so as to feel secure against both Egypt and Rome. The one way to accomplish this was to fuse all the peoples of his kingdom in the universal melting pot of Hellenistic culture. In those days the national culture of a people was strongly bound up with its religion, with the cult of the gods. So Antiochus issued a decree that all the peoples of his empire were to serve the Grecian gods and to become Greeks. It was especially important for Antiochus to Hellenize the province of Judah and to make it an organic part of his kingdom, in order to feel secure about the Egyptian border.

All the peoples of the kingdom accepted and obeyed the edict of Antiochus, except the Jews. Antiochus, therefore, sent a mighty army into Palestine to root out the cult of the Jewish God with force, and to eliminate the observance of distinctive Jewish laws and ways.

This produced the greatest crisis in the Jewish life of that time. The Temple service was halted and God's House was turned into a Grecian temple. It was forbidden, under penalty of death, to observe any of the precepts of the Jewish religion. There were many martyrs, the first martyrs for freedom of conscience known in world history.

It was the war between the political parties and their leaders that brought about the critical situation under Antiochus Epiphanes; and it was this situation that led to a revolt against the tyrannic rule of the Syrian kingdom and against the leadership of the aristocratic Syrian party in Judah. The old parties were failures and a new, national party arose, which declared: Jews are concerned with neither Syrian nor Egyptian interests, but only with strictly Jewish interests. This national party was under the leadership of Judah Maccabee and his brothers of the Hasmonean family.[250]

A New Kingdom Is Born... The victories of Judah Maccabee and his volunteer army did not at once lead to great results. At first they only sought to re-install the Temple service, which had been interrupted for three solid years. On the twenty-fifth day of the month of Kislev they re-dedicated the altar in the Temple with a great ceremony, and decreed that an eight-day festival, commencing with that day, be observed yearly.

The Hasmoneans, however, were not content with this small achievement. They soon prevailed upon the Syrian government to recall Antiochus' decree against the Jews, and to re-establish Jewish religious autonomy. After that they deposed the aristocratic, Hellenized Jews from the inner administration of the land, and they themselves took over the role of the ruling party. And when the Syrian kingdom became torn and weakened through inner dissension, the Hasmoneans took the opportunity to erect a new, independent Jewish kingdom in Palestine.

The independent Jewish kingdom of the Hasmoneans lasted only temporarily, less than one hundred years, before the Roman world empire swallowed it up. But the kingdom had far-reaching results for the Jews. They became, through it, a renascent people. For centuries since the Babylonian exile, they were a small and weak community in the little land of Judah. Had Jews remained in that position they would have become a people suffering from arrested growth, exactly as the Samaritans and the Karaites became. It was only through the revolt and victory of the Hasmoneans that the latent forces of the people were aroused, and the various trends in Jewish spiritual life attained distinct forms. Jews grew enormously in numbers and power during that period; they extended their dominion over all of Palestine and also migrated in large numbers over the then known world.

In this way, through the victory of the Hasmoneans, the

Jews developed new powers and possibilities to exist as a people. Chanukkoh, today, stands for two ideals: first, for the achievement of religious liberty and, secondly, in the minds of large masses of Jewry, for a revival of a sentiment for the national development of the Jewish people.

xxii. Chanukkoh ‡ IN EARLY DAYS

Character of the Festival...We, thus, know with certainty in what period and through what events Chanukkoh was decreed as a universal festival for Jews. It is neither clear nor certain, however, what type of festival Chanukkoh was at that time, what its character was, and with what rites it was observed. The oldest historical sources that deal with the festival and the period are the two Books of the Maccabees.[251] The First Book relates:

"Then said Judas and his brethren, 'Behold, our enemies are discomfited: let us go up to cleanse and dedicate the sanctuary.'

Upon this all the host assembled themselves together, and went up unto mount Zion.

And when they saw the sanctuary desolate, and the altar profaned, and the gates burned up, and shrubs growing in the courts as in a forest, or in one of the mountains, yea, and the priests' chambers pulled down, they rent their clothes, and made great lamentation, and cast ashes upon their heads, and fell down flat to the ground upon their faces, and blew an alarm with the trumpets, and cried toward heaven.

Then Judas appointed certain men to fight against those that were in the fortress, until he had cleansed the sanctuary.

So he chose priests of blameless conversation, such as had pleasure in the law, who cleansed the sanctuary, and bare out the defiled stones into an unclean place.

And when as they consulted what to do with the altar of

burnt offerings, which was profaned, they thought it best to pull it down, lest it should be a reproach to them, because the heathen had defiled it: wherefore they pulled it down, and laid up the stones in the mountain of the temple in a convenient place, until there should come a prophet to shew what should be done with them.

Then they took whole stones according to the law, and built a new altar according to the former; and made up the sanctuary, and the things that were within the temple, and hallowed the courts.

They made also new holy vessels, and into the temple they brought the candlestick, and the altar of burnt offerings, and of incense, and the table.

And upon the altar they burned incense, and the lamps that were upon the candlestick they lighted, that they might give light in the temple.

Furthermore they set the loaves upon the table, and spread out the veils, and finished all the works which they had begun to make.

Now on the five and twentieth day of the ninth month, which is called the month Kislev, in the hundred forty and eighth year,[252] they rose up betimes in the morning, and offered sacrifice according to the law upon the new altar of burnt offerings which they had made.

Look, at what time and what day the heathen had profaned it, even in that was it dedicated with songs, and citherns, and harps, and cymbals.

Then all the people fell upon their faces, worshiping and praising the God of heaven, who had given them good success.

And so they kept the dedication of the altar eight days, and offered burnt offerings with gladness, and sacrificed the sacrifice of deliverance and praise.

They also decked the forefront of the temple with crowns of gold, and with shields; and the gates and the chambers they renewed, and hanged doors upon them.

Thus was there very great gladness among the people, for that the reproach of the heathen was put away.

Moreover Judas and his brethren with the whole congregation of Israel ordained that the days of the dedication of the altar should be kept in their season from year to year by the space of eight days, from the five and twentieth day of the month Kislev, with mirth and gladness." [253]

In this account Chanukkoh is no more than the holiday of the re-dedication of the Temple, but it does not state what character the festival had at the time.

Another account is given in the Second Book of Maccabees. There we are told:

"Now Maccabeus and his company, the Lord guiding them, recovered the temple and the city; but the altars which the heathen had built in the open street, and also the chapels, they pulled down.

And having cleansed the temple they made another altar, and striking stones they took fire out of them, and offered a sacrifice after two years,[254] and set forth incense, and lights, and shewbread.

When that was done, they fell flat down, and besought the Lord that they might come no more into such troubles; but if they sinned any more against him, that he himself would chasten them with mercy, and that they might not be delivered unto the blasphemous and barbarous nations.

Now upon the same day that the strangers profaned the Temple, on the very same day it was cleansed again, even the five and twentieth day of the same month, which is Kislev.

And they kept eight days with gladness, as in the feast of

the tabernacles, remembering that not long afore they had held the feast of the tabernacles, when as they wandered in the mountains and dens like beasts.

Therefore they bare branches, and fair boughs, and palms also, and sang psalms unto Him that had given them good success in cleansing his place.

They ordained also by a common statute and decree, that every year those days should be kept of the whole nation of the Jews." [255]

Here we have a different account from the one given in the First Book of Maccabees. Chanukkoh is not only the festival of the re-dedication of the Temple, but is also a second Sukkos and it is observed, as Sukkos is, with the singing of *Hallel* and the carrying of the *lulov*.

In neither of the two accounts, however, is there anything said about the name of the festival, and neither one mentions the kindling of the Chanukkoh lights. They say only that the lamps of the Menorah were kindled. But this was no special Chanukkoh ritual; the lamps of the Menorah were kindled every day of the year in the Temple. The burning of special lights in honor of the festival is first mentioned about two centuries later. The first one to speak of it is Josephus Flavius. Following the account in the First Book of Maccabees, he tells of the renewal of the Temple services, and then he adds, "From that day to this we observe this festival, and call it 'Lights.'" Josephus also strives to give a reason for the name of the festival because freedom glowed and lighted up Jewish life unexpectedly.[256]

We see from this that in Josephus' time, in the generation of the destruction of the second Temple, the Chanukkoh lights were not yet an old or deep-rooted ceremony and the custom was not yet generally understood. An explanation for the lights was still being sought. This is further demonstrated from the fact that in those days there was no specification for the number of lights to be kindled each day of the festival; it was still a matter of controversy between the followers of the school of Hillel and the school of Shammai. Shammai's followers declared that the festival must start with the kindling of eight lights, steadily diminishing the number till there was only one light on the last day; Hillel's followers held the opposite view, that it was to begin with one light and end with eight.[257]

All the citations and facts quoted here prove that at the time of the second destruction of Jerusalem, Chanukkoh already had a long history behind it and had passed through various phases in its evolution. We cannot be certain what these phases were, for we know so little about the inner Jewish life of that time. From what we do know we can assume that Chanukkoh went through the following stages:

It was first observed as a festival of joy, with the singing of *Hallel* and the waving of palm branches, just as Sukkos. It was made a second Sukkos because, in the three years that the Temple service was halted, it was impossible to observe Sukkos. This explains several Sukkos-traits that remain in the festival to this day, as the eight-day duration of the holiday and the inclusion of *Hallel* in the daily religious services during the festival.

If Chanukkoh were to become a universal festival for all Jews and for all time, it could not remain a second Sukkos. It was, therefore, made the festival of the re-dedication of the Temple and the name Chanukkoh (dedication) was given to it. The festival was thus bound up with various events and observances of olden days, and ancient sanctity was given to it. Various dedication observances are mentioned in the old sacred books. Moses, the Pentateuch tells us, held a dedication service when he erected the Tabernacle. Solomon held a festival of dedication when he opened the Temple. The Jews held another such festival when they finished the erection of the second Temple. Nehemiah also held a dedicatory festival when he finished the wall about Jerusalem.[258] In this way a fitting motive was found for the observance, yearly, of a dedicatory festival, in honor of the resumption of the Temple service, which had been halted for three years. Even in the Pharisaic circles such a festival could be observed, though they were opposed to the Hasmoneans, and were against the observance of their victories.

The explanation would be quite simple, were it not for the Chanukkoh lights. This ritual, which in time became the main observance of the festival, is the most difficult and beclouded point in the history of Chanukkoh.

Kindling the Lights . . . We know that Josephus was the first writer to mention the Chanukkoh lights and he attempted to tie them up with the story of Chanukkoh. In Josephus' time it was not yet decided whether to begin the festival with one light and end with eight, or to begin with eight and end with one. To these we can add the following facts:

Nothing is said in the Mishnah about the kindling of Chanukkoh lights. There is much about Purim and the Book of Esther, but silence regarding Chanukkoh. The name of the holiday is mentioned a few times, but no more. Once, in passing, the Chanukkoh lights are mentioned, but there is no law ordering the kindling of them. The Gemoro, which discusses and interprets the Mishnah, does deal with the Chanukkoh lights, but only in the name of the *Amoraim*, the interpreters, without referring to the Mishnah.[259] We get the impression, then, that the Chanukkoh lights were not popular with the *Tannaim*, the teachers of the Oral Law whose teachings are contained in the Mishnah; they were not eager to deal with the problem.

The very fact that legends were created in an effort to connect the festival with the lights arouses suspicion. Had this connection existed from the beginning, from the time that Chanukkoh became a festival, there would have been no need to invent tales about them.

All these facts call for explanations and, in accordance with what we know of the custom, there can be but one explanation—that the Chanukkoh lights, originally, had nothing to do with Chanukkoh, but originated with an older festival that occurred at the same time of the year and that was forced out by the new Chanukkoh festival.

That Chanukkoh took the place of an older festival is no cause for surprise. For, as we have seen, this happened with every other festival of the Jews and of other peoples as well.[260] A new period needs a new festival. But people do not take an ordinary week day and make a festival of it; they take over a day that previously had a festive character. And it is a general rule that the story, the explanation, is always about the new festival, but the ceremonies are carried over from the old festival. A new meaning and interpretation is sought for them, so that they will fit into the new festival.

When we wish to learn something about the older, discarded festival we must turn not to the stories told in connection with the newer festival, but to its rites and ceremonies. What kind of festival, then, was the one that was forced out by Chanukkoh?

The answer to this must be looked for in the main ritual of Chanukkoh, in the lights; and only one answer is possible, that the original festival had to do with fire and light. It was no doubt a nature festival, one of those semi-holidays with a heathenish background that was bound up, not with the official Jewish religion, but with the folk belief as, for instance, the Fifteenth Day of Sh'vot, *Lag Bo-Omer*, and others, to be discussed further on.

The Chanukkoh lights originated in an old nature festival, that was observed in winter by certain Jewish groups, in the season when the days begin to lengthen. In time the lights were eventually tied up with Chanukkoh.[261]

Why the Chanukkoh lights began to play an important role in the generation before the destruction of the second Temple we cannot be certain. It is possible that the lights had some connection with the political situation of that time, after the fall of the Hasmoneans.[262] But that is not certain. We can only say with certainty that in the first generations after the destruction, the Chanukkoh lights had no ancient, sacred tradition; it was during this period that the attempt was first being made to sanctify them.

The Flask of Oil...In order to imbue the Chanukkoh lights with a religious aura, with a sacred tradition, the legend of the flask of oil was created.

"What is Chanukkoh?" the Gemoro asks, and the answer given there is that the Greeks, when they occupied the Temple, defiled all the oil that was stored therein. When the Hasmoneans won, they searched the Temple and found only one small flask of oil bearing the seal of the High Priest, containing only enough oil to light the Menorah for one day. A miracle occurred, and this oil lasted for eight days. The next year these days were declared a festival, with *Hallel* and thanksgiving to God.[263]

The question of the Gemoro, "What is Chanukkoh?" does not imply that the Amoraim did not know what Chanukkoh meant. They knew very well what Chanukkoh was. What troubled them was the question of the Chanukkoh lights, and how the kindling of the lights was connected with the festival. In answer to this question they gave the legend of the flask of oil. The legend does not seek to explain the festival, but the reason for kindling the lights. At the same time, the legend gives the answer to another question, why the festival lasts eight days instead of seven. In those days it had long been forgotten that Chanukkoh was originally observed as a second Sukkos.

The above legend was an easy one to create and present, for the theme behind it is a universal one, and is met in the folk tales of all peoples. The Greeks, for instance, also relate that the bit of oil poured into the lamp near the statue of the goddess Athena, on the Acropolis, burned for an entire year. Amongst Jews the same theme, that of the miracle of the flask of oil, is also found in the tales of Elijah and Elisha.[264]

But not in all Jewish circles were the Chanukkoh lights explained by the miracle of the flask of oil. In some circles they were explained otherwise. "Why are lights kindled on Chanukkoh?" the Midrash asks, and the answer is:

"When the Sons of the Hasmonean, the High Priest, defeated the Greeks they entered the Temple and found there eight iron spears. They stuck candles in these spears and kindled them." [265]

Here the question about the Chanukkoh lights is asked explicitly. But exactly as in the tale of the flask of oil this tale of the iron spears at the same time gives an answer to the second question, why Chanukkoh lasts eight days. The oil burned eight days and the number of spears found was eight.

The same Midrash, in dealing with Chanukkoh, in general, states that it is a commemoration of the re-dedication of the Temple by the Hasmoneans, who made war against the Greeks and defeated them, that it was observed in the same manner as the dedication the Jews held in the wilderness when they finished the Tabernacle.[266]

Elsewhere the two questions are asked separately. The first question asked is why Chanukkoh is observed for eight days; the answer is that it took the Hasmoneans eight days to erect and whitewash the new altar and to install the new sacred utensils. Then the reason for the kindling of lights is asked; to which the reply is given that, when the Hasmoneans entered the Temple, they held eight iron spears in their hands, and they covered them with wood, in which they kindled lights.[267]

A unique presentation of the Chanukkoh lights is given in *Al Ha-nissim*, the special prayer that is recited during the festival. The great accomplishments of Mattathias and his sons are told there in simple and beautiful language; but the legends of the lights are not mentioned in the prayer. The author of this prayer speaks of the lights without reference to miracles. They are kindled, he says, because at the time when the Jews cleansed the Temple and re-instituted the regular Temple service, they kindled lights in the courts of the sanctuary. But the two Books of the Maccabees do not mention lighting lamps in the courts, in addition to the lighting of the Menorah in the Temple. This was obviously originated in those Jewish circles that sought to eliminate the miracle-tales in connection with the Chanukkoh lights.

It is extraordinary, however, that Jews usually spoke of Chanukkoh and the Chanukkoh lights according to the version found in the Gemoro, and not in accordance with the prayer, *Al Ha-nissim*. Possibly this is because the miracle of the flask of oil was more appealing to the imagination of the people than the natural, straightforward account of the victories of Judah Maccabee and his brothers; or else because the people paid more attention to the Gemoro than to the actual meaning of the prayers they used.

Later Developments...Chanukkoh is a young festival, without deep roots, and therefore the attitude toward it changed greatly in the course of time.

Had Chanukkoh been only a political, national holiday, a reminder of the victory of the Hasmoneans, it would surely have disappeared, exactly as other festivals that originated in the same period disappeared. The holiday, however, soon became a religious festival, in commemoration of the re-dedication of the Temple, and for that reason was able to continue its course even after the Pharisees became antagonistic to the Hasmonean rulers.

It was not possible, however, to make Chanukkoh entirely a religious festival. In observing the re-dedication of the Temple there was incidentally a reminder of the political background of the holiday, the revolt of the Hasmoneans and their great victory. This was the very reason for the lack of popularity the festival had in the time of the *Tannaim*. Shortly after the destruction of the Temple after the great rebellions against Rome which had led to such gory catastrophes, the Jews did not want to be reminded of the revolt of the Hasmoneans. In general, the Jews resigned themselves, politically, and wanted to forget wars and rebellions. The spiritual leaders, the teachers of the Torah, became the rulers of Jewish life, and they obviously did not wish to commemorate any festival that harked back to revolt, especially to the revolt of the Hasmoneans. For the later Hasmonean rulers were Sadducees and waged a bloody war against the Pharisees. The *Tannaim*, the spiritual leaders of the Jews after the destruction, followed the Pharisaic trend and formed from it Rabbinic Judaism.

The greatest opponent of Chanukkoh was Rabbi Judah the Patriarch, compiler and editor of the Mishnah. He sought, in general, to establish friendly relations between the Jews and the Romans, and was anxious that Jews forget the past. Had it depended entirely upon him he would have also abolished Tishoh B'Ov and Purim. However, these two days were very popular with the Jews, were engraved in their hearts, and Rabbi Judah could not abolish them. Chanukkoh, however, was not very popular, and Rabbi Judah sought to make it even less so by practically ignoring it in the Mishnah.[268]

Despite this, Chanukkoh did not disappear. Of course, observance was centered about the miracle of the flask of oil, thus strengthening the religious character of the festival, but it was impossible to obliterate entirely the political, national background. We have already learned that in many quarters the miracle of the flask of oil was neglected and the true story of Chanukkoh, with its historic, religious, and national import, was told.

In one way the legend of the flask of oil helped to sanctify Chanukkoh and to preserve it as a festival. In another way, though, it did much to becloud the true importance of the occasion. Later, therefore, protests against the miracle tale began to be heard in many Jewish circles.

As far back as the seventeenth century a strong protest was lodged against the practice of basing Chanukkoh on a miracle, thus neglecting the main importance of the festival, the victory of the Hasmoneans.[269] The protest against the miracle of the oil became even stronger during the *Haskalah* (Enlightenment) period. A great debate regarding it was carried on in the Jewish press of the nineties of the nineteenth century.[270]

The miracle of the oil became in recent times increasingly unpopular; on the other hand, the festival of Chanukkoh grew in popularity. With the spread of the Zionist sentiment the importance of Chanukkoh increased in Jewish life. The close of the last century and the beginning of this century saw a new epoch in the history of Chanukkoh. The festival emerged from the mistiness in which it had been obscured for two thousand years, during which it existed as a semi-holiday. It is being called by a new name, too, the Hasmonean Festival, or the Festival of the Maccabees. It is observed now also in those Jewish circles where the religious festivals play an unimportant role.

Chanukkoh is rapidly becoming one of the greatest of Jewish festivals.

Anticipation...The two months between Sukkos and Chanukkoh drag along, gray and cloudy, without sunshine and without a trace of festive joy. This time of the year is especially drab and monotonous for the school children. Day after day, they trudge through the muddy streets on their way to the *Cheder*, where they study and repeat the same lessons over and over again. And how much Torah can be studied during the short winter days! The children, therefore, must also go to *Cheder* in the evening. With lanterns in their hands they make their way to the *m'lammed*, the teacher, for another few hours of study.

In this way two solid months pass, till the days of Chanukkoh come, bringing with them a bit of festive light and joy into the *Cheder* and the home.

In Cheder...About a week before Chanukkoh the discipline in the *Cheder* begins to weaken. There is less strain in the actual teaching, and the teacher appears not to notice the lads playing when they should be studying.

When the first day of the festival comes, and with it the first Chanukkoh light, all discipline ceases. During Chanukkoh, the school is open only half-days, and during the half-day there is more frolicking than teaching. The children play, and the teacher not only lets them play, but joins them in their games. They play many games, but the most popular is spinning *dreidlech*, leaden tops.

Pouring the lead for these tops was begun some weeks

earlier. They are cast in wooden forms. There are a few handy lads about, who know just how to whittle the forms and to cast the leaden tops. Most of the work is in the whittling of the forms. These consist of four sections, in each of which is whittled a letter of the Hebrew alphabet. There is a *nun* (N), *gimmel* (G), *he* (H), and *shin* (SH). If the top falls with the *nun* uppermost then the cast means nothing (nisht); if the *gimmel* is on top, then the player has won all (gants); if the *he* is on top, then the player wins half (halb); and if the *shin* shows, the player loses (stell or shlecht).

The day before Chanukkoh the teacher tells the children the story of the flask of oil and other Chanukkoh tales as well. He tells of the battles of Mattathias and his sons against the Greeks, and the story of Hannah and her seven sons. The children listen intently, breathlessly.

Toward Evening...It is cold and wet outdoors, but the *Bes ha-Midrosh*, the House of Study, is light and warm. The evening prayers are the regular, week-day prayers and the atmosphere is as on ordinary days, except for the Chanukkoh lights which the sexton kindles in the large menorah, and which spread a festive spirit about the room, a spirit which is heightened by the addition to the services of the *Al Ha-nissim* prayer.

The worshipers go home after the evening services. The Chanukkoh lamp, shining and bright, awaits them, and the children wait eagerly for the first candle to be kindled.

After the kindling of the lights, the family gathers about the table. Usually there is a goose prepared for the occasion, a goose that was bought weeks before and fattened and stuffed with dumplings. There may be a potato pudding as a special treat, but it is regarded as specially meritorious to eat pancakes made of cheese and other cheese delicacies during Chanukkoh.

After the meal the family starts to play. They spin tops, but in the main, all play cards. The table is opened as wide as possible, and about it gather all the members of the family, relatives, friends, and neighbors. They play cards, they drink tea, and they talk and frolic in honor of Chanukkoh.

The outstanding Chanukkoh night is that on which the fifth candle is lit, especially for the children. As this is the evening when families gather and the children are given Chanukkoh-money. Special food is served, either pancakes or pudding. The children eat pancakes and count their coins, and consider themselves fortunate.

xxiv. Chanukkoh = CUSTOM & CEREMONY

The Lights...No rich ritual grew up about Chanukkoh. The only ceremonial of the festival lies in the kindling of the lights. Originally the lights were kindled only in the home. At a later period they were also kindled in the synagogue. In the olden days they were kindled at the left side of the door leading to the street, opposite the *mezuzoh*. If one lived in an upper story and had no door leading to the street, the lights were placed in the window.

The benediction recited over the Chanukkoh lights stems from the time of the *Amoraim*. During the Middle Ages the song, Rock of Ages, appeared amongst the Ashkenazic Jews.[271]

Cheese Dishes...The custom of eating cheese delicacies on Chanukkoh is an old one. We find it practiced in the fourteenth century, but it originated, apparently, in a much older period. The custom is as old, perhaps, as the Chanukkoh lights. Pancakes made with cheese were used. From this developed the custom of eating pancakes of all kinds.

During the Middle Ages Jews explained this custom by connecting it with the story of Judith, which they linked with the story of Chanukkoh. Judith, according to legend, was a daughter of the Hasmoneans, who fed cheese to the leader of the Jewish foes; he became very thirsty and consequently drank much wine. When he became drunk, she beheaded him. For this reason, it was said, Jews eat cheese delicacies at Chanukkoh.[272]

The Dreidel... The custom of spinning *dreidel* tops on Chanukkoh is very widespread. The top is called a *trendel* or *trenderel* by the Jews of Germany, Bohemia, and Hungary. In some places it is called a *werfel*. The tops are made with four wings, each of which bears a letter, *nun* (N), *gimmel* (G), *he* (H), and *shin* (SH). The *dreidel* was also associated with Chanukkoh and the letters were interpreted as an acrostic of the sentence, *Nes Godol Hoyoh Shom* (A great miracle happened there). It has been proved that, originally, the *dreidel* was not connected with Chanukkoh in any way. The German Christians also had the custom of spinning a three-winged top on Christmas Eve, each wing of which bore a letter.[273] The Germans did not originate the game but borrowed it from the Greeks and the Romans.

Games and Cards... Chanukkoh was never a festival of revelry as was Purim.

It was the custom in the Middle Ages to while away Chanukkoh evening with jests, puzzles, charades, and such. This was especially true in the *y'shivos*, the Talmudic academies.[274]

Playing cards on Chanukkoh is not a new Jewish custom. Many rabbis protested against it, but obviously without success. Levy Yitschok, the famous Chassidic rabbi of Berditchev, was, in general, a champion of the Jews before God and man, and he also defended Jews in this respect. He claimed that Jews played cards on Chanukkoh evenings in order to accustom themselves to stay up late, so that they could study more Torah. But still, he was also against the custom.

Theatricals... In past times it was also customary to present theatricals on Chanukkoh. We know that in the seventeenth century, and in the beginning of the eighteenth, it was the custom to present plays not only on Purim, but also on Chanukkoh, in the German ghettos.[275]

In the Orient it was still a custom, as late as the seventeenth century, for Jews to masquerade during Chanukkoh, men donning women's clothes and parading through the streets.[276]

It appears, however, that the theatricals of Chanukkoh were merely borrowed from Purim, and were, therefore, never as widespread as the Purim theatricals.

The Scroll of Antiochus...In the Middle Ages it became the custom, in some Jewish communities, to read publicly in the synagogue on Chanukkoh the Scroll of Antiochus or, as it is also called, the Scroll of the Hasmoneans. This book is not an exact historical record, but merely an outline of the events in connection with the revolt and victory of the Maccabees, in legendary form, with the facts and chronology confused and with a large admixture of fiction.

It was written originally in Aramaic in late Talmudic times, and was later translated into Hebrew and into many other languages which Jews spoke. It was the Hebrew translation which became popular and which was read in the synagogue. The custom, however, has died out.[277]

XXV. Purim = ITS ORIGINS

Introduction...Purim, like Chanukkoh, is a lesser festival, and comes on the fourteenth day of the Jewish month Adar. The fifteenth day of Adar is called Shushan Purim (the Purim of Susa), and the thirteenth day of Adar is the Fast of Esther.

Like Chanukkoh, Purim is also a day of deliverance. On Chanukkoh the deliverance of Judaism is observed; on Purim the deliverance of the Jews is celebrated.

The Book of Esther...There are five books of the Bible, known in the ritual of the synagogue as "Scrolls," which are read on five holidays. The Song of Songs is read on Pesach, the Book of Ruth on Shovuos, Lamentations on Tishoh B'Ov, Ecclesiastes on Sukkos, and the Book of Esther on Purim. Of these five books, three (the Song of Songs, Ruth, and Ecclesiastes) have no real relation to the festivals on which they are read. The fourth book, Lamentations, is connected with Tishoh B'Ov, but the bond is not so close that it would be impossible to separate them. The situation is entirely different regarding Purim and the Book of Esther, which are so closely associated that they could not exist without each other. Purim cannot be understood without the Book of Esther, and the Book of Esther gives the *raison d'être* for Purim.

We cannot, therefore, begin to talk about the origin and the history of Purim without first making clear what the Book of Esther is.

The Story...The story told in the Book of Esther is a remarkable one. The actual events related there never happened. In the time spoken of, in the days of King Ahasuerus, no such events occurred as are described in the book, nor could they possibly have happened then. This is the opinion held by practically all students of the Bible.[278] Yet the Book of Esther is more truthful than many really truthful books. For the story in the Book of Esther happened a countless number of times and keeps on happening to this very day.

The opinion that the events described in the Book of Esther are not historical is based on many premises, some of which follow.

It could never have happened that Ahasuerus, or any other Persian king, would allow the Jews to slay, in his own land, 75,000 of his subjects, nor would he let them slay eight hundred in his capital.

As far as we know, from the Greek historian Herodotus, neither Esther nor Vashti was the queen of Ahasuerus. Herodotus lived in the period mentioned in the Book of Esther (the fifth century, B.C.E.) and was in a position to know better than any others the situation and the events in the Persian court. According to Herodotus, a Persian king had to choose his wife from one of the seven highest aristocratic Persian families. So Esther could never have become queen of Persia. Besides, according to Herodotus, Ahasuerus' queen was Amestris, the daughter of a Persian general.

The historical authenticity of Mordecai and Esther, the two main figures in the book, is entirely doubtful; for their names closely resemble the names of the god Marduk and the goddess Istar of the Babylonians.[279] This does not eliminate the possibility that there was, in the court of King Ahasuerus, a Jew with the Babylonian name, Mordecai. But there is a suspicion that the creator of the Book of Esther wove a theme from Babylonian mythology into his book.

The author of the Book of Esther obviously lived centuries after the time of which he wrote, and his knowledge of the period was vague. Mordecai, he relates, was expelled from Jerusalem in the exile of Jeconiah, King of Judah. This happened in the year 597 B.C.E. In the third year of the reign of Ahasuerus, that is, in the year 482, Mordecai must have been over one hundred and fifteen years old. But in the Book of Esther he is presented as a young man, and he rides his steed through the streets of Shushan. It is obvious that the writer of the Book of Esther knew little of the chronology of the Persian period and imagined that Ahasuerus was the direct successor of Nebuchadnezzar.[280]

Another point of suspicion is the fact that, throughout the Book of Esther, the word "God" is not mentioned, despite the fact that throughout the Bible nothing takes place without God's intervention. We get the impression that the writer was somewhat afraid to mention the name of God in his book. Even in situations where the use of the word is called for he does not mention it directly. For instance, Mordecai says to Esther, "For if thou altogether holdest thy peace at this time, then will relief and deliverance arise to the Jews from another place—." In such a situation it would have been more fitting to say: "—then God will eventually help His people." This can only be explained on the assumption that the author wrote his book as an explanation of an old, heathen festival, in which it would have been distasteful to include God and piety, as conceived by Jews.

But most curious of all is the fact that Mordecai, in the book, is descended from King Saul, and Haman descends from Agag, king of the Amalekites, whom Saul defeated.

It appears, then, that six hundred years after the battle between Saul and Agag their great-great grandchildren met in the court of King Ahasuerus and re-lived the life and death struggle between Israel and Amalek.

In all, it is easy to see that we have to deal here, in the Book of Esther, not with a true story of historical events, but with phantasy and poetry; the war between Mordecai and Haman is only an allegory that presents, in guarded speech, the war that Jews must carry on, from time to time, against the enemies that seek to destroy them.

The Book of Esther, then, is not a book of history, but a historical novel, that relates a tangled and lengthy tale of ancient days.

There were many historical novels written by the Jews of old. Three of them, Ruth, Jonah, and Esther, are included in the Bible. Other historical novels, such as Judith and Tobias, were never incorporated into the sacred books, but were preserved in their Greek versions.

The story of the Book of Esther is, then, a poetic, literary creation of a Jewish novelist, who lived during the time of the second Temple. Only as such can it be truly understood and appraised. Since it is a historical novel, we must not be surprised that the themes on which it is based are universal ones, present in other tales of the period.

Motifs of the Book of Esther ... The main motif of the Esther romance is that of the woman who, through her beauty, captures the heart of the enemy and thereby saves her people from catastrophe. Exactly the same motif is found in the story of Judith, a book that was a product of the same period.

Since Judith is not included in the Bible, and is not familiar to all, an outline of the story is here presented:

Nebuchadnezzar, King of Assyria, demanded of all the peoples in western Asia that they help wage war against the king of the Medes. This demand was also made of the inhabitants of Palestine. The peoples of western Asia, however, decided to disregard the order and Nebuchadnezzar sent his general, Holofernes, with a great army to punish these nations. Holofernes laid waste the countries and profaned their sanctuaries, so that all peoples would bow to Nebuchadnezzar, and consider only him as their god.

In Palestine, at that time, Jews had returned from exile and had rebuilt the Temple in Jerusalem. When the Jews heard that Holofernes and his army were already in the valley of Jezreel, they fortified the hill country of Ephraim. They took special pains to fortify the pass between the hills at the town of Bethulia, to keep Holofernes from marching on Jerusalem. Holofernes besieged the town and cut off the water supply, causing great suffering among the inhabitants. People lay in the streets faint with thirst; the last bit of water was about to be used; it seemed that nothing could save the city from the hands of the foe.

In Bethulia, however, there lived a rich and lovely widow by the name of Judith, and she undertook to save the city. After offering prayers to God, she dressed in her loveliest raiment and, escorted by a slave, made her way to the camp of the enemy. She convinced Holofernes that she escaped from the city in order to show him the road to Jerusalem. Holofernes believed everything she told him, and became greatly enamoured of her beauty.

Judith stayed in the enemy camp for three days, and Holofernes invited her to a wine-feast. Judith accepted the invitation and, after the feast, remained alone with him in his tent. He was very drunk, and Judith proceeded to execute her plan. She beheaded Holofernes with his own sword, placed the head in a sack, and carried it back with her to the city, where she was met with songs of joy and hymns to God.

The next morning when the foes saw the head of their leader impaled on the walls of the town, they became panic-stricken and fled in wild disorder. The Jews followed and slaughtered many of them, and Judith was acclaimed the saviour of her people.

That is the outline of the story and it is apparent that we have here a typical, historical novel, in which the writer has confused various historical facts and persons. Nebuchadnez-zar, the king of Babylon who destroyed Jerusalem, becomes, in the story of Judith, the king of Assyria, and the Jews, the story relates, had in his time returned from exile and re-built the Temple.

Holofernes is a historical person. There actually was a general by that name who led a great army to overthrow Palestine. But it was not in Nebuchadnezzar's time, but in the time of the Persian king, Artaxerxes the Third, who ruled shortly before Alexander the Great. There was, at that time, a great revolt against Persia in Syria and in Egypt, a revolt that Artaxerxes put down with a bloody hand. The commander of the Persian army was called Holofernes. Jews took part in this revolt, and it is possible that Holofernes besieged a town by the name of Bethulia, near the valley of Jezreel.

The story of Judith, then, has a much greater historical basis than the story of Esther. But only the background on which the story is based is historical, not the facts. For history tells us that Holofernes did not lose his head in the above war, but scored a great victory.

We see the confusing of various historic personages, facts, and periods that the writer of Judith brought into his tale.

To these he added the theme of the beautiful woman who conquers the foe with her beauty; in that way he built his Judith romance.

The story of Judith is practically the same as the story of Esther, told in a different way. In the one Holofernes is the Jewish enemy; in the other, Haman. In the one, Ahasuerus is the king; in the other, Nebuchadnezzar. In one the Jewish foe is hung as the result of a wine-feast; in the other he is beheaded. The main point of difference is the fact that Esther is a story of the Jews in the lands of the Diaspora, while Judith is a novel of Jewish life in Palestine.

The Book of Esther, however, is not built on the Esther theme alone. A great role is played by Mordecai, the Jew who sits in the court of the king and wins favors for his people. This theme was a universal one in the Jewish literature of the time of the second Temple. In addition to the Book of Esther we meet this theme in the story of the three servants of King Darius, a tale told in the Third Book of Ezra.[281]

The story, in a few words, is as follows:

Zerubbabel, grandson of Jeconiah and the builder of the second Temple, was, according to the legend, one of the body-servants of King Darius, the father of Ahasuerus. Darius, on one occasion, after a victory over an enemy, gave a feast for all the nobles of Persia and Media. After the feast all went to sleep, including Darius.

In the middle of the night Darius awoke and could sleep no more. So he began to talk with his body-servants. Each one was asked to give an answer to the question: What is the strongest thing in the world? He who gave the cleverest answer would receive costly regal gifts and, in addition, become second to Darius in the kingdom. One said that wine was the strongest thing in the world. The second said that the king's might was strongest. The third, Zerubbabel, said that woman was strongest but, above all, "truth beareth away the victory."

Zerubbabel was acknowledged the cleverest and the king offered to give him anything he desired. And Zerubbabel asked for only one thing, permission to re-build the Temple in Jerusalem. Darius at once gave him the necessary permission, as well as many other privileges, and Zerubbabel returned to Jerusalem with the exiled Jews of Babylonia and built the second Temple.

It is perhaps unnecessary to state that the above story is a legend, in which the role of Nehemiah is transferred to Zerubbabel, but the legend is, at all events, an ancient one. According to many authorities it is older than the story of Esther.

It has just been said that Nehemiah's role, in the legend, was transferred to Zerubbabel. We know for certain that Nehemiah held a high position in the court of Artaxerxes the First, and that he won the king's permission to build a wall around Jerusalem. It is possible, then, that all the stories about court Jews of those times were but a reflection of Nehemiah's role in the court of Artaxerxes the First. There may have been other prominent Jewish officials in the court of the Persian kings. It is not impossible to believe that there was a high Jewish official by the name of Mordecai in Ahasuerus' court.

We meet another theme in the Book of Esther that is dealt with in another Jewish book of those days, the theme of the ruler who, to begin with, hated Jews and desired to destroy them, but who later changed his attitude and became the Jews' best friend. We find this theme in the Third Book of the Maccabees.

In this book a story is told of the Jews in Egypt and of the king who wanted to slaughter them all; but, through a miracle from heaven they were saved from death. The king in this tale is Ptolemy the Fourth, the time about fifty years before the Hasmonean revolt, and the place Alexandria.

The king of Egypt, the book tells us, marched into Jerusalem after his victory over Antiochus the Great, and began to enter the Holy of Holies in the Temple. The Jews prayed to God and He answered their plea; at the threshold the king was stricken, and fell to the earth, stunned and paralyzed. Ptolemy returned to Egypt in a great rage and sought to revenge himself on the Jews. He took all civil rights away from them and had all the Jews of Egypt, fettered in chains, brought to Alexandria and confined in the Hippodrome. He then ordered that five hundred elephants be plied with liquor and then goaded on against the Jews. But on the day designated the king overslept and awoke too late to give the necessary order. The next day the king lost his memory and forgot all about it. On the third day the decree was about to be carried out, but the Jews prayed and called to God, and He sent two angels from heaven who threw such fright into the king and his army that they became petrified, unable to stir. Instead of attacking the Jews, the elephants turned on the soldiers and trampled them. The king then became angered at his councilors, had all the Jews freed of their chains, and told them to hold a seven-day festival at his cost, a festival which was observed yearly.

Practically the same story, in a different text, is told by Josephus Flavius in the second part of his book against Apion. According to Josephus this incident occurred somewhat later, under Ptolemy the Seventh, in the time of the Hasmonean ruler, John Hyrcanus. The king's sweetheart begged him not to harm the Jews, as Esther did of Ahasuerus. Josephus' tale is recognizably the older one, because it is based on historical events and situations; the text in the Third Book of the Maccabees is a later version.

We have here a story, in two versions, very similar to the story in the Book of Esther, the locale changing from the Shushan of Ahasuerus' time to the Alexandria of the Hasmonean period.

We have considered now those themes in the Book of Esther which are found in other Jewish stories. There is one theme in the book, however, which is found, not in Jewish stories, but in the Persian-Arabic tales of the thousand-and-one nights. For in the first chapter Esther plays the same role as does the grand vizier's daughter, Scheherazade in the Arabian Nights, a story-teller to the king.

In the introduction to the Arabian Nights the king weds a different girl each day, and the next morning orders the grand vizier to put her to death. He is certain that not only his wife, whom he lost through unfaithfulness, is false, but that every woman is false to her husband. And the only way to be sure of a woman's faithfulness is to kill her on the day after the wedding. For this reason, the king married a different girl every day for three years, and had her slain the next morning, till Scheherazade, the beautiful and clever daughter of the grand vizier, risks her life and enthralls the king with the tales that she tells him for a thousand-and-one nights. When the tales are ended Scheherazade shows the king the three children she bore him during that time, and he decrees that she be allowed to live for the sake of her sons.

Students have long recognized that this story is based on the same theme as that of Esther and Ahasuerus. Ahasuerus, too, marries a different girl each day and sends her away the next morning, refusing to see her again—till Esther finds favor in his eyes and remains with him forever. Ahasuerus, too, whiles away the nights with stories that are related to him. In addition, there is this similarity in the two tales: Both Esther and Scheherazade, through their effect on the king, bring help and salvation, Scheherazade to the maidens of her land, and Esther to her people.

The story of Scheherazade is not Arabic, but Persian. One must not assume, however, that the two stories influenced each other, but rather that the two stories originate from one source, from an ancient Persian tale.

Its Historical Background...We have discussed thus far the literary themes on which the story of Esther is built. But the writer of the book also had to have a historical background on which to build his novel. He had to have in mind a certain historical period and certain historical events similar to the incidents that he relates in his book. It is certain that he would not be able to tell the story of Haman did he not have in mind a definite enemy of the Jews who sought to overthrow them and, in the course of his struggle against them, lost his head.

The Haman story consists of two separate themes, each of which may have its own historical background. One theme, that of the struggle between Haman and Mordecai is really fiction and could never have happened as it is related, though it may be founded on an actual happening in the life of the Jews in Persia. It is possible that in the court of Ahasuerus there was a Jew-hating grand vizier, who came to a disastrous end through a court Jew by the name of Mordecai; and that the Jews of Persia commemorated this unimportant episode and later exaggerated it through fantastic tales.

The same cannot be said of the other theme in the story of Haman, that in which he seeks to slaughter all the Jews and is finally hanged, while the Jews slay thousands of their enemies. That, as has been pointed out before, could not have happened in the Persian epoch. The question, then, is: What kind of historical connotation and what historical events are reflected in this episode? There are various interpretations given by scholars.

Graetz contends that this episode reflects the period of Antiochus Epiphanes and the woes suffered by the Jews of that time. Most students of the Bible are of the opinion that the Book of Esther reflects, in imaginative form, the events in Palestine during the time of the Syrian king, Demetrius, the nephew of Antiochus Epiphanes.

Demetrius had sent his general, Nicanor, with a great army, against Judah Maccabee and his followers. Nicanor was a confirmed Jew-hater, and he threatened to burn the Temple to ashes if the Jews did not surrender Judah and his adherents. The First Book of the Maccabees states: "The king sent Nicanor, one of his honorable princes, a man that hated Israel and was their enemy, and commanded him to destroy the people." [282] This reads very much like Ahasuerus' order in the Book of Esther.

The decisive battle between Nicanor and Judah Maccabee came on the thirteenth day of Adar, the same day on which Haman, according to the Book of Esther, strove to slaughter all the Jews. Not only was the entire army wiped out, but Nicanor himself fell on the battlefield, and the Jews beheaded him and exhibited his head in Jerusalem.

This day, the thirteenth day of Adar, was a festival for Jews in the days of the second Temple, and was called *Nicanor Day*. It was the day which marked, for them, the conversion of grief to joy and of mourning to festivity, the day on which their greatest foe was defeated.

Many scholars claim, therefore, that the writer of the Book

of Esther had Nicanor and Judah Maccabee in mind when he told the tale of Haman and Mordecai, a tale in which Haman suffers Nicanor's fate. And the day on which, in the Book of Esther, Jews settle accounts with their foes is the same day on which Nicanor's army was wiped out.

It seems logical to assume that Haman's defeat, as well as the death of Holofernes through Judith, is a reflection of the defeat and death of Nicanor.

This theory did not originate with modern Bible critics. The Jewish homiletical preachers of the Middle Ages recognized it quite a while ago, and, therefore, combined the story of Judith with the story of Chanukkoh, and told it with the expressions and phraseology of the Book of Esther.[283]

The Book of Esther, and the story of Judith also, thus point to the Grecian period of Jewish history. Even the situation of the Jews in the world, as contained in Haman's charges to Ahasuerus, is more fitting to the Grecian period than to the Persian,[284] though this cannot be said with certainty. For the Book of Esther was written as a historical explanation for the Purim festival, and the origin of Purim is very obscure. We cannot be certain who wrote the Book of Esther, where it was written, or under what circumstances it was written.

xxvi. Purim = IN SEVERAL SETTINGS

Current Theories...From all that has been said it is clear that Purim did not have its source in the story told in the Book of Esther; on the contrary, the Book of Esther was created as an explanation for the festival.

What happened to other Jewish festivals and to the holidays of other peoples also happened to Purim. Purim as the new festival of the salvation of the Jews was decreed for a day that had long been observed as somewhat of a holiday. The ceremonies and customs of the old festival remained, but they took on new meaning and added significance.[285]

What kind of festival was Purim before it became the popular festival of Jewish salvation?

Many theories and hypotheses were advanced in answer to the above question. But none of them is well founded or entirely satisfactory, and not worthy of thorough examination here. From all the conjectures we may accept the following:

Purim originally appeared amongst the Jews of Persia, and was adopted by them from their non-Jewish neighbors. Persian Jews observed, in common with their neighbors, a festival which was celebrated yearly in the middle of the last winter month, in the same way, that Jews of today observe, to a certain extent, the general New Year in the middle of the winter. It also seems that Purim, from the beginning, had the characteristic of a spring masquerade, and was a festival of play and frolic, of merriment and mischief, of abandon and wine-drinking. This festival was very popular with the Jews of Persia and Babylonia and, in time, it spread to the Jews of

Palestine. It seems, from certain passages in the Talmud, that the Palestinian Jews were at first opposed to observing Purim. It was some time before they gave up their opposition.[286]

The above is all that we can unravel from the tangled snarl that Purim and the Book of Esther present to us. When we go further we enter the field of hypothesis.

We do not know, for instance, what character the Purim festival had at the time it spread into Palestine, whether it was still a heathen, Persian-Babylonian festival, or whether it had already become Judaized and given a historical background. Even if we accept the premise that it was already a historical festival when it began to spread amongst the Jews of Palestine, we do not know what type of historical festival it was. It is possible that it was already based on the Book of Esther. It is also possible that even before the book was written, Purim had been linked with some event in the history of the Persian Jews. In the old days Purim also bore the name, *Mordecai Day*.[287] It is, therefore, possible that the heathen festival became for the Jews of Persia a *Mordecai Day* in which they celebrated the victory that a high Jewish official in the court of Ahasuerus had scored over his enemy. It is also possible, however, that the festival was named, *Mordecai Day*, from the account in the Book of Esther.

More important is the fact that we do not know the relationship between this *Mordecai Day* and *Nicanor Day*. These were two festivals that must have aroused much rivalry. They came on succeeding days, *Nicanor Day* on the thirteenth of Adar and Purim on the fourteenth, and they both had practically the same content, the victory of the Jews over a great foe who sought to annihilate them. The stories told in connection with the two days were almost identical, with merely a change of names.

It does not seem logical that the same Jewish circles that decreed the thirteenth of the month as *Nicanor Day* in observance of Judah Maccabee's victory over Nicanor should observe, on the next day, Mordecai's victory over Haman. It seems more likely that *Nicanor Day* was a political holiday of the Hasmonean dynasty and Purim was set up as a rival holiday by the Pharisees, who were opposed to the Hasmonean rulers. That does not preclude the possibility that there were Jewish circles that had no interest in politics and, therefore, observed both *Nicanor Day* and Purim.

Even in the matter of date we must assume that Purim was influenced by *Nicanor Day*. It seems that originally Purim was celebrated on the fifteenth day of the month; it was only later that its observance was ordered a day earlier for the inhabitants of the villages. Apparently it was difficult for peasants to celebrate one day, work the next, and resume the festival on the day after. That could be done, if at all, only in the larger towns. The date of the festival was, therefore, changed for the inhabitants of the villages and the small towns from the fifteenth day of Adar to the fourteenth. It is possible that even in this detail there was a political motive, that the opponents of the Hasmoneans slyly set Purim a day earlier so that it should become a still stronger rival to *Nicanor Day*.

These, after all, are no more than hypotheses. The origin of Purim cannot be stated with certainty.[288] We know only that after the destruction of the second Temple *Nicanor Day* disappeared, while Purim continually grew more popular.

Festivals Follow Tribulations...We have seen that every historical epoch of Jewish life produced holidays and festivals in answer to the needs and demands of the time. So, in the last centuries of the second Temple, one of the richest epochs in all Jewish history, new festivals sprang up. But these were different from the festivals that had originated in the beginnings of Jewish history. In the days of the second Temple the Jewish nation was subject to severe trials; more than once the country found itself in great danger from advancing hostile armies, sent against it by the Greco-Syrian rulers. Usually the Jews were victorious against these armies; they defeated them, revived the Jewish kingdom, and spread its rule over all of Palestine.

These great accomplishments of the Hasmonean period, having made such an impression upon Jewish life, demanded recognition and celebration, and during that period three festivals celebrating Jewish deliverance originated: Chanukkoh, *Nicanor Day*, and Purim. At the same time three new Jewish books appeared, each of which, in its own way, told a story of the deliverance of the Jews from their enemies. These three books appeared separately, in three centers of Jewish life: the Book of Esther originated in Persia; the Book of Judith appeared in Palestine; and the Third Book of the Maccabees was written in Alexandria.

Of these three festivals of Jewish deliverance one, *Nicanor Day*, has entirely disappeared. Popular as the day may have been at one time, it apparently lost its hold on the masses with the end of the Hasmonean dynasty, and after the destruction of the second Temple Jews certainly had no desire to observe a day which commemorated a victory over a Grecian general. The Chanukkoh observance retained its status because of the religious character of the festival. Purim, although it had no religious significance, survived and forced out its nearest rival, *Nicanor Day;* it overshadowed Chanukkoh itself. To this day it is the most joyous festival of Jewish deliverance.

Had Jewish history taken another path, had Jews led a

peaceful existence and not dwelt in continual fear of their enemies, then perhaps Purim, too, would have lost its popularity in time. The everlasting attacks upon Jews, the hostility and enmity visited upon them in the lands of the Diaspora, helped to keep the day dear to them. Wherever Jews lived there arose new Hamans to persecute and enslave them. Purim gave them courage in the darkest hours and hope that eventually they would see the downfall of their enemies.

The Book of Esther has always been for Jews an allegory depicting the Jewish life and Jewish lot among the nations. It is a book in which not just one period is depicted, but all periods; it is a book that remains forever new because Jewish enemies will not allow it to grow old. It is a book that breathes of love for Jews, of the tie that unites the Jews, the Jew of the masses to the one who has attained kingly honors.

It is not strange that such a festival, connected with a book that tells of the indestructibility of the Jewish people appealed to all Jews in all times, and was beloved by young and old. There is a second reason for its great popularity—Purim is the only worldly holiday that Jews possess, the only festival not imbued with religious solemnity. The pious Jew was preoccupied day after day with serious thought and earnest endeavor. Even Sukkos, the festival of joy, took on, in time, an earnest and serious character. The Jew had very little opportunity to express the playful, light-hearted side of life. This expression the Jew found in Purim, the day when all is joyful, when one can revel and be a good fellow.

Thus, bearing in mind the fact that long ago the day on which Purim was celebrated was a spring carnival; adding to that the allegory inherent in the Book of Esther, with which the festival was later identified; we can see why Purim became the popular and beloved holiday that it now is.

Purim will not die as long as prejudice and hatred of the Jew exist anywhere in the world.

Special Purims...Purim became the symbolic name for Jewish deliverance, and whenever a Jewish community was saved from a horrible fate, from pogrom or exile which a Haman-like ruler tried to impose, the community would celebrate, yearly, the day of rescue as a special, local Purim, in the same manner as the universal Jewish Purim.

There were also special family Purims. It often happened that a certain Jewish family was saved from disaster, and it remained a tradition in that family to observe a yearly Purim on the anniversary of their day of deliverance.

There were many such special Purims, three of which can be considered here, for they are the most noted. Two are local and one is a family festival.

A very noted local Purim is the one of Egypt, which is already more than four hundred years old. It occurred in the year 1524. The governor of Egypt, a rebellious despot, at that time rose up against his sovereign, Sultan Suleiman II. The Jews remained faithful to the sultan and the governor imprisoned many of the Jewish leaders of the Cairo community and announced that he would massacre all the Jews on a certain day. On that very day an uprising against the governor broke out and, in the end, he was the one who lost his head. This happened on the twenty-eighth day of Adar and the Jews of Egypt, since then, have observed that day as a Purim, during which they read a book, specially prepared, telling how they were saved.[289]

The second noted Purim of a Jewish community is the "Wintz Purim" of the Frankfurt Jews, which occurred at the beginning of the seventeenth century. The economic situation in Germany which was very bad at that time, was blamed on the Jews. An organized movement against the Jews began in Frankfurt-am-Main, the leader of which was a baker by the name of Wintz Hans Fettmilch. In the year 1614 this Haman of Frankfurt organized a raid on the Jewish ghetto. Jewish homes were sacked and the Jews were driven from the city. But the emperor intervened, and Fettmilch and his followers were arrested. On a certain day, the twentieth of Adar, the leaders of the pogrom were sentenced; the Jews of Frankfurt returned to their ghetto and were compensated for the damage they had suffered. This day was celebrated by the Frankfurt Jewish community as "Wintz Purim" until the second half of the last century.[290]

The best instance of a family Purim is the "Gunpowder Purim" of the family of Rabbi Abraham Danzig, the noted author of *Chaye Odom* (Life of Man), the most popular religious code among the Jews of Eastern Europe. There was a great gunpowder explosion in Wilna, on the fifteenth day of Kislev, in the year 1804. Thirty-one people lost their lives through this explosion, and many houses were wrecked, among others the home of Rabbi Abraham Danzig. He and all the members of his household were dangerously wounded, but all survived and recovered. So he decreed that his family was to fast on that date every year, the fast to be followed, in the evening, with a Purim feast at which festival lights were to be kindled and special prayers and Psalms chanted.[291]

The S'fardim ... On the days before Purim the S'fardic Jews in Palestine are occupied with baking many sweets for the festival. The day preceding Purim a coin is put aside for a special charity, a memento of the half-shekel that Jews once paid as a tax to the Temple. Toward evening all go to the synagogue, dressed in festive clothing, each man bearing a scroll of the Book of Esther under his arm. The S'fardic Jews have no mechanical noise-makers for the occasion; they merely stamp their feet as certain passages are read. Lately, however, the S'fardic children in Jerusalem have been purchasing Haman-rattles from the Ashkenazim. After the reading of the Book of Esther the congregation stamps again, making riotous and boundless noise. This stamping is for Haman and Zeresh and their children.

The S'fardic Jews rise very early the next morning for the synagogue services. Breakfast is eaten hurriedly so that it will be completed before the beggars begin to go from house to house asking for alms.

Minchoh, the afternoon service, is held early, after which the Purim feast is held. Neighbors and friends bring all their delicacies and drinks to one house, and all feast together. Wine and brandy flow like water. The men put on impromptu masquerades, wearing their coats inside out, and carrying brooms in their hands. They sing Purim songs in Hebrew and Spanish and they dance and revel far into the night.

Among Persian Jews...Purim is celebrated with great splendor by the Jews in Persia, the land where the festival was cradled.

For weeks beforehand preparation is made for the festival. The dealers sell special Purim-goodies, and in the religious school, the children pore over the Book of Esther, *Tikkun Purim*,[292] and all the other writings that have any relation to the festival. Purim songs are sung in every Jewish household. The children are especially occupied with the coming festival. The older ones spend their days copying the entire Book of Esther in printed letters. And all the children, big or small, are busy in their spare time with the creation of a human effigy. One sews the hands, a second the feet, a third the head, and a fourth the trunk. The individual parts are filled with straw and rags and are then sewed together, the finished figure being a veritable Haman to hang on Purim.

There is a festive spirit in the synagogue on the Saturday before Purim. On that day a *Piyut* from a *Tikkun Purim* is recited and, at the end of the reading of the Torah, when the reader recites the words, "Thou shalt blot out the remembrance of Amalek from under heaven,"[293] the worshipers beat their fists on the tables and walls.

A highly exalted spirit rules the afternoon of that Sabbath. The synagogue is filled from wall to wall and the preacher gives a sermon based on *Targum Sheni*.[294] He relates and presents vividly the beautiful legends of this folk book, and the congregation listens, enthralled.

The Fast of Esther (see p. 266), amongst the Persian Jews, is as strictly observed as is Yom Kippur. Even the sick fast on that day. The children who are too young to fast have to be forced to partake of food.

In the evening, at the reading of the Book of Esther, the noise is deafening every time Haman's name is mentioned. The children use no rattles; they shoot off fireworks instead.

For the Persian Jewish children Purim is a lovely festival. They masquerade at night, after the reading of the Book of Esther, donning colorful clothes and painting their faces; thus attired they go from house to house, dancing and singing and clapping their hands.

Purim morning is even more joyous. Directly after the reading of the Book of Esther the children are given Purim money by their parents and relatives. Then they prepare to hang Haman.

A pole is set up in the middle of the courtyard, and on it is hung the Haman-effigy. It is then doused with oil and set afire. The children stand about, clapping their hands and calling out, "Haman, the wicked; Haman, the wicked." [295]

A generation or so ago, it was still the custom amongst the Jews of the Caucasus to burn Haman. When the master of the house came home from the synagogue he found a piece of black wood that his wife had put in the kitchen. He asked what it was and his wife answered that it was Haman. He would grow very angry, stamp his feet, and order his wife to throw it at once into the fire and burn it.[296]

xxvii. Purim = IN EASTERN EUROPE

The Preceding Sabbath...Although it is not yet Purim the spirit of the festival permeates the air. This feeling is especially evident at the services in the synagogue. It is the Sabbath on which Jews recall Amalek, Israel's oldest enemy. After the regular portion of the Torah, that passage of the Bible is read which says, "Remember what Amalek did unto thee by the way as ye came forth out of Egypt." The Haftoroh, the portion of the Prophets that is recited, is from the Book of Samuel and tells of Saul's war against Agag, king of the Amalekites.

After midday the rabbi gives his annual sermon on the subject of Purim. He twists and turns and juggles words throughout his sermon. He sermonizes on the prophet Samuel and on King Saul, tells about Agag and Haman, Mordecai and Esther, and each year he gives a new interpretation of a certain passage in the Book of Samuel, or the Book of Esther.

The Day Before ... The thirteenth day of Adar, the day before Purim, is the Fast of Esther. Since it is not a strictly ordained fast, very few people observe it.

The chief pre-festival sign is the pre-occupation of the women. They bake *hamantaschen*, three-cornered cakes generally filled with poppy-seed, and prepare sheets of dough for *kreplech*, a three-cornered pastry filled with meat. The children are busy, too, buying tin and wooden rattles and other noise-makers to use when Haman's name is pronounced in the reading of the Book of Esther.

Toward Evening...The *Bes ha-Midrosh* is well-lighted and filled with people, dressed in week-day clothing. It is not really a holiday, but an occasion of joy and a revelry.

The time for evening prayers is near. The grown-ups chatter, the youngsters wander about with rattles in their hands, the sexton goes among the congregation, bearing a plate, in which each man drops coins as a reminder of the "half-shekel" tax for the Temple. The passage of the Bible which tells that every man over twenty must pay a tax for the sanctuary, repeats the words "half-shekel" three times.[297] It is, therefore, necessary to give three coins to represent the three half-shekels. These are three half-rubles, a goodly sum of money, which very few Jews of the town can afford to give. But provision is made for that. A little packet bearing three silver half-rubles is carried around in the sexton's plate. Each man throws a copper coin into the plate, then picks up the packet of half-rubles and restores it to the plate. By picking up the packet it becomes his, and when he returns it to the plate it is as if he contributed three silver half-rubles from his own pocket.

The children can barely wait for the end of the evening prayers and the beginning of the reading of the Book of Esther. The first two chapters go by, and all is quiet and orderly. At the beginning of the third chapter, as soon as the reader pronounces the name of Haman for the first time there is a terrible tumult and outbreak. From every side there is rattling and beating, till the sound is deafening. The quiet, orderly children stand near their parents, dutifully twirl their tin or wooden rattles, and dutifully stop upon order. The wilder and less disciplined lads of the town stand at the door, armed not with rattles alone, but with logs of wood, which they beat without pause. The pious Jews become angry and shout to them to halt, but the lads pay no attention to them.

The service is repeated the next morning, but the beating and rattling is not as noisy and unrestrained as it was the night before.

Many times the young men form a troupe and rehearse for months to present a play at Purim, usually "Joseph and His Brethren," or "The Kingship of Saul." This is quite an occasion in the town and all go to see the theatrical offering.

The Day of Joy . . . After returning from the synagogue in the morning, *hamantaschen* are served for breakfast. The noon meal of the day generally consists of soup and *kreplech*.

There is no special holiday air about the town. The shops are open and the usual daily work is done; yet, it is not an ordinary week day. Everyone is in a festive mood. People take sips of liquor during the day and nibble at the various delicacies baked for Purim.

Looking out into the street one sees people bearing *shalach-monos*, food delicacies sent to friends as Purim gifts. The doors of the houses keep opening and closing, as a steady stream of paupers, following at each other's heels, come for their Purim alms.

The children wait impatiently for the appearance of the Purim-players, who go about the town, from house to house, presenting the story of Esther. They go singing through the streets, and a crowd of children follow them about. The actors are pious Jews, men of the masses, who become actors just for the day. They paste on flaxen beards, wear paper crowns, and outfit themselves with swords and epaulettes as they play the roles of the heroes of the Book of Esther. The actors are all men, even the roles of Vashti, Esther, and Zeresh are taken by males.

The Feast...After the evening prayers all sit down to the Purim feast. It is very much like the *Simchas Torah* feast, but the exalted festivity of the latter holiday is missing.

Families come together. The great, white, braided loaf baked specially for the occasion, covers a large part of the table. All eat and drink and are merry in honor of the day.

Shushan Purim...The day after Purim is known as *Shushan Purim*, the Purim of Shushan, the capital of the old Persian kingdom. According to the Book of Esther the Jews of Shushan celebrated the victory over Haman a day later than did the other Jews.

Purim is not considered a major festival. But for the children even *Shushan Purim* is a bit of a holiday. To begin with, there is no school on that day, enough in itself to make any day a festival. Then there are still cakes to be eaten, the left-overs from the day before, which are called "Purim crumbs."

No Special Ritual...Purim was in the beginning, and it remained, no more than a joyous occasion, a revelry. No ritual was, therefore, evolved to give it holiday atmosphere or spiritual exaltation.

On Chanukkoh, Hallel is chanted and lights are kindled. Purim has not even these rituals. The only thing that could be considered a religious rite is the reading of the Book of Esther. But the Book of Esther, as previously stated, has no religious content and can arouse no pious thoughts. In addition, the reading of the book is accompanied by noise and tumult, which does not comport with a religious ceremony. Above all, the Book of Esther, which explains the Purim festival and orders all to observe it, does not provide any form of religious ceremonial to accompany it. It only orders the observance of the fourteenth and fifteenth days of Adar with revelry, with exchange of gifts, and with giving charity.

Purim, then, has no religious observances or ceremonials. Instead, it has many folk customs associated with it. Practically all the customs of Purim originated when it was still a heathen observance, a nature festival, before it became the festival of Jewish deliverance. The Book of Esther is newer than any of the Purim customs.

Reading the Book of Esther...In the beginning the Book of Esther was read only once, on the fourteenth of Adar. It was later, in the time of the *Amoraim*, that the reading on the evening before was also instituted. The benedictions before and after the reading also come from the Amoraic period.

During the period of the *Tannaim* it was a point of issue whether to read the Book of Esther from the very beginning; whether to start from the second chapter, in which Esther and Mordecai are introduced; or whether to begin the reading with the third chapter, where Haman enters the story. The reading of the entire book became the accepted usage.

At one time there were Jewish communities where the book was also read on the fifteenth of Adar, *Shushan Purim*. There were also communities in which the book was also read on the evenings of the two Sabbaths preceding Purim, half during one evening and the second half the following week.

The Book of Esther is regarded as a letter to be read, and, therefore, the scroll bearing the story is rolled entirely open while it is being read.

Beating Haman...Beating Haman is a very old custom. We know that in the Middle Ages Jews would write the name of Haman or draw his likeness on two slabs of stone and then beat and rub them together till the likeness or the name was entirely rubbed out. It was also a custom at one time to write the name of Haman on the soles of one's shoes and to stamp hard every time Haman's name was mentioned.

It is assumed that the custom of erasing Haman's name led to the custom of "beating" Haman; however, the opposite is the truth, from the custom of "beating" Haman arose the custom of erasing his name.

The beating and noise of Purim originally had nothing to do with Haman; it comes from ancient times, when Purim was still a nature festival, bound up with the passing of winter and the approach of spring. It is an ancient belief with people that at the time when the seasons change the evil spirits have great power and strive to do mischief to all. One of the surest safe-guards against these spirits was noise. The beating and noise-making of Purim originally had the same significance, as the noise-making on New Year's Eve at present. It was only later, when Purim attained historic significance and was bound up with the Book of Esther, that the beating was interpreted as the beating of Haman. Haman is further bound up with Agag and Amalek, and of Amalek it is written that its name be blotted out. In this way the general beating became a Haman-beating, and from the beating of Haman was evolved the custom of erasing his name or likeness, in order to prove the truth of the passage about the blotting out of the name of Amalek.

The Fast of Esther...The custom of fasting on the day before Purim first spread after the compilation of the Talmud. The first we hear of the custom is in the eighth century.

It is not correct to assume from that, as many do, that the custom first arose at that time. It would never have occurred to the Jews of the Gaonic period to fast the day before Purim, were it not already an old custom. We must rather assume that the fast of the day before Purim is as old as the revelry of Purim, that originally they both belonged together, that the fast was a preparation for the revelry of the next day. While Jews observed *Nicanor Day* on the thirteenth of Adar, it was impossible to observe the fast on that day. Later, when *Nicanor Day* had been forgotten, the thirteenth of Adar became popular again, and was bound up with the fasting of Esther, which is related in the book bearing her name. This tie-up is not very consistent, for Esther's Fast was observed in the month of Nisan.[298] In Palestine, however, *Nicanor Day*, was remembered longer than in other lands, and the Fast of

Esther was held, therefore, not before, but after Purim.[299]

This explains, too, why the Fast of Esther is so strictly observed by the Persian Jews. They obviously never observed *Nicanor Day* and, from oldest times, they observed the fast of Purim as punctiliously as they did the revelry of Purim.[800]

Shalach-Monos...As old as any of the other Purim customs is the custom of *shalach-monos*. This custom of sending food delicacies to friends was practiced, originally, not only at Purim, but on every festival. The Bible tells us that Ezra read the Torah to the Jews in Jerusalem on the first of Tishri, and they were overjoyed with it and made it an occasion of joy, with feasting and *shalach-monos*.[301]

In the Book of Esther, *shalach-monos* is decreed together with the sending of gifts to the poor, and the two are often combined. The pauper sends some little thing as a form of *shalach-monos*, and receives in return a sizable coin.

Burning Haman...Not all of the old customs of Purim were preserved to this day. One old custom has been extinct amongst western Jews for a long time, the custom of making an effigy of Haman, which is hung and then burned. The custom is practiced now only by the oriental Jews.

This custom, like all other customs of Purim, originally had nothing to do with the tale told in the Book of Esther; it was bound up with the season of the year, with the passage from winter to spring. Among Christians it was a custom in many places to make a straw figure of "Prince Carnival," and to burn, behead, or stone him. We deal here with remainders and echoes of the mythology of ancient peoples. Among Jews this was eventually bound up with the Book of Esther, and the human effigy that was burned became Haman. Through its connection with the story of Haman this custom would have remained popular with the Jews, were it not for the opposition of Christians.

As far back as the fifth century the charge was made against Jews that they burned a cross and a figure of Jesus on Purim. This slander often led to attacks upon the Jews by their Christian neighbors. In time, under the pressure of the Christians, the custom disappeared in Christian lands.

Despite this, it was still the custom several centuries ago for the Jews of Frankfurt to erect a waxen house on the *bimoh*, with waxen figures of Haman, his wife, Zeresh, and the hangman; this was all ignited as soon as the reader began the Book of Esther. The Christians condemned this practice, for they assumed that the Jews, with their Haman on the gallows, were deriding Jesus on the cross. In this way the custom disappeared; in some such way, too, did the practice of lighting ten memorial candles on Purim, for Haman's ten sons, also disappear.

Purim Masquerade...It is ordinarily assumed that the Purim masquerade originated amongst the Jews of Italy, through the influence of the Christian carnival, and that from Italy it spread to Jews of other lands.

It is more logical to assume, however, that the masquerade belonged to Purim from the very start, together with the noise-making. Both the noise-making and the masquerading were originally safeguards against evil spirits, against whom it was necessary to guard oneself at the change of the seasons. It would be truer to say that the Purim Mask and the Christian carnival both have the same heathen origin, with the season of the year and the approach of spring, and both later took on new significance. The Catholic carnival was bound up with Christianity and the Purim Mask with the story of Esther.

We can grant, however, that under the influence of the Christian carnival the Purim Mask, beginning with the fifteenth century, took on new forms and added popularity.

Under the influence of the Christian carnival, with its jester-Pope, there arose the custom, in certain Jewish communities, of choosing a Purim-king; from this Purim-king there was evolved the Purim-rabbi. The custom of choosing a Purim-rabbi was till very recently a practice in the Talmudic academies.

The Purim-rabbi was given complete freedom of speech, and was permitted to speak as sharply as he liked about all, even the rabbi of the town, the head of the academy, or the influential men of the town. He was usually a sharp-witted person and quite a joker, and generally gave a sermon which was a satire and a parody on the Gemoro, on certain prayers, and on other deeply-rooted Jewish institutions.

He would, for instance, ask the question: Why is it said in the Talmud that the generation of Jews who were with Moses in the desert do not have a share in the hereafter? To which his answer would be that the Jews in the desert quarreled for years, with Moses and with God, about water, and never asked for a bit of wine. Such bad taste deserved punishment and that was why they lost their share in the hereafter.

In such ways Purim gave rise to a rich Jewish literature of satire and parody.[302]

Purim Drama...In this period of the Purim-rabbi and the Purim-jester, the period of lusty and jovial Purim celebrations (the fifteenth and sixteenth centuries), there began to evolve the Purim drama and the Purim theatre.

We have seen that theatrical pieces were often presented at Chanukkoh. But the real theatrical season in the ghetto was Purim. There were plays of a general nature presented at Purim, but the main theme of drama was the story of Ahasuerus. The custom of dramatizing the Book of Esther at Purim became so widespread and popular that it survives to this very day.[303]

Purim Delicacies. . . First place in the food delicacies of Purim is shared by the *kreplech* and the *hamantaschen*.

The word *kreplech* obviously comes from the German and, like many other forms of Purim observance, was taken over from "Shrove Tuesday" of the Christians and made a part of Purim.[304] From Purim, it must be assumed, the custom of eating *kreplech* was carried over to the day before Yom Kippur and to Hoshano Rabboh. A jesting explanation was evolved as to the reason for eating *kreplech* on those three widely different days. *Kreplech* are eaten, it is said, whenever beating is done: the day before Yom Kippur, when men have themselves flogged; Hoshano Rabboh, when willow branches are beaten; and Purim, when Haman is beaten.

The *hamantaschen* are also of German origin. Originally they were called *mohn-taschen*, *mohn* meaning poppy-seed, and *taschen* meaning pockets, and also signified dough that is filled with other foodstuffs. The people, therefore, related the cake to the Book of Esther and changed the *mohn* to *Haman*. In time the interpretation arose that the three-cornered cakes are eaten because Haman wore a three-cornered hat when he became prime-minister to Ahasuerus. The three corners were also interpreted as a symbolic sign of the three patriarchs, whose merit aided the Jews against Haman.

Beans, cooked and salted, are also eaten at Purim, and are

also related to the Book of Esther. They are eaten, it is said, because Esther did not want to eat anything that was not kosher, and therefore ate only beans and peas at the court of Ahasuerus, exactly as did Daniel and his comrades at the court of Nebuchadnezzar.[305]

XXIX. The Minor Festivals

Folk Religion...We have dealt thus far with those Jewish festivals that are regularly celebrated in the home and in the synagogue, those holidays which left their impression on the Jewish year and without which it is impossible to conceive of Jewish life. In addition to these holidays, there are other festivals, minor ones, which we must mention and discuss. These have no elaborate ritual and they play no important part in Jewish life. They play a great role, however, in the scientific presentation of the Jewish festivals. They help us to understand how festivals, in general, originated and developed.

Such minor festivals are: *Rosh Chodesh*, *Lag Bo-Omer*, *Chamishoh Osor B'Ov*, *Chamishoh Osor Bi-Sh'vot*, and others.

One must not assume that the major festivals were always great and important and that the minor festivals were always of little significance. They became major or minor festivals in the course of time. Their origins are practically identical, and in their beginnings they were all of equal importance.

Festivals became major festivals when they were included as a part of organized religion. They became minor and unimportant when no place was found for them in organized religion. In that case they retained their status only as a part of the folk religion or folk belief.

Organized religion is the product of a people who have an organized government; such people have temples and priests which are often a part of the state. Organized religion has established rites and ceremonials, and priests, and theologians as its representatives and teachers. But side by side with such organized religion there has always existed a folk religion, which is not organized, has no temples, no priests, no fixed precepts; it consists of old beliefs and customs, generally not in the spirit of the official religion. The folk belief is in the background, but it plays a great role in the lives of the masses, those who are little influenced by the new thoughts and trends of the times.

It can be said that organized religion has its basis in the "law," while folk religion follows the usages of custom. There is no clear, sharp boundary between the two; there never was.

As a rule, organized religion was hostile to folk religion and tried to suppress it. But the folk belief was often stronger and many times succeeded in breaking or changing the law.[306] From time to time the leaders of the official religion have had to accede to the masses of the people and were forced to give official sanction to the folk belief. For instance, for a long time the great rabbis of Jewish history battled against *Kaporos*, the custom of killing a fowl on the day before Yom Kippur as an expiation for the sins; but the custom was so deeply rooted in the life of the people that eventually the rabbis had to abandon their disapproval.

A good example is also Purim. In the old days Purim was not observed officially; it was only a part of the folk religion. In time it became recognized by the leaders of the official Jewish religion to such an extent that the Book of Esther was included among the sacred books.[307]

Rosh Chodesh ... A prolonged conflict took place between the official Jewish religion and the custom of observing *Rosh Chodesh*, the first of the month, synonymous with the appearance of the New Moon.

There was a time when *Rosh Chodesh* was a major festival, much more important than the weekly Sabbath.[308] The observance of *Rosh Chodesh* was obviously bound up with old heathen customs and was a reminder of the cult of the moon-god; it, therefore, aroused the antagonism of the teachers and leaders of the official religion. That, perhaps, explains why the older laws of the Pentateuch, written in the period before the Babylonian exile, make no mention of this observance.[309]

The mass of the folk, however, insisted on treating *Rosh Chodesh* as a festival, and they could not be discouraged from this observance. One reason for its importance resided in the fact that the date of all the Jewish festivals depended on the New Moon. After the return from the Babylonian exile a compromise was reached; *Rosh Chodesh* was not recognized as a full festival, during which labor was forbidden, but special sacrifices were arranged on that day in the Temple.[310] To this day Jews perform a special ritual to welcome the new month: there is a special prayer in the synagogue on the Sabbath before the New Moon, and there is a ceremony sanctifying the New Moon by a special benediction to be recited in the open air when the New Moon appears.

This blessing of the New Moon is an old custom. In the old days the Sanhedrin, the central Jewish authority, would proclaim the New Moon and a ceremonial was enacted. Later, when the Jewish calendar was definitely established,[311] it became the custom to announce the arrival of the New Moon on the Sabbath preceding it, after the reading from the Torah in the synagogue. This Sabbath is still known as the "Sabbath of Blessing," for the important part of the ceremony was no longer the announcement of the New Moon, but the reciting of the benediction.

A much older custom than that of blessing the first day of

the month is that of "sanctifying the moon," which is still done by Orthodox Jews upon the appearance of the first phase of the moon. We have to assume that this custom is a remainder of ancient days, when people gathered in the open when the new moon appeared, danced in its honor, and performed various ceremonies.[312]

About the sixteenth century a custom spread amongst very pious Jews to fast the day before each New Moon, calling the day *Yom Kippur Koton*, minor Day of Atonement.[313] One must not suppose that the custom sprang up suddenly; we must assume that there was a fast in connection with the festival of the New Moon in the very oldest times, and this was just a revival.[314]

In east European communities *Rosh Chodesh* was, and still is, a half-holiday for the Jewish school children. For the women of the community, however, it was almost a full holiday on which they did not work.[315] We have to assume that this, also, had its origin in very ancient times when *Rosh Chodesh* was a full holiday for all, men and women. The men allowed themselves to be influenced by the leaders and teachers of the official religion and gave up the observance to a great extent; but the women, who were not influenced so much by the official theology, and generally retained old customs longer than their men folk, could not and would not accept the arguments of the teachers, and continued to observe the day as a full holiday.[316]

The custom remained; but a new interpretation was given to it. When the golden calf was set up in the wilderness, it was said, the women of Israel refused to give up their golden earrings for it; God, therefore, rewarded them by giving them forever an extra holiday each month.

In former times the *T'kufoh* was announced and observed

by Jews just as they observed the New Moon. The *T'kufoh* is the cycle, the season of the year, and refers to the days known in English as the solstice and equinox, those days when the sun is either at the Tropic of Cancer, the Tropic of Capricorn, or the Equator. In other words, they mark the longest day of the year, the shortest day of the year, and the two days when day and night are practically of equal length.

In early times, the occurrence was announced in the synagogue on the previous Sabbath. Not only the day but the very moment on which the sun reached its furthest or nearest point was announced. A superstition connected with it forbids the drinking of water half an hour before and after the moment of the *T'kufoh*. If the water has been salted it may be used, but all freshly drawn water must not be drunk, as it is considered very dangerous to drink at that time, unless a piece of iron is placed in the water.[317]

The custom has largely disappeared amongst European Jews, though there is a likelihood that it still prevails there in some circles of Jewish life. In the Orient, however, Jews still practice the custom and the beadle goes about the courtyards on the day of the occurrence, warning Jews that the moment of the *T'kufoh* is at hand.

Lag Bo-Omer . . . Lag Bo-Omer has already been mentioned in connection with Shovuos.[318] It is an ancient, heathen festival taken over by the folk religion of the Jews of old, a festival that obviously had kinship with the forest and with the season of the year.

In later years an effort was made to Judaize this folk festival by connecting it with some event in Jewish history. On that day, it was said, the scourge of death ceased amongst the thousands of pupils of Rabbi Akiba. But this historic interpretation is so forced and so baseless that there is no need even to examine it.[319] Another historic connection was, therefore, attributed to *Lag Bo-Omer*; it was declared that this was the day on which the manna began to fall from heaven.[320]

An old custom bound up with *Lag Bo-Omer* is that of children going to the forest, bearing archers' bows.

The Kabbalists connected *Lag Bo-Omer* with the name of Rabbi Simeon ben Jochai, the legendary father of Jewish mysticism, and declared that on that day, just before his death, he revealed his mysteries to his disciples. The "fire-observance" held yearly in Palestine at his grave, on *Lag Bo-Omer*, has really nothing to do with Rabbi Simeon ben Jochai, but is an ancient, heathen, light-ceremonial.[321]

Two Chamishoh Osor Festivals...The two *Chamishoh Osor* festivals, *Chamishoh Osor B'Ov* (the fifteenth of the month of Ov) and *Chamishoh Osor Bi-Sh'vot* (the fifteenth day of Sh'vot) belong to the group of minor ordinary festivals. Both were originally primitive nature observances of the Jewish peasants of old. *Chamishoh Osor B'Ov* is midsummer day, and *Chamishoh Osor Bi-Sh'vot* midwinter day. *Chamishoh Osor Bi-Sh'vot* was always recognized as a nature festival, as the New Year of the trees, and no historic interpretation was ever sought for it.[322] The origin of *Chamishoh Osor B'Ov* was completely forgotten, however, and for that reason historic interpretations were later proposed for the day.

In the time of the second Temple *Chamishoh Osor B'Ov* was the festival of the wood-offering. It was the last day for bringing wood for the altar where burned the eternal fire. The wood had to be perfectly dry, so that it would not smoke, and after *Chamishoh Osor B'Ov* the sun was not as hot and the trees were not as dry as earlier in the summer.[323]

Chamishoh Osor B'Ov would have remained the festival of the wood-offering, and no historic interpretation would have been sought for it, had it not been for a tradition recorded in the Mishnah that linked the day with Yom Kippur. These two days, according to the Mishnah, were, in olden times, the merriest of festivals among the Jews, days on which maidens danced in the vineyards.[324] This quotation in the Mishnah caused much mental twisting and turning to the *Amoraim* of the Gemoro, the interpreters of the Mishnah, who strived to give historic significance to *Chamishoh Osor B'Ov*. Some of the results were: the fifteenth of *Ov* was once a great festival for on that day the last of the generation that went into the desert with Moses died; that was the day on which Benjamin was re-admitted into the tribes of Israel;[325] and other such interpretations.

We can assume that the connection between *Chamishoh Osor B'Ov* and Yom Kippur resided in the fact that they were observances, respectively, of the beginning and the end of the grape harvest.

It is customary to eat fruit on *Chamishoh Osor Bi-Sh'vot*, especially fruit that grows in Palestine, notably, St. John's Bread. After the destruction of the Temple, when there was no longer need for the wood-offering, there were no concrete customs practiced on *Chamishoh Osor B'Ov*, and for that reason it is the least important of the minor festivals.

Other Minor Festivals...Isru-Chag is considered somewhat of a festival. This is the name given to the day after a festival. There are three *Isru-Chags*, the days after Pesach, Shovuos, and Sukkos.[326]

The seventh day of the month of Adar is noted as the anniversary of the death of Moses.[327] In many Jewish communities the fifteenth day of Kislev is the day of the *Chevroh Kadisho*, the burial brotherhood, who observe it with fasting, *s'lichos*-prayers, and a feast in the evening. The twentieth day of Sivan was observed in some regions in Eastern Europe as a fast day, to commemorate the slaughter of the Jews by Chmelnitzki, in the years 1648-1649.

There are other Jewish folk-festivals. Many of these are observed only in certain regions. Many other minor festivals have been entirely forgotten.

*Social Festivals...*Festivals, in general, have an important social significance. For each festival there are products to be purchased in the way of food and clothing, and thus commerce and trade are fostered. Festivals also serve as social levelers of the various classes in society, serving, in some measure, to remove class distinctions. The poor as well as the rich, the servant as well as the master, rest from their toil. All, with few exceptions, don festive clothes, eat holiday delicacies, and feel more free and exalted.

This is true of all festivals, but the Jews of earlier times created special social festivals that served to lighten the pressure of economic need among the poor and oppressed classes. The Sabbath was a festival, a day of rest, with such a motive.[328]

*Sh'mitoh and Jubilee...*The Sabbath idea attained a further evolution in *Sh'mitoh*, the year of release. Just as the days were divided into weeks so were the years, and, exactly like the seventh day, the seventh year was declared holy as the year of *Sh'mitoh*, decreed for social reform.

There was a twofold *Sh'mitoh* law, one referring to land, the other to money. According to the law of the Pentateuch, Jews were forbidden to till the soil of their land every seventh year, and anything that grew wild was to be harvested by the poor. In addition, there was to be a moratorium on all debts.[329]

This idea of a year of release was enlarged in the law of the year of Jubilee, which made holy the fiftieth year as the end of a period of seven *Sh'mitohs*. In this fiftieth year every slave was to be given his freedom, and every impoverished peasant was to regain the heritage that he was forced to sell.

How faithfully the laws of *Sh'mitoh* and Jubilee were enforced in practical life is not certain. It seems that the law regarding release from debts was not followed. The laws commanding the peasants to let their fields lie fallow, it seems, were observed in the days of the second Temple.[330] But we do not know if all Jews observed them or only Jews of certain circles. The Jubilee law, with its grandiose scheme for bringing social and economic equality among Jews, certainly remained only a social Utopia. At any rate, the laws regarding the Sabbath, *Sh'mitoh*, and Jubilee are a monument to the Jewish ideal of social justice, even in ancient days.

Questions

SABBATH

1. Is there any foundation to the assertion that the Sabbath had its origin in Babylon? On what is that assertion based? What are the main differences between the Jewish Sabbath and the Babylonian *Shabattum?*

2. Why did the Sabbath attain a new importance in the Babylonian exile? What is the relation of the Sabbath to the Synagogue?

3. What were the two elements on which the Sabbath was based? How did these two elements function among the Jewish sects which were conservative and among the Pharisees who were progressive? What part do these aspects play in the Sabbath of the present day?

4. What do you think of the saying which the Gospels ascribe to Jesus, that "the Sabbath was made for man and not man for the Sabbath"? Was Jesus really the originator of this saying? In what version was it current among the Pharisees?

5. What part of the Sabbath celebration came last in the history of the Sabbath?

6. Which factors broke down the rigorous observance of Sabbath rest in the 19th century? Why was it that until the 19th century Jews found no difficulty in resting completely on the Sabbath?

7. What is the usual explanation given to the custom of throwing a piece of dough into the fire? What new light has modern historical and anthropological research thrown on the origin of this custom?

8. Why do women cover their eyes when reciting the benediction over the Sabbath candles?

9. What is the origin of the belief in the Sambatyon? How was it related to the belief in the ten lost tribes and in the children of Moses?

10. What do you know of Eldad the Danite, the Jewish traveler

of the ninth century, and his tales of the Sambatyon and the lost tribes?

11. How does the Sabbath function in our own day in the United States? What changes would you introduce into our Sabbath customs in order to help it function better among the Jews of America?

PESACH

1. What are the pastoral characteristics of the Pesach ceremony?
2. What historical explanation was given in later times for the use of bitter herbs and the *charoses?*
3. Why and how did the reform under King Josiah change the entire character of Pesach?
4. How did the Exodus from Egypt become connected in the Jewish mind with the belief in the Messiah?
5. What stage in the evolution of Pesach does the Pesach of the present day Samaritans represent?
6. What new features were added to the celebration of Pesach night in the later period of the second Temple?
7. In what respect does Pesach retain its original character to this day?
8. What is the origin of the *Seder?* Was it originally a ritual?
9. How was Elijah associated with the Seder night?
10. What part did the Haggadah play in Jewish folk lore and in Jewish plastic art?

SHOVUOS

1. Why is the name of this holiday Shovuos (weeks)? What was the older, more precise name of this festival? Why is it also called "the day of the first-fruits"? What other sort of *bikkurim* were brought to Jerusalem between Shovuos and Sukkos?
2. Why didn't Shovuos play any great role among the holidays in ancient times?
3. What were, and still are, the different dates for Shovuos among different groups of Jews?
4. When did Shovuos become the festival of the giving of the Torah?

5. What name is given to the days between the second day of Pesach and Shovuos? Why?
6. What are the popular explanations given for the use of "greens" and "dairy dishes" on Shovuos?
7. Is Shovuos as old as Pesach?
8. What ceremony does Reform Judaism emphasize on Shovuos? Why?

TISHOH B'OV

1. What national catastrophies in Jewish history are connected with Tishoh B'Ov?
2. What light does the ancient joyous festival of the fifteenth day of Ov throw on the origin of Tishoh B'Ov?
3. Which are the national days of mourning in the Jewish calendar? When are they first mentioned?
4. What was the attitude of the Prophet Zechariah toward these fasts?
5. What was the attitude of Rabbi Judah, the Patriarch, to Tishoh B'Ov?
6. What do we mean by the "Three Weeks" and the "Nine Days"?
7. What is the name of the Sabbath before Tishoh B'Ov and of the Sabbath following it?
8. What is the relation of the "Messiah" to Tishoh B'Ov?
9. How does Tishoh B'Ov function in our day? How does its observance vary among different groups within Jewry?

THE DAYS OF AWE

1. What is the basic difference between the Jewish and the general calendar? Why does it have an intercalation of an entire month?
2. Why is Rosh Hashonoh, the Jewish New Year, designated as the first day of the seventh, and not of the first month?
3. Why are some Jewish New Year customs continued until Hoshano Rabboh?
4. Why was an extra day added to the festival as a "second holiday of the Diaspora"? Why did Reform Judaism abolish the "second day"?

5. Why was Rosh Hashonoh observed for two days even in Palestine?
6. What interpretations were read into the blowing of the Shofar on Rosh Hashonoh? What explanation was given to the custom of blowing the Shofar on the New Moon of Elul?
7. Why is the *piyut* of *Un'saneh Tokef* so popular and appealing?
8. In what respects did Jewish life and ideas undergo a profound change after the Babylonian exile?
9. Is it right to call Yom Kippur a day of mourning?
10. What was the effect of the destruction of the second Temple on Yom Kippur? Did it lessen its importance? What was the attitude of Rabban Jochanan ben Zakkai towards it?

SUKKOS

1. What are the older names for Sukkos found in the Bible?
2. What was the part which Sukkos played in the time of the independent Jewish kingdom?
3. In what respect did Sukkos retain its original character?
4. What was the reaction of the great Prophets to the hilarity of the ancient Feast of Ingathering?
5. In what respect did Sukkos change and in what respect did it retain its character and its ritual after the destruction of the second Temple? In what respect did the Synagogue take over the role of the Temple in the Sukkos ritual?
6. When and how did Simchas Torah arise?
7. What are some of the theories on the origin of the Sukkoh?
8. Why does not the connection with the wanderings in the desert constitute a satisfactory explanation?
9. Which ideas were read into the Sukkoh in later times?
10. Which meanings were later attached to the "four species" used on Sukkos?
11. What primitive idea is behind the custom of eating honey or syrup with the first slice of bread on Rosh Hashonoh? Why is it eaten until Hoshano Rabboh?
12. What was the origin of the custom of Tashlich and how was it reinterpreted later?
13. What was the origin of the custom of *Kaporos* and what was the attitude of the great rabbis in the Middle Ages toward this custom?

CHANUKKOH

1. What was the character of the Chanukkoh celebration at the beginning of its institution? Was it originally called Chanukkoh?
2. How does Josephus designate Chanukkoh and explain the lights?
3. What was the controversy between the followers of Shammai and of Hillel about the Chanukkoh lights?
4. What was the attitude of Judah, the Patriarch, toward Chanukkoh?
5. What different tales and explanations were given for the Chanukkoh lights? What inference concerning the origin of the lights may we draw from these?
6. Why did Chanukkoh become in recent time a popular festival?
7. What sort of games and entertainments were and are now popular during the Chanukkoh days?

PURIM

1. What stories similar to Esther were composed in the latter days of the second Temple? In what respects do they differ from the story of Esther?
2. What historical events are mirrored in the Book of Esther?
3. What other day was celebrated by the Jews in latter times of the second Temple as a day when they were saved from an enemy who sought to exterminate them? What is the relation of that day to Purim?
4. What, in view of the above, may we assume to be the origin of the story of Esther?
5. What minor local Purims do you know in Jewish history?
6. What special features does Purim have among the oriental Jews?
7. What is the relation between Purim and the Christian Carnival?

THE MINOR FESTIVALS

1. Why are the Minor Festivals called minor?
2. What were their origins?
3. What do you know of New Moon in the olden times? Why was it reduced to a minor holiday?

4. How is the New Moon observed today among Orthodox Jews?
5. What was the origin of Lag Bo-Omer? What historical associations were attached to it?
6. How has Lag Bo-Omer been observed in Palestine to this day? What is the origin of such observance?
7. What is the origin of the two Chamishoh Osor festivals and what is the relation between them?
8. What Jewish customs were connected with the T'kufoh?
9. What do you know of Sh'mitoh and Jubilee? To what extent were they actually observed?

Notes

All Talmudic tractates quoted in the following notes refer to the Babylonian Talmud, unless preceded by a Y, indicating Yerushalmi.

The transliteration of Hebrew and Aramaic names of books is here different from that in the text and follows more closely the scientific transliteration accepted by most scholars.

[1] Isa. 1:13; Hos. 2:13; Amos 8:5. Cf. also Isa. 66:23. All critical scholars agree that this chapter is of post-exilic times, when the Sabbath was beyond any controversy the seventh day of each week, and still it is coupled here with New Moon. This seems to support the scholars who maintain that the mention of New Moon and Sabbath together cannot be used as proof that Sabbath designated originally the full moon.

[2] See Morris Jastrow, *Hebrew and Babylonian Tradition*, pp. 134-195; Hugo Gressmann, *Mose und seine Zeit*, pp. 462-463. See also the controversy on this topic between Johannes Meinhold and Karl Budde in *Zeitschrift fuer die alttestamentliche Wissenschaft*, 1930, pp. 121-145. See also Abram Menes, *Die vorexilischen Gesetze Israels*. About days of rest among different peoples of various stages of culture see Hutton Webster, *Rest Days*.

[3] Exod. 23:12; cf. also Deut. 5:13-15.

[4] This refers only to the so-called Former and Latter Prophets. The Pentateuchal laws cannot be taken as the starting point in the investigation of Jewish life in pre-exilic times. No one can tell with any certainty to what extent the written laws were then actually observed. Besides, modern criticism has demonstrated the difficulty of establishing the time of their authorship. Both the extent of observance and the time of authorship can be discussed only in the light of the knowledge we derive from the Former and Latter Prophets. These books of the Bible and not the Pentateuch must therefore be the starting point in any investigation of the history of the Sabbath or of any other institution in Jewish life of biblical times.

[5] When the Shunamite asks her husband to send her one of the servants and one of the asses that she may run to the man of God, he wonders at it because it is neither New Moon nor Sabbath. This implies that on the Sabbath it would be the expected thing to do. II Kings 4:22-23.

[6] II Kings 11.

[7] Amos 8:5.

[8] Ezek. 20:12-13, 16, 21, 24; 22:8.

[9] Gen. 17:9–14; Exod. 31:12–17; Lev. 19:1–3.

[10] Neh. 13:15–22. Cf. Jer. 17:19–27 which is according to modern critics an interpolation from a post-exilic editor of the book.

[11] Neh. 10:32.

[12] Exod. 31:14–15; 35:2; Num. 15:32–36.

[13] Isa. 56:6.

[14] *See* p. 5 and p. 8.

[15] Isa. 58:13.

[16] I Macc. 2; II Macc. 6; Josephus, *Ant.* XIV, 4, par. 2; XXIII, 9, par. 2. Pompey conquered Jerusalem on a Sabbath according to Dio Cassius.

[17] Yoma 85 b; Mekhiltha on Exod. 31:13–14.

[18] Berakhoth 57 b; Shabbath 10 b; Betsah 16 a.

[19] Erubin 43 b.

[20] Taanith 24 b–25 a. Samuel Krauss, *Tal. Arch.* I, 104.

[21] Shabbath 35 b; Mishnah Sukkah, V, 5; Tosef. Sukkah IV, 11–12; Josephus, *War*, IV, 9 par. 12; Ismar Elbogen, "Eingang und Ausgang des Sabbats" in *Israel Lewy Festschrift; Der Juedische Gottesdienst* (by the same author); Louis Ginzberg, "The Sabbath in Ancient Times" in *United Synagogue Record*, Vol. I, No. 1; A. Berliner, "Die Juedische Speisetafel" in *Jahrbuch fuer Juedische Geschichte und Literatur*, 1910.

[22] A. Berliner, *Aus dem Leben der deutschen Juden im Mittelalter*; Moritz Guedemann, *Geschichte des Erziehungswesens und der Kultur der Juden in Deutschland waehrend des XIV. und XV. Jahrhunderts*, chap. iv; Israel Abrahams, *Jewish Life in the Middle Ages*.

[23] Ismar Elbogen, *Der Juedische Gottesdienst*; A. Z. Idelsohn, *Jewish Liturgy*.

[24] Ps. 119.

[25] It is the usually accepted view that the custom of throwing a piece of dough into the burning oven arose after the destruction of the second Temple as a substitute for the first of the dough which was to be given to the priest (Num. 15:19–21). However, from the Mishnah (Challah IV, 8) it may be inferred that it was customary to throw a piece of dough into the fire even in the days when the first of the dough was still being given to the priest. One should take into consideration the fact that this custom also prevails among the Mohammedans. It may therefore be assumed that the contrary is true: the practice of giving the first of the dough to the priest superseded an older custom of throwing it into the fire as an offering to the evil spirits. It seems, however, that the older custom was in vogue here and there along with the new one, but after the destruction of the second Temple its practice became general and it assumed a new meaning: that of being a substitute for giving it to the priest. *See* Heinrich Lewy, "Kleine Beitraege zu Bibel und Volkskunde" in *Monatsschrift*. 1931, pp. 28–29.

[26] S. Krauss, "Aus der Juedischen Volkskueche" in *Mitteilungen zur Juedischen Volkskunde*, 18. Jahrgang, Heft 1–2; *see also* article "Barches" in *J.E.*

[27] Louis Ginzberg, "The Sabbath in Ancient Times" in *United Synagogue Record* Vol. I, No. 1.

[28] Shabbath 118 b–119 a. *See* A. Sulzbach, "Der Fisch als Symbol" in *Jeschurun* II, p. 506ff.

[29] A. Berliner, *Aus dem Leben der deutschen Juden im Mittelalter*, p. 60. *See also* article of S. Krauss as in note 26.

[30] *See Halochoth Gedoloth*, herausgegeben von Dr. J. Hildesheimer, p. 85; *Responsen des Rabbenu Tam*, Dr. F. Rosenthal, pp. 81–82. It seems from this that the custom of reciting the benediction over the candles sprang up in the Gaonic period in antagonism to the Karaites who prohibited having light on the Sabbath. Cf. note 189.

[31] שולחן ערוך אורח חיים, רס"ן.

[32] Pesachim 112 b.

[33] Tosafoth Pesachim 105 a; Jacob Z. Lauterbach, "The Ceremony of Breaking a Glass at Weddings" in *Hebrew Union College Annual* II; Heinrich Lewy, "Zum Daemonenglauben" in *Archiv fuer Religionswissenschaft*, Vol. XXVIII, pp. 243–244. *See also* article "Habdalah" in J.E. To this category of customs belongs also the scanning of the fingernails (*see* p. 26). The explanation usually given for it is merely a forced later interpretation. According to ספרא דחנוך quoted by ר' אברהם בן הגר"א מווילנא, רב פעלים, p. 65, scanning the fingernails before the light of a fire at the departure of the Sabbath was a safeguard against witches, that they do no harm during the entire week. It was believed that these same witches picked up the fingernails of men, dropped on the ground, for the purpose of witchcraft.

[34] Ps. 19:9.

[35] Ps. 39:5.

[36] Shabbath 30 a–b, also 117 b and 119 b.

[37] The first version is according to Josephus, *War*, VII, 5, par. 1; the second version is according to Pliny in his *Natural History*, XXXI, 2.

[38] Sanhedrin 65 b.

[39] Exod. 32:10.

[40] W. Bacher, *Die Agada der Tannaiten* I, 290–291; I. Markon, "Das Land Schabat" in *Wohlgemut Festschrift*.

[41] According to the earlier version of the story of the Exodus, Moses begged Pharaoh to give the Children of Israel permission to go out into the wilderness in order that they might observe their feast in honor of God. In the later version it was altered to just the opposite, that they held their feast because they went out from Egypt. It may be worthwhile to mention that according to a Midrashic interpretation of the Bible, Lot baked matsos for the three angels because that episode happened during Pesach. *See* Rashi on this passage.

[42] Even in as late a book as Jubilees (*see* note 98) it is told that if Pesach will be correctly observed, no plague will come during the year (Chap. 49). Parallels among other peoples: Samuel Ives Curtiss, *Primitive Semitic Religion Today*, p. 181; Paul Volz, *Die biblischen Altertuemer*, p. 102. See

also Hugo Gressmann, *Palestinas Erdgeruch in der israelitischen Religion,* p. 27ff.

[43] Two different explanations for the meaning of the word Pesach are offered even in the Pentateuch. According to one (Exod. 12:13) Pesach means to spare, to save: וּפָסַחְתִּי עֲלֵכֶם is translated in תרגום אונקלוס: וְאֵיחוֹס עֲלֵיכוֹן; cf. Isa. 31:5. *See* Rashi on Exod. 12:13, also תנ'ך עם פירוש מדעי. According to a second explanation (Exod. 12:23) Pesach means to skip, to pass over. But both are later interpretations and are untenable. Because the name was used more for the sheep or goat that was sacrificed and eaten at the festival, than for the festival itself: וְשָׁחֲטוּ הַפֶּסַח, שמות י'ב, כ'א; מבחת פסח, דברים ט'ז, ב; כי אכלו אֶת הַפֶּסַח, דברי הימים ב, ל, יח. Also in the usage of the language in Mishnah: הַפֶּסַח שֶׁשָּׁחֲטוֹ שֶׁלֹּא לִשְׁמוֹ, הַפֶּסַח נִשְׁחָט בְּשָׁלֹשׁ כִּתּוֹת, אֵין צוֹלִין אֶת הַפֶּסַח. We therefore have to seek the etymological origin of Pesach in the ceremonies that were connected with the sacrificial lamb; and because these very ancient ceremonies are not known to us, the origin of the name, Pesach, remains obscure. Modern investigators of the Bible have presented various theories on the subject. According to one, Pesach originally meant, "the skipper," and was a name for the young, skipping lamb. According to a second theory, the name Pesach is derived from a certain sacred, limping dance which was performed around the lamb. A third theory seeks to connect the word with the phase of the moon. But these are all mere hypotheses. The assumption that the lamb was the first-born and that Pesach was originally the festival in which the first-born of the flock was offered to God, is also an hypothesis, though a plausible one.

[44] Deut. 16:7. This Deuteronomic law, which seeks to give to the Pesach festival an entirely new character by centralizing it in the Temple of Jerusalem (*see* further on page 46), prescribes only the celebration of Pesach eve and ignores the Chag ha-matsos on the fifteenth day of the month (cf. with Lev. 23:5-7). For if the Pesach-lamb could be sacrificed and eaten only in the Temple in Jerusalem, the peasants could not stay on, at the beginning of the harvest, to observe a second holiday.

[45] The origin of the precept of eating matsos and the prohibition of chomets is very obscure. The traditional explanation of the Pentateuch, that it is a reminder of the haste with which the Children of Israel left Egypt, is contradictory and untenable. For it is told in the same chapter that God enjoined the Israelites to eat the flesh of the Pesach-sacrifice with unleavened bread and bitter herbs before the Exodus took place (cf. Exod. 12:8, 39). The later Jewish tradition was therefore not content with this old explanation and, turning to the designation of matsos as bread of affliction (Deut. 16:3) it explained it as "the bread of affliction which our fathers ate in the land of Egypt." Thus, according to this later interpretation, the matsos are not a reminder of the deliverance, but rather of the slavery in Egypt. These two contradictory declarations about matsos, at the beginning and end of the Haggadah, have been a source of great disturbance to commentators on the Haggadah. Modern, scientific biblical research has also erred on this point. Modern critics have missed the mark, because most of them seek to explain why matsos were eaten at the beginning of the cutting of the grain, and thus fail entirely to explain the

removing of the leaven, that "there shall no leavened bread be seen with thee, neither shall there leaven be seen with thee, in all thy borders" (Exod. 13:7). That great dread of the least bit of chomets can surely not be explained as the product of the precept to eat matsoh. Besides, it is a precept to eat matsos only on Pesach eve; on all the other days of the holiday it is merely prohibited to eat chomets. This Talmudic law was doubtless no innovation, but an old tradition. From all this it is evident that we must not confuse the precept of eating matsoh on Pesach eve with the prohibition of chomets for seven days. The former is quite understandable. We do not have to go far to seek an explanation for the precept to eat the Pesach sacrifice with matsos (Exod. 12:8), for other sacrifices were also offered with unleavened bread (Lev. 2:4-11). Besides, matsos were, in olden times, and they are, among the Bedouins of today, an ordinary food when bread is baked in haste (Cf. Gen. 19:3 and I Sam. 28:24). What we have to seek is an explanation for the removal of leavened bread. There can be no doubt that this custom grew out of primitive beliefs connected with the beginning of the cutting of the grain. But the explanation that it was a removal of the remnants of the last year's crop, as offered by Julian Morgenstern "The Origin of Massoth and the Massoth-Festival," in *American Journal of Theology*, XXI, 274–293, misses the mark. It was not the remnants of the previous crop, grain and flour, that had to be removed, but leaven and things containing leaven only. So the origin of this was evidently a fear, a dread of leaven, on the part of primitive people at the time when they began to cut the grain. *See* the treatise of Eerdmans on the origin of matsos, in *Orientalische Studien, Theodor Noeldeke zum Siebzigsten Geburtstag*, pp. 671–679. *See also* Frazer, *The Golden Bough*, "Adonis Attis Osiris," I, 272.

[46] Exod. 23:14-19; 34:18-26. Cf. Lev. 23 and Deut. 16. *See also* sections in this book on Shovuos and Sukkos.

[47] Deut. 16:11.

[48] Menachoth 62 a. It is evident from this that the waving of the omer was originally a safeguard against crop failure.

[49] That Pesach and the Festival of Unleavened Bread were originally two distinct festivals, distinct in name as well as in character, is evident from the Pentateuchal sources (*see* Lev. 23:5-6 and Num. 28:16-17). That Pesach was merely a family festival is evident from Exod. 12:43-46, where it is prescribed that no alien, sojourner or hired servant is to take part in the Pesach. A purchased slave could participate only after he was circumcized and thus became a member of the family. Pesach and Chag ha-matsos were never amalgamated among the Samaritans and remained two distinct holidays. *See* Moses Gaster, *The Samaritans*, p. 173, בזה המועדים השנים לא נעשה בהן מלאכה. *See also* J. A. Montgomery, *The Samaritans*, p. 40.

[50] Exod. 12:25-27; 13:14.

[51] II Kings 23:22-23. Later the Jews reconciled the two modes of observing Pesach of Exod. 12 and Deut. 16 with the explanation that the older form was prescribed for the Exodus only פסח מצרים, whereas the newer form was prescribed for the future פסח דורות. *See* Mishnah Pesachim IX.

[52] Mic. 7:15.

[53] *See* Midrash Rabbah, Mekhiltah and Yalkut on Exod. 12:42.

[54] The number given for the population of Jerusalem and the pilgrims which is found in the Talmud and Josephus is an impossible and fantastic exaggeration. Considering the area of Jerusalem in those days the number of permanent dwellers is estimated at from eighty to ninety thousand—S. Klein, *Juedisches Lexikon*. Some scholars give a minimum estimate of 50,000 and a maximum of 100,000. More details in Joachim Jeremias, *Jerusalem zur Zeit Jesu*, erster Teil: "Die wirtschaftlichen Verhaeltnisse," pp. 89–97.

[55] Yoma 12 a.

[56] Aboth V, 5.

[57] Cf. with the tale told in Midrash Lamentations of the pepper merchant who came to Jerusalem with a caravan of two hundred camels heavily laden with pepper.

[58] Pesachim 116 a.

[59] It is called, in the Talmud, ירושלים דדהבא also עיר של זהב. According to the very plausible theory of Joachim Jeremias it was a kind of golden souvenir which the goldsmiths of Jerusalem sold to the pilgrims.

[60] Cakes of leavened bread belonged to this sacrifice of thanksgiving (Lev. 7:13). Such could not be offered during the week of Pesach and there were thus many such offerings accumulated on the second day before Pesach. The eating of these was forbidden on the next day, the day before Pesach. But the priests could not consume so many challos in one day. So, many of these loaves became disqualified on the morning before Pesach and had to be burned.

[61] Pesachim 65 a.

[62] Pesachim 65 b.

[63] Taanith 19 a.

[64] Josephus, *Ant.* XVIII, 2, par. 2.

[65] Mishnah Pesachim X, 6.

[66] According to the latest census there are now one hundred and eighty-two Samaritans in Palestine (Census of Palestine, E. Mills, 1931).

[67] Exod. 12.

[68] They burn everything that came in contact with the Pesach sacrifice, in order to fulfill the precept, "that which remaineth of it until the morning ye shall burn with fire" (Exod. 12:10). We have to presume that this custom of the Samaritans was also prevalent among the Jews of ancient times.

[69] About the Samaritans in general: Moses Gaster, *The Samaritans;* J. Montgomery, *The Samaritans;* Rudolf Kittel, *Geschichte des Volkes Israel*, 3. Band, 1929, pp. 680–683; Ernst Sellin, *Geschichte des israelitisch-juedischen Volkes*, II, 1932, pp. 169–172. About the Pesach of the Samaritans: Warren J. Moulton, "Das samaritanische Passahfest" in *Zeitschrift des deutschen Palestina-Vereins*, 1904; Joachim Jeremias, *Die Passahfeier*

der Samaritaner. See also J. N. Schofield, "The Samaritan Passover" in *Pal. Exploration Fund Quarterly Statement*, April, 1936. About the Falashas: Jacques Faitlovitch, *Quer durch Abessinien;* I. Scheftelowitz, "Sind die Falaschas Juden?" in *Monatsschrift*, 1923, pp. 244–249.

[70] Exod. 12:34.

[71] Exod. 12:39; Deut. 16:3.

[72] טשארני, ספר המסעות No. 75; 1903, צבי כשדאי, המליץ.

[73] יעקב משה טולידאנו, נר המערב. Cf. p. 60.

[74] About the Maggid of Dubno *see* further p. 84.

[75] *See* pp. 68–69.

[76] Pesachim 37 a.

[77] Maharil. Cf. p. 72.

[78] This is the older version of the questions in Mishnah Pesachim X.

[79] There will be four great empires up to the coming of the Messiah, according to the Book of Daniel; four rivers go out from Eden; Zechariah saw four horns in his vision (2:1); Daniel saw four great beasts in his vision (Chap. 7).

[80] Mal. 3:23.

[81] יהא מונח עד שיבוא אליהו, פרשה זו אליהו עתיד לדורשה, תשבי יתרץ קושיות ואיבעיות.

[82] This is the interpretation of the Gaon of Wilna.

[83] *See* p. 70. This custom is already mentioned in Y. Baba Bathra I, 4.

[84] *See* above p. 55.

[85] חיים קנאללער, דבר יום ביומו.

[86] This is obviously the sense of אין מפטירין אחר הפסח אפיקומן, משנה פסחים, י:ח, for the Tosephta says explicitly כגון אגוזים ותמרים וקליות. Cf. also Pesachim 119 b. *See* הפטיר in Levy's *Woerterbuch*, IV, 31, and אפיקומן in Jastrow's *Dictionary*, p. 104.

[87] As early as the third century of this era, the Babylonian Jews were confused about the definition of the word afikomon. *See* the controversy on this in Pesachim 119 b. It seems, however, that the word was better remembered in Palestine, for an Amora in the Palestinian Talmud defines it as "kinds of song" מיני זמר.

[88] Exod. 12:17. The sense of this passage is that Jews were to guard the feast of matsos. Instead, Jews took it literally as an injunction to guard the matsos themselves. However, the role of the afikomon in the folk-belief is still obscure, and there is no clear explanation for the fact that magic power is ascribed to it and it is used as a form of charm. Isidor Scheftelowitz is of the opinion that the afikomon acts as a talisman in the folk-belief because it is a left-over from a food that had been used at a religious ceremony, and therefore has magic power. This, however, does not explain why just the afikomon is used in this manner, and not the left-overs from any other religious feast. *See* the treatise of I. Scheftelowitz, "Juedischer Volksaberglaube," in *Zeitschrift fuer Missionskunde und Religionswissenschaft*, 1930, No. 9.

[89] *See* Koheleth 9:8; Mishnah Taanith IV, Sota I; Y. Rosh Hashanah I, 3. But *see also* Jacob Z. Lauterbach in *Hebrew Union College Annual*, 1927, p. 185, note.

[90] It is taken from the Mekhiltha.

[91] More details about the history of the Haggadah are to be found in the Revised Union Haggadah. *See also* George A. Kohut, "Passover Rhymes and Their Parallels" (reprint from the *Jewish Exponent*, Philadelphia, 1903).

[92] Exod. 34:22; Lev. 23:15–17; Num. 28:26. This, however, must not be confounded with the first-fruits of the trees, that were brought into the Temple with great parade. These first-fruits were not brought at Shovuos, but from Shovuos until Sukkos. Besides, the first-fruits of the trees were an offering of the individual Jew and his household, whereas the Bikkurim-bread was an offering of the entire community. In very ancient days, by the way, the Bikkurim-bread was sometimes brought, not to the priest at the sanctuary, but to the man of God. *See* II Kings 4:42.

[93] *See* about the Bomoh, pp. 41–42.

[94] Even in later, Talmudic times, Shovuos is still referred to as the concluding festival of Pesach. It is called in the Talmud and Midrash "Atseres shel Pesach" or, briefly, "Atseres."

[95] Lev. 23:15–16.

[96] Modern critics of the Bible have advanced different theories about the original meaning of "the morrow after the Sabbath." One theory is that the calendar was so arranged in the very old times that the fourteenth of Nisan always came on the Sabbath. The morrow after the Sabbath, therefore, was both Sunday and the fifteenth day of the month. There is another theory that Sabbath here signified not the seventh day of the week, but the fifteenth day of the month, the full moon (*see* p. 4). In that case "the morrow after the Sabbath" referred originally to the sixteenth day of Nisan, the same date for which the Pharisees later set the offering of the omer. Some other theories have also been advanced but they are all mere hypotheses.

[97] The Falashas interpret "the morrow after the Sabbath" to mean the morrow after the last day of Pesach, not after the first day of Pesach, as the Pharisees interpreted it. (There was no eighth day of Pesach in the old days.) According to the Falashas, therefore, the omer was offered on the twenty-second day of Nisan. For more about the Falashas *see* preceding text on pp. 64–65.

[98] The Book of Jubilees is a Midrashic amplification on Genesis that was written in Hebrew in Palestine during the latter time of the second Temple. But the Hebrew original was lost. What remained was an Ethiopian translation of the book, which was copied from a Greek version. This Ethiopian version of the Book of Jubilees was discovered in Abyssinia about the middle of the nineteenth century. Later, there were also found fragments of a Latin translation. The date that the Book of Jubilees fixes for Shovuos is very close to the date observed by the Falashas. Both are based on the premise that "the morrow after the Sabbath" refers to the day after Pesach. The difference between them is entirely a matter of the

calendar. According to the Book of Jubilees the months of Nisan and Iyar each have twenty-eight days; according to the Falashas these months have thirty and twenty-nine days. So Shovuos, according to the Book of Jubilees, comes on the fifteenth day of Sivan and, according to the Falashas, on the twelfth day of that month. *See* Book of Jubilees, chaps. 6 and 15.

[99] *See* Book of Jubilees, chap. 6.

[100] Such a tie-up came very easily, for it is stated in the Bible that the Jews entered the desert of Sinai in the third month after they had left Egypt, Exod. 19:1. Ezekiel ignores Shovuos, 45:18–25.

[101] Exod. 19.

[102] The Leviathan is the primordial ocean, the primeval waters from which the world was created, represented as a gigantic sea-monster, not only by the Jews, but also by the Babylonians. The Behemoth is a similar mythological conception that grew up among Jews under the Persian influence. In the belief of the ancient Persians the Behemoth was a celestial ox, which would be slaughtered by the Messiah. *See* I. Scheftelowitz, *Die altpersische Religion und das Judentum*, pp. 207–208, *also*, by the same author, *Alt-Palaestinensischer Bauernglaube*, pp. 27–28. *See also* article "Leviathan" in *J.E.*

[103] The *Tikkun* for the eve of Shovuos is a special book, a form of anthology which contains fragments, the beginning and the end, of all the books of the Bible and of all the Orders and Tractates of the Talmud; also bits of the Zohar and, in addition, prayers and "piyutim" referring to the 613 precepts.

[104] Read about Lag Bo-Omer in the chapter on the Minor Festivals.

[105] ‎בעצרת על פרות האילן, משנה ראש השנה, פרק א‎.

[106] ‎יעקב משה טולידאנו, נר המערב, ירושלים, תרע״א‎.

[107] II Kings 25:8; Jer. 52:12. *See also* Taanith 29 a.

[108] Josephus, *War*, VI, 4, par. 5. Cf. Taanith 29 a. and Y. Megillah I, 5. The Karaites, by the way, observe the tenth day of Ov instead of the ninth.

[109] This is the accepted, traditional explanation, which in truth explains nothing. For Tishoh B'Ov was not first declared a national day of mourning after the destruction of Bether, but was such for a long time preceding that event. Had the mourning for the destruction of the first Temple come upon the seventh or tenth day of the month, its date would not have been changed after the destruction of Bether. On the contrary, the destruction of Bether may have served as a stimulus to further observe the old custom to fast and mourn on the ninth day of Ov, regardless of the fact that the second Temple went down in flames on the tenth day of the month. There remains then the question: Why was the ninth of Ov observed, since ancient times, as a day of mourning? That the day was a fast day even before the destruction of the second Temple can be seen from the reminiscence of Rabbi Eleazar ben Zadok, Taanith 12 a. This Tanna was a merchant in Jerusalem in the years preceding the destruction of the second Temple. *See* W. Bacher, *Die Agada der Tannaiten* I, pp. 46–47 and Weiss, *Dor*, II, 121. We must assume, therefore, that Tishoh B'Ov

as a day of mourning is not only older than the destruction of Bether and of the second Temple, but is even older than the first destruction of Jerusalem. Tishoh B'Ov was obviously a primitive nature festival, a festival of the folk-belief, in the time of the Jewish kingdom. Jews, it appears, observed a nature festival in those ancient days, in the month of Ov, in the middle of summer, that lasted seven days. It began, as did many other festivals, with a day of fasting on the ninth day of the month, and ended with a joyous revel and dance procession in the vineyards on the fifteenth day of the month (Chamishoh Osor B'Ov). It was only later, in the time of the Babylonian exile, that Tishoh B'Ov was bound up with a historic event, with the destruction of the Temple, and was thus changed from a heathenish folk-observance to a national day of mourning. This also explains, by the way, why the Mishnah says that "on the ninth of Ov it was decreed that our ancestors should not enter the Holy Land" (Taanith IV, 1). Who or what forced the Tannaim of the Mishnah to tie up Tishoh B'Ov with the tale of the messengers? More, the Mishnah does not present this explanation in broad, homiletical phrases, but states it simply, as if giving an old tradition. This points to the fact that the explanation for Tishoh B'Ov comes from a much older period than the Mishnah, from a time when people still remembered that the fast of the ninth day of Ov was older than the destruction of the first Temple, and they therefore sought to connect it with the period in the wilderness. See more about Chamishoh Osor B'Ov on pp. 277–78. Cf. *also* with p. 122 and p. 266. *See* Julian Morgenstern, "The Three Calendars of Ancient Israel," in *Hebrew Union College Annual*, 1924.

[110] *See* Taanith 29 a, *also* Rabbah, Tanchuma, and Yalkut on Num. 14:1.

[111] I Sam. 7:6; I Kings 21 (Jezebel obviously availed herself of the privilege to call a general fast day for the land in the name of Ahab); Jer. 36:9; Joel 1–2.

[112] II Kings 25:1; Jer. 39:1; 41.

[113] Zech. 7–8.

[114] Megillah 5 b. It seems from this that Rabbi Judah the Patriarch also sought to minimize the observance of the fast of the Seventeenth of Tammuz. He was not enthusiastic about Purim either, for the tale of the Book of Esther does not tend to promote an atmosphere of friendship between Jew and Gentile. *See* Weiss, *Dor*, II, 180.

[115] Kinoh was originally the name given by Jews to any ode of mourning. In the Talmud the Book of Lamentations is referred to as Kinos. Now, however, Kinos refer specifically to those Jewish songs of mourning which Jewish religious poets composed in the Middle Ages. Many of these Kinos do not hark back to the destruction of Jerusalem, but to later calamities that the Jews suffered. On the eve of Tishoh B'Ov, after the reciting of Lamentations, only a few Kinos are chanted, but mainly they are chanted the next morning, after the regular prayers. The number of these Kinos grew so great in time, that they became a separate book.

[116] Maharil.

[117] Midrash Lamentations 1, 57.

[118] Jer. 50–51. These prophecies of certain anonymous prophets who lived toward the end of the Babylonian exile were, by the way, never fulfilled. Cyrus captured Babylon, but he did not destroy it, Babylon remaining one of the capitals of the Persian Empire.

[119] Lev. 23:24; Num. 29:1. The term Rosh Hashonoh is used in the Bible only once, however, in reference to the tenth day of Tishri, Ezek. 40:1.

[120] In a cycle of nineteen years, the third, sixth, eighth, eleventh, fourteenth, seventeenth, and nineteenth years are leap years.

[121] According to a Babylonian tradition of Gaonic times, it was Hillel II (in the IV Century c.e.) who fixed the Jewish calendar and established its rules. However, these rules of Hillel II were only one phase in the history of the Jewish calendar, which was not completed before the sixth-seventh century. The last point of contention regarding the Jewish calendar arose about a thousand years ago, in the beginning of the tenth century, between Saadia Gaon of Babylonia and Aaron ben Meir, a noted head of an academy in Palestine. See Henry Malter, Saadia Gaon, pp. 70–71 and חיים יחיאל בארנשטיין, מחלקת ר' סעדיה גאון ובן מאיר.

[122] It seems that in the old days Jews changed the calendar many times and had various methods for equalizing the lunar and the solar year. See Morgenstern, "The Three Calendars of Ancient Israel," "Additional Notes," "Supplementary Studies" (Hebrew Union College Annual, 1924, 1926, 1935).

[123] See Betsah 4 b.

[124] Exod. 23:16; 34:22.

[125] Exod. 12:2.

[126] Exod. 23:14–19; 34:18–26; Lev. 23; Deut. 16.

[127] See note 119. It is also possible that in ancient days, from the time that Jews first settled in Palestine, they had, in various circles and for various purposes, two New Years: one in the fall and one in the spring. In the Mishnah (Rosh Hashanah I, 1), the first day in Nisan is designated as the New Year for kings and festivals, and the first day in Tishri as the New Year for years, Sh'mitohs and Jubilees. But which of these is the religious and which the civil New Year is not clear. Josephus, however, distinctly says that the religious New Year of the Jews comes in Nisan, and the civil in Tishri (Ant. I, 3, par. 3). The Karaites actually observe the first day of Nisan as Rosh Hashonoh.

[128] See Num. 10:10 and Lev. 23:24; cf. also Mishnah Rosh Hashanah III. More of this in the chapter on the blowing of the shofar.

[129] When Ezra reads forth the Torah in Jerusalem on the first day of Tishri the Jews burst into tears, and he tells them not to weep and mourn on this holy day, but to go home to feast and drink, to send portions of food to the poor, and to be festively joyous (Neh. 8). Hence we see that the first of Tishri was, in Ezra's time, somewhat of a festival. But what type of holiday it was, whether it was in observance of the New Year, or the New Moon of the seventh month, we are not told. Among the Samaritans, to this very day, the first of Tishri is not the New Year,

but the beginning of the season of repentance. *See* J. Montgomery, *The Samaritans*, p. 41; M. Gaster, *The Samaritans*, p. 173 יום ראש החודש השביעי.

[130] In the Apocryphal literature there is no mention of Rosh Hashonoh. Nor is it to be found in Philo or Josephus. For Philo the first day of Tishri is a form of introduction to the month of festivals. *See Die Werke Philos*, II, pp. 159–160 (ed. Cohn). For Josephus, too, the first of Tishri was a special form of New Moon, *Ant.* III, 10, par. 1 and 2. Cf. S. Krauss, *Talmudische Archaeologie*, II, 417–418 and Schuerer, *Geschichte des Juedischen Volkes*, new edition, I, 32–35.

[131] Tannaitic literature consists of Mishnah, Tosephta, the Baraitas and parts of the Midrashim.

[132] *See* p. 156 ff.

[133] *Malchiyos* is a prayer which stresses the one-ness of God, King of the world; *Zichronos* stresses God as Creator and Judge of the world and His relation to mankind; *Shofaros* adds the thought of God as the Deliverer, the thought of the great Shofar to be blown when the Messiah comes, as the signal of redemption. More about this in I. Elbogen, *Der Juedische Gottesdienst*, and A. Z. Idelsohn, *Jewish Liturgy*.

[134] "Piyut" is a hebraized form of the same Greek root-word that gave us "poet." In the Midrashim we already meet the expression, דברי פיוטין for imaginative concepts, for fictional tales (Bereshith Rabbah 85, 3). Later the name "Piyut" was used to designate the religious poetry which was added to the services for the festivals and outstanding Sabbaths, after the regular prayers had been established and accepted by all Jews. The prayers are therefore the same in the prayer books of all the Jews of the world (with the exception of the Reform Jews), but not so the piyutim. And there is not the same obligation to recite the piyutim as there is for the prayers. At any rate, Piyut is the general name for the synagogal poetry that is chanted in the services. But usually only one part of this poetry is thus designated, the songs of praise to God. The supplications have a separate name, *S'lichos*. The subject is treated in detail in the above mentioned books of Elbogen and Idelsohn.

[135] Judging by its simple language and clear style, this bit of piyut is a very old one, from the time before the Crusades. It is attributed to a legendary Jewish martyr, Amnon of Mayence. The story of Amnon is found in the traditional machzor, in Hebrew, and is very popular among Jews. Frug, the great Jewish-Russian poet, composed an historical poem on this theme (in Russian, also available in the Hebrew translation of Kaplan). The Yiddish poet Sharkansky dramatized the story of Amnon, and the play had great success on the Yiddish stage of America. The legend, however, has no historic worth. The piyut appeared in connection with the remembrances of the persecution of Jews in the time of the Crusades. *See* I. Elbogen, *Der Juedische Gottesdienst*, A. Z. Idelsohn, *Jewish Liturgy, also* article "Amnon of Mayence," *J.E.* I, 525. A translation of this prayer appears on pp. 147–148.

[136] *See* about Pesach on pages 39–40; about Rosh Chodesh *see* the chapter on the minor festivals; about the festival of the shearing of the sheep, *see* I Sam. 25, and II Sam. 13.

[137] *See* pp. 40–43.

[138] *See* p. 42.

[139] *See* pp. 86–87.

[140] The festivals bear this character only in the laws of the Priestly Code, which are, in the main, a product of the period that began with the Babylonian exile.

[141] We can see from the Bible that the tenth day of Tishri was originally the beginning of the year. Ezekiel specifically designates that day as Rosh Hashonoh, 40:1. There can be no doubt that בראש השנה means here "in the day of the New Year," and not, as some seek to interpret it, in the beginning of the year. For it was on New Year and not on an ordinary day that Ezekiel had his prophetic vision, in which he saw a new Jerusalem and a new Temple. (The Baal Shem Tov, by the way, had his "Ascension of the Soul," during which he rose to Heaven and conversed with the Messiah, on Rosh Hashonoh. *See* ספר החסידות by אברהם כהנא pp. 73–75.) It is for this reason, because the tenth of Tishri was the New Year, that it is designated in the Bible as the day on which the Jubilee year is to be announced (Lev. 25:9). That there was something wrong about the Jubilee year starting on the tenth of the month was recognized even by the Rabbis of the Talmud, who struggled to find an explanation for it, Rosh Hashanah 8 b.

[142] Ezekiel (45:18–25) apparently knew nothing of any Yom Kippur on the tenth of Tishri. He designated two days in the year to atone for the sins committed against the sanctuary; the first days of the first and seventh months. (The expression, בשבעה בחודש in sentence 20, should be read, according to the Septuagint בשביעי באחד לחודש.) Ezekiel's suggestion was, by the way, not accepted in detail. We can also infer from Neh. 8 and 9, that the institution of Yom Kippur did not yet exist in Ezra's time. For, after the first day of Tishri, when Ezra read forth the Torah, we are next told of Sukkos, without any mention of Yom Kippur in between. But greater proof is the fact that a fast, like unto Yom Kippur, is held on the twenty-fourth day of Tishri, according to chapter 9. Were the tenth of Tishri already Yom Kippur at that time, it would have been impossible to have another such day on the second day after Sukkos. But still we can not arrive at any definite conclusions from the Book of Nehemiah. For in the Books of Ezra and Nehemiah the chapters do not follow each other in consecutive order. We do not know, therefore, if chapter 9 in Neh. is the continuation of chapter 8. It is also possible that Neh. 9 is the continuation of Ezra 10, that the Great Assembly occurred after the Jews parted from their foreign wives, and that "of this month" in Neh. 9:1, means the month of Nisan.

[143] Jews have long recognized that it is a real question as to why Yom Kippur was set for the tenth of Tishri. They therefore sought to create for Yom Kippur an historic explanation. On that day, the homiletical expounders in the Talmud claimed, Moses descended with the second two

tablets and let the Jews know that they were forgiven for the sin of the golden calf: Taanith 30 b; Pirke de Rabbi Eliezer 46. *See also* Rashi on Deut. 9:18 and Maimonides, *Guide*, III, 43. Philo sought to explain it with the fact that, according to his philosophy, ten was the perfect number.

[144] Cf. with note 142. Ezekiel, obviously, does not present here something absolutely new; he seeks to reform an old custom.

[145] There is a theory that this had some connection with the cult of Baal-Adonis-Tammuz. We know from the Bible that this cult was widespread amongst the ancient Jews. Ezekiel describes Jewish women sitting at an open gate of the Temple and bewailing the death of Tammuz, Ezek. 8:14. *See also* Zech. 12:11. But here the god carries the Aramaic-Babylonian name, Hadad-Rimmon, (cf. II Kings 5:18). This god was the personification of the vegetation, which dies suddenly at the end of summer, and his death was mourned and bemoaned, especially by the women. It must be understood, however, that regarding this point we are in the domain of conjecture.

[146] Mishnah Taanith IV, 8. This is obviously a remembrance from older times. It is impossible to assume that such a joyous dance procession occurred in Jerusalem in the later days of the second Temple.

[147] *See Die Werke Philos* (ed. Cohn) II, pp. 161–163; I. Elbogen, *Studien zur Geschichte des juedischen Gottesdienstes.*

[148] Josephus, *War*, V, 5, par. 9; Mishnah Yoma I.

[149] אבן שתיה. It was interpreted that from this stone the world began שממנה הושתת העולם. In the first Temple the ark with the Cherubim stood in the Holy of Holies. See D. Feuchtwang, "Das Wasseropfer," *Monatsschrift,* 1910, p. 535.

[150] שהיו נוטלים בדמים ויש אומרים שהיו הורגים זה את זה בכשפים, ירושלמי יומא, פרק א. It is specifically told of the High Priest Joshua ben Gamla, that he attained his rank through money, Yoma 9 a, 18 a.

[151] Most of all it was important that he pour the incense on the burning coals, according to the teaching of the Pharisees, after he stood inside, in the Holy of Holies, and not before he entered there, as the Sadducees taught. See Jacob Z. Lauterbach, "A Significant Controversy Between the Sadducees and the Pharisees" (*Hebrew Union College Annual*, IV).

[152] Yoma 19 b.

[153] The Ineffable Name was not allowed to be uttered outside of the Temple (Mishnah Sotah VII; Sanhedrin X). Jews believed that in the Ineffable Name, when one knew the secret of how to actually pronounce it, resided the power to do magic and to perform miracles. This belief was also held by the early Christians and by the Mohammedans. The ancient Egyptians also believed that with the secret ineffable name of their god Ra one could become a magician. See Erman-Ranke, *Aegypten und Aegyptisches Leben im Altertum*, p. 301.

[154] The scapegoat was obviously not a sacrifice to the *Azazel*, but was a means to send the sins into the wilderness, into a place of contamination, where the evil spirits dwell. There, in the unclean places, in the waste-

lands, dwelt, according to the folk-belief, the satyrs, imps in the shape of goats. There, too, Lilith made her home. (Cf. Isa. 34:14, and Lev. 17:7.) To this waste realm of Lilith and the Seirim, the *Azazel* also belonged. We do not know for certain, however, the interpretation of the name *Azazel*, nor do we know what part it played in the folk-belief of the ancient Jews, for it is mentioned in the Bible in no other connection except with the ceremonial on Yom Kippur. In the later days of the second Temple the *Azazel* was bound up with the tale of the fallen angels, and, according to one version, was their chief. It appears that the sending away of the goat to the *Azazel* was an old, heathenish custom, one of many heathen customs that seeped through into the Jewish New Year observance. For the Babylonians followed a similar custom in their New Year observance, Heinrich Zimmern, "Das babylonische Neujahrsfest" (*Der Alte Orient*, Vol. XXV, Heft 3, p. 11); *also* Robert William Rogers, *Cuneiform Parallels*, p. 196. The custom was apparently beloved by the folk, and it could not be discarded. It was therefore taken into the official Jewish religion and in that way made harmless, for it became no more than a symbolic ceremony. A *Soir* as a sin-offering was sacrificed to God, and the scapegoat merely symbolically represented the forgiving of the sins of the people. An original theory regarding the scapegoat is offered by the English Bible critic, T. K. Cheyne. According to him Jews originally sacrificed the goat to the satyrs (Lev. 17:7; cf. *also* Deut. 32:17). In order, however, to wean the folk away from sacrificing to these spirits, the religious leaders of the Jews created the figure of *Azazel*, a legendary name of a fallen angel, and directed that the goat be sent to him, instead of bringing it as a sacrifice to the spirits of the desert. *See* Cheyne's article in *Zeitschrift alttestamentliche Wissenschaft*, 1895, pp. 153–156.

[155] The priests (and the Levites) were divided into twenty-four shifts, service sections. Each shift performed the Temple service for one week and was divided into seven smaller shifts, one for each day.

[156] A red ribbon or thread was a charm against evil spirits among all peoples. *See* I. Scheftelowitz, *Alt-Palaestinensischer Bauernglaube*, p. 63. *Also* in *Die altpersische Religion und das Judentum*, by the same author, pp. 78–80. Originally the goat was apparently sent to the desert and was there released free in the wasteland (Lev. 16:22). There was fear, obviously, that it might return. It is even possible that this eventuality happened. It was therefore arranged that the goat was to be killed by being pushed over a cliff.

[157] He recited Lev. 16 and 23:26–32 from the Torah-scroll, and then recited Num. 29:7–11, by heart (Mishnah Yoma VII). This synagogue was situated in the "hall of hewn stones" where the Sanhedrin held its sessions, Mishnah Tamid I. *See* Samuel Krauss, *Synagogale Altertuemer*, pp. 66–72.

[158] "Chazan hakneseth." In those days chazan referred to the sexton of the synagogue.

[159] Aboth de R. Nathan IV. The passage of the Bible is quoted here from Hos. 6:6.

[160] Due to the fact that the two days of Rosh Hashonoh were considered as one, it did not seem proper to recite the benediction Shehecheyonu on the second night, as if the day were a separate one. Jews overcame this by putting a new fruit on the table, over which the benediction was recited the second night.

[161] See pp. 99–100.

[162] Hos. 14:2.

[163] Rosh Hashanah 16 a–b.

[164] Weiss, Dor, III, 156, contends that Rabbi Judah ben Ilai was the one who originated the idea that Rosh Hashonoh was a "Day of Judgment." Weiss would not have said this, had he known that, among the Babylonians, New Year's Day was a day of judgment even a thousand years before the time of King David. In one detail, however, Weiss is correct, that in the time of Rabbi Akiba's disciples this thought had not yet been accepted by all Jews. For Rabbi Jose says that "a man is judged every day" and Rabbi Nathan says that "a man is judged every hour."

[165] In ancient times Jews already had the idea that there were books in heaven, lists on which all are entered (Exod. 32:32; Isa. 4:3; Dan. 7:10 and 12:1; Ps. 69:29; 139:16; Mal. 3:16). However, we must not conclude that these Babylonian ideas first entered Jewish life during the Babylonian exile. This may have happened quite a bit earlier, through the medium of the Assyrians, or still earlier, through the medium of the Phoenicians. For Exod. 32:32 belongs to the oldest portions of the Pentateuch and, consequently, to the older days of the kingdom.

[166] Details regarding the Babylonian New Year observance are to be found in Heinrich Zimmern, "Das babylonische Neujahrsfest," (Der Alte Orient, Vol. XXV, Heft 3); Alfred Jeremias, Handbuch der Altorientalischen Geisteskultur.

[167] This custom is already mentioned in Responsa of the G'onim.

[168] See S. Krauss, "Aus der Juedischen Volkskueche" in Mitteilungen zur Juedischen Volkskunde, 18. Jahrgang, Heft 1–2.

[169] The relationship between the primitive shofar and the artificial trumpet in the early religious ceremonial of Jews is not certain. Naturally, in the Temple, silver trumpets were blown, and it is possible that on Rosh Hashonoh, too, artificial trumpets were blown, rather than the shofar. See Sol B. Finesinger, "The Shofar" in Hebrew Union College Annual, 1931–32.

[170] Cf. Judg. 7:18–22; I Sam. 1:13; I Kings 1:39; II Kings 9:13; Isa. 58:1; Jer. 4:19; Amos 3:6.

[171] Lev. 23:24 and Num. 10:9–10. See also about the bells on the High Priest's robe in Exod. 28:35.

[172] Die Werke Philos, (ed. Cohn), II, 160–161.

[173] Rosh Hashanah 16 a–b. This saying of the Talmud was thus interpreted. We must assume, however, that in the expression "to confound Satan" there still resides the primitive idea of chasing away the evil spirits with noise. This primitive idea, by the way, explains why the general New

Year is greeted by clanging of bells and blowing of horns and general noise-making. Cf. pp. 265–266.

[174] *Machzor Vitry* by R. Simchah, a pupil of Rashi.

[175] 7:19.

[176] Rashi on Shabbath 81 b.

[177] Jacob Z. Lauterbach, "Tashlik" in *Hebrew Union College Annual,* 1936; I. Scheftelowitz, *Alt-Palaestinensischer Bauernglaube,* p. 41.

[178] Responsa of the G'onim 8.

[179] Berakhoth 6 a.

[180] *See* about encirclings on pp. 206–207.

[181] *Shibbole Haleket* (XIII Century).

[182] J.Q.R. 1892, pp. 387–389.

[183] The custom to send the Kaporoh fowl to the poor is mentioned already in the 13th century (*Shibbole Haleket*). Details regarding the Kaporoh fowl among different peoples: I. Scheftelowitz, *Das stellvertretende Huhnopfer. See also* Jacob Z. Lauterbach, *Jewish Studies in Memory of George A. Kohut.*

[184] *Machzor Vitry.*

[185] Is first mentioned in *Shne Luchoth Habrith* by R. Isaiah Halevi Hurwitz (XVI Century).

[186] The time of the G'onim was from the seventh to the eleventh centuries.

[187] It is to be found neither in Alfas nor in Rambam.

[188] The S'fardim and the oriental Jews, to this day, use the older version, and add to it the newer version.

[189] It is the very plausible theory of Posnansky and Krauss that Kol Nidre appeared in Palestine during the warfare between the Rabbinic Jews and the Karaites, for the latter were opposed to the remission of vows. *See* S. Krauss, "Das Problem Kol Nidre" in *Jahrbuch der Juedisch-Literarischen Gesellschaft,* 1928. *See also* I. Davidson, "Kol Nidre" in *Am. Jewish Year Book,* 1923. Cf. note 30.

[190] A. Z. Idelsohn, "The Kol Nidre Tune" in *Hebrew Union College Annual,* 1931–32.

[191] *See* p. 113.

[192] Exod. 23:16; 34:22; Lev. 23:34, 39; Deut. 16:13, 16; Judg. 21:19; II Kings 8:2; Isa. 31:29; Ezek. 45:23, 25; II Chron. 7:8. In Mishnah also, Sukkos is called, shortly, Chag. From Exod. 32:5, 9 and Ps. 42:5; 107:27 it is inferred that Chag originally denoted the religious dance, the procession of the festival.

[193] Pesach is only mentioned once in connection with Josiah's reform, II Kings 23:21–23. Cf. above p. 46. The Book of Chronicles belongs to the beginning of the Greek period and cannot be taken in consideration regarding Jewish life during the independent kingdom.

[194] Judg. 9:27.

[195] We are not sure even about the month. It seems, however, that during the earlier days of the Jewish kingdom, the fall festival was observed in the eighth month, and not in the seventh. This is clearly seen in First Kings. According to chap. 6:38, Solomon's Temple was finished in the eighth month. The dedication, however, according to chap. 8, was held in the seventh month. It is not possible that after the Temple was completely finished that the dedication was delayed for eleven months. (Cf. Yalkut on First Kings, 184.) The only explanation for this is that the older version actually told that the dedication came in the month Bul. Later, however, in Judah, the festival was transferred from the eighth to the seventh month, and the text was changed in the detail regarding the dedication, and declared to have occurred in the seventh month (8:2). Since Jeroboam imitated the festival of Judah, he also observed the holiday in the eighth month (I Kings 12:32–33). But a Judean writer of later times could not imagine that the festival was originally observed in Cheshvan, and he added a note to the text that the wicked Jeroboam devised the festival month "of his own heart." *See* Hugo Gressmann, *Die aelteste Geschichtsschreibung und Prophetie Israels*, p. 243. It is therefore also possible that Pesach was originally observed a month later, in Iyar, and that the Second Pesach of Num. 9 was originally the date of Pesach for all. At the same time that the autumn festival was changed, the Pesach festival was set for one month earlier. The original Pesach, that of Iyar, thus remained a holiday only for those who were ritually unclean in Nisan.

[196] Isa. 5:1–2; 16:10; 24:7–11.

[197] *See* p. 46.

[198] Judg. 21:19–21; I Sam. 1.

[199] I Kings 8:2; Isa. 30:29. Chag means here not Pesach, but Sukkos.

[200] Amos 5:21–27; Hos. 9:1; Isa. 28:7–8.

[201] *See* pp. 119–120.

[202] Lev. 23:43.

[203] *See* p. 46.

[204] *See* p. 89.

[205] Josephus, *War*, II, 19, par. 1.

[206] Josephus often tells of onslaughts by robbers. He also related that the Babylonian Jew, Zamaris, whom Herod had colonized in Batanea, aided the Babylonian pilgrims against robbers' raids (*Ant.* XVII, 2 par. 2). *Also* cf. Mishnah Shekalim II, where there is a discussion regarding money that is sent for the Temple and is lost or stolen along the way.

[207] S. Krauss, *Tal. Arch.*, II, 323.

[208] Josephus, *Ant.* XVIII, 9, par. 1.

[209] Mishnah Taanith I, 3.

[210] Aboth de Rabbi Nathan, 2nd version, chap. 27.

[211] Ps. 42:5.

[212] In contrast to the first tithe, which belonged to the Levites, the second tithe had to be used up by the owner himself in Jerusalem.

213 Mishnah Bikkurim III.

214 Ps. 87:2.

215 Ps. 84:2, 3, 11.

216 Ps. 122 and 125.

217 Rosh Hashanah 31 b; Sukkah 37 a, 41 b; Betsah 5 a.

218 Zech. 14:16. Cf. 8:20–23; Isa. 2:2–4; Micah 4:1–3; Isa. 56:6–7.

219 The pouring of water on the altar was apparently a talisman for rain (Rosh Hashanah 16 a.). It is not mentioned in the laws of the Pentateuch. The Sadducees were therefore against it. Apparently it was made part of the ceremonial after the victory of the Pharisees in the days of Queen Salome Alexandra. But we cannot tell how old the ceremony is. It appears that it was an ancient custom of the Jewish folk-belief which, for certain reasons, was not codified and taken into the official Jewish religion. We may assume that originally the water was poured upon the earth, as a talisman for rain, and only later, when it was made a part of the official ritual of the Temple, was it changed to a water-offering for the altar. See D. Feuchtwang, "Das Wasseropfer," Monatsschrift, 1910, p. 535ff. See also I. Scheftelowitz, Alt-Palaestinensischer Bauernglaube, p. 93–95.

220 Isa. 12:3.

221 They wanted to be certain of it because, as told above, the Sadducees were opposed to the custom and the Hasmonean ruler, Alexander Janaeus once poured the water on the earth (cf. Josephus, Ant. XIII, 13 par. 5 and Sukkah 48 b.). From the expression in משנה סוכה ,ולמנסך אומרים לו הגבה ידך it appears that ordinarily not the High Priest, but an ordinary priest, poured the water on the altar. See A. Buechler, Die Priester und der Kultus, p. 113.

222 See pp. 128–129.

223 The interpretation and the meaning of the expression Simchas Bes Hashoevoh is not certain. For this was a fire-observance which had nothing to do with the ceremony of drawing and pouring the water on the altar. This ceremony occurred in the morning, while the Simchas Bes Hashoevoh was a night observance. According to the interpretation of one of the Amoraim השואבה was put down in error for some other word. See Joseph Hochman, Jerusalem Temple Festivities.

224 Tosephta Sukkah IV.

225 Pss. 120–134.

226 This refers to Ezek. 8:16. We learn from this that the fire-observance of Simchas Bes Hashoevoh, originally, before it was Judaized, had a close relationship to the worship of the sun. We must not assume, however, that this arose among Jews through Hellenistic influence, as some scholars contend; it rather had to do, originally, with the worship of Baal-Adonis-Tammuz. See the above mentioned book by Joseph Hochman. Cf. also with note 145.

227 This concluding festival of the eighth day was added later, obviously after the Babylonian exile. We see this when we compare I Kings, 8:65–66

with II Chron. 7:8, 10. According to the older account in the Book of Kings the festival lasted seven days, but according to the later account in Chronicles it lasted eight days.

[228] Yoma 21 b.

[229] See I. Elbogen, Der Juedische Gottesdienst and A. Z. Idelsohn, Jewish Liturgy. Hoshano Rabboh certainly did not become suddenly a "Day of Judgment" in the Middle Ages, a sequel to Rosh Hashonoh and Yom Kippur. We must assume that it had some of this character from the oldest times. For it is told already in Midrash Tehillim that on Hoshano Rabboh is the גמר חתימה. But why Hoshano Rabboh is a conclusion to Yom Kippur has thus far not been explained. ובחג נידונין על המים (Mishnah Rosh Hashanah I) is no explanation. See, however, explanation given above on p. 122.

[230] See p. 115.

[231] The name, Simchas Torah, is mentioned the first time by R. Hai Gaon (died 1038).

[232] See note 103. The Tikkun of Hoshano Rabboh, which is usually bound in one with the Tikkun of Shovuos, consists of selections from Deut., Ps., and bits of Zohar.

[233] See note 102.

[234] This was already seen by the Rabbis of the Talmud, and therefore, according to some of them the sukkos of the desert were not booths, but "clouds of glory," basing it on Isa. 4:5–6. See Sukkah 11 b. See also Rashi and Ibn Ezra on Lev. 23:43.

[235] See Die Werke Philos (ed. Cohn), II, 165–166, and Maimonides, Guide III, 43.

[236] This idea was tied up to the expression "temporary dwelling" with which the sukkoh is designated in the Talmud.

[237] See p. 171.

[238] Neh. 8. The part of the Pentateuch that is here referred to is the calendar of the festivals in Lev. 23. For in no other part of the Pentateuch is anything said about sitting in sukkos. But the text of the decree regarding sukkos, as it is quoted in Neh. 8, is not identical with Lev. 23. It seems from this that the text of Lev. 23 was changed, in several details, after Ezra's time.

[239] So it appears from Hos. 12:10.

[240] There is also the theory of Hugo Gressmann that the sukkos on the roofs originally had to do with the worship of Baal-Adonis-Tammuz, and were only later Judaized. This theory answers all questions. See Gressmann, "The Mysteries of Adonis and the Feast of Tabernacles," in The Expositor, 9. Series, 1925, 3, pp. 416–432. Also "Tod und Auferstehung des Osiris" in Der Alte Orient, Vol. XXIII, Heft 3, p. 17. See also Rudolf Kittel in Orientalistische Literatur-Zeitung, 1924, No. 7. Cf. also note 145. However, according to the tablets of Ras-Shamra, which were recently excavated, the sukkoh has a Canaanite origin and was connected with the Baal worship. See Theodor Herzl Gaster, "The Combat of Aleyan-Baal

and Mot" in *Journal of the Royal Asiatic Society*, 1934, pp. 677–714, especially p. 680. The Canaanites performed a ritual drama at their autumn festival. Part of this was the enthroning of Aleyan-Baal, a banquet of the gods, and the erection of a sukkoh for the gods. The sukkoh is called מצלל. The Hebrew word סוכה is translated in תרגום אונקלוס: מטלל מצלל.

241 Lev. 23:40; cf. Neh. 8:15.

242 It was only later that Lev. 23:40 was interpreted to mean these four species. In Neh. 8:15, there is no mention of "the fruit of goodly trees," and הדס and עבות עץ are two separate species. Cf. Lev. Rabbah 30, 14.

243 Taanith 2 b.

244 *See* Rabbah and Tanchuma on Lev. 23.

245 Sukkah 44 a.

246 In this same way, instead of pouring water on the field, they poured it later on the altar as an offering to God. *See* note 219. *See* I. Scheftelowitz, *Alt-Palaestinensischer Bauernglaube*, pp. 90–95.

247 Taanith 23 a.

248 *See* the above mentioned book of Scheftelowitz, pp. 52–53. *See also* הקפות ועיגולים (חורב, ניו יארק, תשרי, תרצ׳א) 75–77, *also* מיכאל היגער, מסכת שמחות.

249 A. Buechler, *Die Tobiaden und die Oniaden*

250 Most critical scholars of today contend that the nom de guerre Maccabee, which Judah possessed, designated "the hero," "the hammerer," from מקבה or מקבת a hammer. Cf. with name of Frankish ruler, Charles Martel ("Martel"=hammer). In Talmudic literature the Maccabean family is known as בני חשמונאי or בני חשמוני and also בית חשמונאי. In many parts of Josephus the family also bears this name. In the Second Book of Maccabees, Mattathias' name is not mentioned. Not Mattathias, but Judah begins the uprising in that account, and it appears that this is the historical truth. In the first Book of Maccabees (chap. II, 1) we read, "Mattathias, the son of Jochanan, the son of Simeon." It is a conjecture of Wellhausen that Mattathias' grandfather bore the name Hasmon and that the son of Simeon was erroneously written down for the son of Hasmon.

251 There are, in all, four Books of Maccabees. But as a source for the history of the Maccabees, only the first and the second books can be considered. These are two separate books that tell the story of the Maccabees from two different viewpoints. Originally they were written in two separate languages: the First Book of Maccabees in Hebrew and the Second in Greek. They were both preserved, however, in Greek, for the Hebrew original of the First Book was lost.

252 Reckoned according to the Seleucid era, which began with the first of October in the year 312 B.C.E. We gather from this that the rededication of the Temple services occurred in the year 165 B.C.E.

253 First Macc. chap. IV.

254 Scholars generally consider that this is an error, that it should be three instead of two.

255 II Macc. chap. X.

[256] Josephus, *Ant.* XII, 7, par. 6–7.

[257] Shabbath 24 b.

[258] Num. 7:1, 10–11, 84, 88; I Kings 8:63; Ezra 6:16; Neh. 12:27.

[259] Mishnah Baba Kamma VI, 6; Shabbath 21 b.

[260] *See* pp. 38–43, 86–88, 119, 174.

[261] We see this implication specifically from the following Baraita in עבודה זרה דף ח, עמוד ב: תנו רבנן לפי שראה אדם הראשון יום שמתמעט והולך אמר אוי לי שמא בשביל שסרחתי עולם חשך בעדי וחוזר לתוהו ובוהו וזוהי מיתה שנקנסה עלי מן השמים. עמד וישב ח' ימים בתענית ובתפילה כיון שראה תקופת טבת וראה יום שמאריך והולך אמר מנהגו של עולם הוא, הלך ועשה שמונה ימים טובים, לשנה האחרת עשאן לאלו ואלו ימים טובים, הוא קבעם לשם שמים והם קבעום לשם עבודת כוכבים. *Also* cf. the explanation regarding the fire-observance in the Second Book of Maccabees, chap. I.

[262] According to the theory of Samuel Krauss this happened under Herod. It seems logical that Herod would not allow the observance of a Maccabean victory, but he did allow the observance of the old folk custom to kindle lights at that season of the year. In that way, the Chanukkoh lights, which, in time, the people bound up with the events of the Maccabean uprising, saved the Chanukkoh festival from extinction. This, however, is no more than a conjecture. *See* Krauss' article on Chanukkoh in *Revue des Etudes Juives*, XXX, 24. *See also* Oliver Shaw Rankin, *The Origins of the Festival of Hanukkah*.

[263] שבת דף כ"א, ב: מאי חנוכה שכשנכנסו יונים להיכל טמאו כל השמנים שבהיכל וכשגברה מלכות בית חשמונאי ונצחום בדקו ולא מצאו אלא פך אחד של שמן שהיה מונח בחותמו של כהן גדול ולא היה בו אלא להדליק יום אחד ונעשה בו נס והדליקו ממנו שמונה ימים, לשנה אחרת קבעום ועשאום ימים טובים בהלל והודאה.

[264] I Kings 17:16; II Kings 4:1–6.

[265] פסיקתא רבתי, פרשה ב: ולמה מדליק נרות בחנוכה אלא בשעה שנצחו בניו של חשמונאי הכהן הגדול למלכות יון נכנסו לבית המקדש מצאו שם שמונה שפודים של ברזל וקבעו והדליקו בתוכם נרות.

[266] פסיקתא רבתי פרשה ו: זאת החנוכה שאנו עושים זכר לחנוכת בית חשמונאי על שעשו מלחמה ונצחו לבני יון, ואנו עכשיו מדליקין, וכן בשעה שנגמרה מלאכת המשכן עשו חנוכה.

[267] מגילת תענית, פרק ט: ולמה ראו לעשות חנוכה זו שמונה ימים אלא בימי מלכות יון נכנסו בית חשמונאי להיכל ובנו את המזבח ושדוהו בשיד ותקנו בו כלי שרת והיו מתעסקין בו שמונה ימים. ומה ראו להדליק את הנרות אלא בימי מלכות יון שנכנסו בני חשמונאי להיכל ושמונה שפודין של ברזל היו בידם וחפום בעץ והדליקו בהם את הנרות, והיהי הנרות מתעסקין בהם מנחות דף כ"ח, עמוד ב. Regarding the iron spears there is also mention in כל שמונה ב: שפודים של ברזל היו וחפום בעץ, העשירו ועשאום של כסף, חזרו והעשירו עשאום של זהב.

[268] *See* p. 223 and note 114. The statement is made, in the name of the German-Hungarian rabbi, Moshe Sofer, that Rabbi Judah the Patriarch who traced his ancestry to King David, ignored Chanukkoh because he was incensed at the Maccabeans because they had usurped the kingship that belonged to the descendants of King David. But it is much more probable that he looked askance at the observance of a festival that commemorated a successful Jewish rebellion against the rule of a foreign power.

[269] In חמדת הימים, a book of homilies ascribed by some to Nathan of Gaza, the prophet of Sabbatai Zwi.

[270] This polemic was aroused by an article called מאי חנוכה by Hayyim Selig Slonimski in No. 278, 1891 הצפירה. *See* the book אגדת פך השמן by Samuel Alexandrov.

[271] *See* I. Elbogen, *Der Juedische Gottesdienst,* and A. Z. Idelsohn, *Jewish Liturgy.*

[272] Commenting on the saying in Shabbath 23 a.: אמר ר' יהושע בן לוי נשים, R. Nissim ben Reuben (in the XIV Century), in his commentary on the Alfas says: שרו יונים על כל הבתולות הנשאות חייבות בנר חנוכה שאף הן היו באותו הנס שיבעלו להגמון תחילה וע"י אשה נעשה נס דאמרינן במדרש דבתו של יוחנן האכילה לראש האויבים גבינה לשכרותו וחתכה את ראשו וברחו כולם ועל זה נהגו לאכל גבינה בחנוכה.

[273] A. Landau, "Spiele der juedischen Kinder in Ostgalizien," in *Mitteilungen zur Juedischen Volkskunde,* 1899, Heft 1.

[274] A specimen of these charades is given in *Students Scholars and Saints* by Louis Ginzberg, p. 75.

[275] יצחק שיפער, געשיכטע פון יידישער טעאטער-קונסט און דראמע.

[276] חמדת הימים II in the chap. on Chanukkoh כי לכולם יהיה חליפות שמלות היו לנשים כי על כל נבר יהיו כלי אשה.

[277] *See* M. Gaster, "The Scroll of the Hasmonaeans" in *Transactions of the Ninth International Congress of Orientalists,* II, 3–32. *See also* article "Scroll of Antiochus" by L. Ginzberg, *J.E.* I, 637.

[278] Ahasuerus, the Persian king of the story of the Book of Esther, was the son of Darius I and, on his mother's side, the grandson of Cyrus. He reigned twenty years, from 485 to 465 B.C.E. In Persian he was called Khsayarsha; the Greeks transliterated the name to Xerxes, and the Jews to Ahasuerus.

[279] This fact was already observed by the homilists of the Midrash: רבי נחמיה אומר: הדסה שמה ולמה נקרא שמה אסתר שהיו עובדי אלילים קורין אותה כוכב הנוגה על שם אסתהר, ילקוט שמעוני, אסתר ב, ז.

[280] The author of the Book of Esther obviously regarded Ahasuerus as the successor of Nebuchadnezzar, in the same way that the author of Daniel regarded Darius as the successor to Belshazzar (Dan. 5:30; 6:1).

[281] One of the Apocryphal books that were composed in the days of the second Temple and were preserved in their Greek translation. The name "Third Ezra" comes from the Vulgate Bible, in which the Book of Ezra is designated the First Ezra, the Book of Nehemiah the Second Ezra, and the apocryphic Ezra as the Third Book of Ezra. There is still a Fourth Book of Ezra, an Apocalypse from the time of the destruction of the second Temple.

[282] I Macc. 7:26.

[283] *See* the Scroll of Antiochus and the various versions of מעשה חנוכה and מעשה יהודית in אוצר מדרשים, אייזענשטיין. *See also* p. 234 and note 272. Cf. *also* the prayer Al Hanissim for Chanukkoh and Purim.

[284] A strong argument for the contention that the Book of Esther is a product of the Maccabean period is the fact that Ben Sirach, who lived in the days just before the Maccabean uprising, mentions neither Mordecai

nor Esther in his reckoning of all the great and noted Jews from Abraham
to the High Priest Simeon (chaps. 44–50).

[285] *See* p. 224.

[286] Megillah 7 a.; Y. Megillah I.

[287] At the end of II Macc., where it is enjoined that the victory over
Nicanor is to be observed on the thirteenth of Adar, the day before the
"Day of Mordecai."

[288] The meaning that the name "Purim" originally had is also obscure to
this day. The explanation that the Book of Esther gives for the name was
conceived in later times. For a festival must acquire its name from the
essence of the day, not from an unimportant incident. Of what importance
is it that Haman decreed the day through the throwing of lots? The
various explanations offered by Jewish and Christian scholars for the
name Purim are mere hypotheses and none of them wholly satisfactory.
Cf. about the name Pesach in note 43.

[289] *See* יצחק יחזקאל יהודה, מגלת מצרים (רשומות ה).

[290] שטאפלען in מאקס וויינרייך, מגילת וויניץ.

[291] *See* conclusion of Chaye Adam.

[292] *See* note 103 and 232. Tikkun was a name for all piyutim.

[293] Deut. 25:19.

[294] Second Targum, the most popular and beloved of all the Midrashim,
was composed in Aramaic in the time of the G'onim.

[295] ידיעות החברה העי"י להיסתוריה ואתנוגרפיה, שנה א, שבט – אדר, תר"ץ, גליון נ'

[296] טשארני, ספר המסעות 190–192.

[297] Exod. 30:13, 15.

[298] Esther 3:12ff. *See* Paul Haupt, *Purim. See also* "Purim" by Morris
Jastrow in Hasting's *Encyclopedia of Religion and Ethics.*

[299] Tractate Soferim XVII.

[300] *See* p. 258.

[301] Neh. 8.

[302] *See* Israel Davidson, *Parody in Jewish Literature. See also* about
masquerading on Purim: Morris Jastrow, *Hebrew and Babylonian Tradition,* p. 147.

[303] יצחק שיפער, געשיכטע פון יידישער טעאטער–קונסט און דראמע.

[304] Steinschneider, "Purim und Parodie," in *Monatsschrift,* 47, p. 361
and 470.

[305] This is, understandably, an afterthought. The primitive source of this
custom must be sought for in the primitive character of Purim as a
season festival. For, exactly like beating and masquerading, legumes were
also, in the belief of the peoples, a charm against the spirits. For this
same reason beans are also eaten at a wedding and a זכר שלום. *See* I. Scheftelowitz, *Alt-Palaestinensischer Bauernglaube,* pp. 39–40.

[306] Tractate Soferim XIV.

[307] *See* chapter on Purim.

[308] The day of the New Moon was not known as Rosh Chodesh but Chodesh (I Sam. 20:5, 24; II Kings 4:23; Isa. 1:13; 66:23; Amos 8:5; Hos. 2:13). Chodesh stands here by the side of Sabbath, and it is a day of rest, on which there is no trade. Visits are made to the prophet, the seer, and people gather in the sanctuary to serve God.

[309] Rosh Chodesh is not mentioned among the festivals, neither in Exod. 23:14–19, 34:17–26; Deut. 16, nor in Lev. 23.

[310] Ezek. 46:1–6; Num. 10:10; 28:11–15. Here the Sabbath precedes Rosh Chodesh, whereas in the older, pre-exilic writings Chodesh precedes Sabbath.

[311] See pp. 114–115.

[312] Sanhedrin 42 a.; Tractate Soferim XX, 1.

[313] Cf. p. 143.

[314] See I. Elbogen, Der juedische Gottesdienst. Cf. also p. 266 (in regard to the Fast of Esther).

[315] Y. Pesachim IV, 1.

[316] Women were, in general, the more devoted worshipers of the stars. See Jer. 7:18; 46:9, 15–19.

[317] Mentioned in the name of R. Hai Gaon who opposed it. Ibn Ezra ridiculed it as talk of old women.

[318] See p. 94.

[319] Yebamoth 62 b. The ordinary version reads כולם מתו מפסח ועד עצרת. This has absolutely nothing to do with Lag Bo-Omer. The entire tie-up to Lag Bo-Omer is based on the version עד פרוס העצרת.

[320] This was homiletically inferred from Exod. 15.

[321] Regarding fire-observance among the Jews, see p. 225 and the note.

[322] Mishnah Rosh Hashanah I.

[323] See Neh. 10:35; 13:31; Josephus, War, II, 17, par. 6; Baba Bathra 121 a–b; Taanith 31. About similar festivals among other peoples see M. Zipser, Des Flavius Josephus Werk 'Ueber das hohe Alter des Juedischen Volkes gegen Apion,' p. 127.

[324] Mishnah Taanith IV, 8. See p. 123 and note 109.

[325] Judg. 21.

[326] It is based on Sukkah 45 b. See Rashi on that passage.

[327] It was already marked as a fast in the Gaonic period. In those days the first of Ov was also a fast day in oriental Jewish communities, commemorated as the day of the death of Aaron, Num. 33:38. See Biruni, The Chronology of Ancient Nations, translated and edited by Sachau, pp. 273, 276.

[328] See chapter on the Sabbath.

[329] Exod. 23:11–12; Deut. 15:1–3; Lev. 25.

[330] So it appears from certain passages of Josephus.

Index

a

Afikomon, 67, 75, 82ff., N. 88

America, Sabbath in, 28–30; Pesach in, 76; blood libel in, 58

Amoraim, 14, 15, 19, 223, 234, 264, N. 223

Anniversary, of the death of Aaron, N. 327; of the death of King David, 93; of the death of Moses, 278

Ashkenazim, 31, 32, 33, 162, 166, 168, 187, 234, 257

Azazel, 135, 136, 138, 163, N. 154

b

Barches, Berches, see Challos

Bar Mitsvoh, see Confirmation

Beating, the willows, see willow branches; the waters of a stream by the Marranos and the Jews of Morocco, 60

Behemoth, see Leviathan

Bikkurim, 87, 178, N. 92

Bimoh, 186, 187, 190, 194, 197, 198, 268

Bitter herbs, 44, 54–55, 64, 79

Blood libel, see Pesach and the blood libel

Bomoh, see High places

Book of Esther, and Purim, 237; the word God not mentioned in the, 239; and the story of Judith, 240ff.; a story of the Jews in the Diaspora, 243; allegory inherent in the, 254; does not provide a form of a religious ceremonial, 264; controversy where to begin the reading, 265; to be read as a letter, 265; dramatized, 270; Purim delicacies related to, 270–271; a product of the Maccabean period, N. 284

Book of Lamentations, 96, 101, 102, 104, 106, 237

Book of Maccabees, 218ff., 244, 248, Notes 251, 261

Book of Ruth, 90, 91, 237

Brochoh, see Kiddush

c

Calendar, Jewish, based on a compromise, 114; its history, 114ff.; establishment of the, 115; time of fixation of, N. 121

Cantor, see Chazan

Caucasus, see Jews of the Caucasus

Chagigoh, 52, 56

Challoh, originally thrown into the fire, N. 25

Challos, 13, 21, 23, 31–32

Chamishoh Osor B'Ov, 272, 277–278; linked with Tishoh B'Ov, N. 109; linked with Yom Kippur, 278

Chamishoh Osor Bi-Sh'vot, 225, 272, 277

Chanukkoh, number of days observed, 208; cessation of work by women, 208; today, 217; in the two Books of the Maccabees, 218ff., 227; in Josephus, 221, 223; festival of the lights, 221ff., N. 262; a second Sukkos, 221, 222; the name, 222; observed eight days, 222, 226–227; in the Mishnah and the Gemoro, 223, 225–227; as a nature festival, 224–225; and the flask of oil, 225ff.; controversy about lights, 222; in Midrash and in Al Hanissim, 226–228; as the re-dedication of the Temple, 228; in recent days, 230; delicacies, 232, 233, 234; money given to children, 233; games, 231–232, 235; lights kindled in home and synagogue, 234; connected with story of Judith, 234, 249; theatricals presented on, 235–236

Hoshanos, beating of the, *see* Willow branches

i

Isru-Chags, 278–279

j

Jews of Abyssinia, *see* Falashas
—of America, *see* America
—of the Caucasus, 65ff., 259
—of Germany and Poland, *see* Ashkenazim
—in Slavic countries, *see* Ashkenazim
—of Morocco, 60, 67, 95, 167
—of the Orient, 105, 168, 236, N. 188
—of Palestine, 38, 82, 86, 112, 116, 169, 170, 277
—of Persia, 257ff., 267
—of Spain and Portugal, *see* S'fardim
Josephus, on waging war on the Sabbath, N. 16; on heralding the Sabbath, N. 21; on the Sabbath river, N. 37; on the number of pilgrims in Jerusalem, N. 54; date of destruction of second Temple, N. 108; on the religious New Year, N. 127; on the first day of Tishri, N. 130; High Priest officiating in Temple, N. 148; story of deliverance from Egypt, 245–246; on the wood-offering, N. 323; on Chanukkoh and the Chanukkoh lights, 221, 223; on observing Sh'mitoh, N. 330
Judah the Patriarch, his attitude to Tishoh B'Ov, 100; to the fast of the Seventeenth of Tammuz, N. 114; to Chanukkoh, 229, N. 268; to Purim, N. 114

k

Kaporos, 149ff., 163, 164ff., 273
Karaites, 11, 61, 78, 204, 216, Notes 30, 127, 189
Kiddush, 15, 24, 30, 190, 192, 193, 203

Kinos, 103, 104, 105; name in Talmud for Book of Lamentations, N. 115
Kohanim, *see* priests
Kreplech, 151, 194, 195, 262, 270

l

Lag Bo-Omer, 94, 101, 225, 272, 276–277, N. 319
L'choh Dodi, 20, 30
Leviathan, 92, 196, N. 102
Lilith, 34, 48, 53, 139, 182, 184, Notes 155, 212
Lulov, 180, 182, 185ff., 190, 193ff., 203ff., 221

m

Ma'ariv, 14, 25, 26
Maccabees, *see* Hasmoneans
Malkus, 152, 167
Matsoh, origin of eating, N. 45
Matsoh shel mitsvoh, 68ff.
Matsoh sh'muroh, 69, 70, 74
Matsos, the festival of, 41, 42, 43, 44; interpretations of, 41, 44
Minchoh, 25, 152, 257
M'laveh Malkoh, 27, 30, 35
Mo-os chittim, 70, 81
Musaf, 118, 140, 182

n

New Moon, lost its status as an official festival, 5; a semi-holiday in Jewish schools, 90; Lag Bo-Omer and the, 101; announced by the Sanhedrin, 115; Rosh Hashonoh, the New Moon of Tishri, 115, 117; observed by the Jews in the desert, 119; High Priest officiates in the Temple, 125; of Elul, 143; blessing and sanctifying of, 274–275; observed by women, 275; as a minor Yom Kippur, 275; and Sabbath, Notes 1, 308, 310

o

Omer, 41, 42, 87, 93, 94, 120
Orient. *see* Jews in the Orient

p

Palestine, *see* Jews of Palestine

Palm branches, *see* lulov

Pay'tonim, 18

Persia, *see* Jews of Persia

Pesach, called Passover, 38, 44; a seven and eight day festival, 38; originally a nature festival, 39; a night celebration, 40; the name, 40, N. 43; a family festival, 43, 76, N. 49; joined with Feast of Unleavened Bread, 45, 46; oppression by the Romans, 46, 47, 50, 55, 56, 57; and the blood libel, 57–58; and the Messianic hope, 46, 56, 67, 80; sacrifice of, 39, 43, 44, 46, 47, 51, 52, 56, 61, 79, 84; the Second, N. 195

Pharisees, and Sadducees, difference in their attitude to the Sabbath, 11–12; their controversy about date of Omer and Shovuos, 87–88, Notes 96, 97; the spiritual leaders of the people, 132; in debate with Sadducees, 133, 183, Notes 151, 219, 221; opposed to the Hasmoneans, 223, 228

Philo of Alexandria, on Yom Kippur, 125; on the first day of Tishri, N. 130; on blowing the shofar, 160; on sitting in booths, 200

Piyut, 118, 258, Notes 103, 104

Portion of the Prophets, *see* Haftoroh

Priest, priests, 13, 29, 41, 129–130, 181ff., 273, N. 155

Psalms of Praise, *see* Hallel

Purim, date, 237; a day of deliverance, 237; Shushan Purim, 237, 252, 263, 265; a nature festival, 250, 251, N. 305; also called Mordecai Day, 251, N. 287; a rival to Nicanor Day, 252, 253; compared with Chanukkoh, 237, 253; the popular holiday, 254; masquerading on, 258; money given to children on, 258; Purim parody, 269; Purim-rabbi, 269; Purim-king, 269; theat-ricals, 236, 262, 269–270; an example of folk religion, 273; name, N. 288

r

Reform Jews, their attitude to the Sabbath, 29; observe Pesach only seven days, 38; observe Shovuos one day, 86; selected Shovuos as the day for Confirmation, 90; attitude to Tishoh B'Ov, 101; observe Rosh Hashonoh one day, 112; discarded "second holiday of the Diaspora," 116; prayer book, N. 134; and Kol Nidre, 168–169; observe Sukkos eight days, 170; reinstituted Sukkos as a harvest festival, 188

Rosh Chodesh, *see* New Moon

Rosh Hashonoh, observed by Orthodox Jews two days, 112; no reference to, in the Bible, 113; as a day of judgment, 118; the official New Year, 123; not a festival of the home, 146; name, Notes 119, 141

s

Sabbath, origin, 3; and the Babylonian Shabattum, 4; and the New Moon, 5, 274, Notes 1, 308, 310; in Amos, 6; and the three festivals, 7; and circumcision, 7, 8; in Ezekiel, 8; in the Book of Nehemiah, 8, 9, 27, 29; in the Priestly Code, 9, 10; prohibited by Antiochus, 11; and the Synagogue, 10–11, 18–19; may be profaned in defensive war, 11, when life is endangered, 12; fire or light on the, 11; and the Bes ha-Midrosh, 11, 18; among the Pharisees, 11, 12; among Jewish sects, 11; in the Talmud, 12; walks on, 12; heralding of the, 13–14; and the prophet Elijah, 13, 27, 35; services on Friday night, 14–15; personified as bride and queen, 19–20, 25, 27; Kabbolas Shabbos, 19–20; lighting the candles, 23, 33; adopted by

Christians, 28; new forms of observance, 30; Oneg Shabbat, 30; benediction over the candles, N. 30; prohibited by Hadrian, 36; Shabbos ha-godol, 71; Nachamu, 106ff.; Chazon, 106; before the New Moon, 143, 274; Shuvoh, 149; preceding Purim, 260; a social festival, 279

Sadducees, *see* Pharisees

Samaritans, 11, 60ff., 204, 216, Notes 49, 66, 68, 69, 129

Satan, 155, 160, 161, N. 173

Scapegoat, *see* Azazel

Seder, 47, 59, 67, 68, 74, 77, 79ff., 83

S'fardim, 31, 79, 168, 187, 256ff., N. 188

S'firoh, 88, 93, 101

Sh'mini Atseres, 116, 122, 170, 185, 187, 196ff.

Shofar, on Rosh Hashonoh in tannaitic times, 118; blown in the month of Elul, 143; at conclusion of Yom Kippur, 154; reasons for blowing, 159; relation to artificial trumpet, N. 169

Shovuos, Feast of Harvest, 41, 86ff.; as a one day and two day festival, 85; two loaves of bread offered on, 87, 120, N. 92; Confirmation Day, 86, 89–90; Yom ha-Bikkurim, 87; among various Jewish sects, 87ff.; the festival of the giving of the Torah, 88–89; anniversary of the death of King David, 93

Simchas Bes Hashoevoh, 183ff., 186, 193, Notes 223, 226

Simchas Torah, 116, 170, 187, 190, 195, 196ff., 263

S'lichos, 143, 145, 149, 168, 279, N. 134

Song of Songs, 22, 71, 237

Sukkoh, building the, 154, 189ff.; inviting guests in the, 192; decorating the, 204; origin, N. 240

Sukkos, Feast of Ingathering, 41; the greatest Jewish festival in olden times, 42, 171, 175; the most joyous of the holidays, 46, 171, 175; attitude of the prophets to, 173; reasons for sitting in, 175, 200ff.

t

Taatscher, *see* Challos

Tannaim, tannaitic, 14, 118, 156, 224, 228, 229, 257, 258, 265, N. 131

Targum, chanted on the Sabbath, 24

Targum Sheni, stories of, read on the Sabbath preceding Purim, 258

Tashlich, 148–149, 160ff.

T'chinoh, 21, 23, 26

Tikkun, 92, 93, 194, Notes 103, 232, 292

Tishoh B'Ov, day of catastrophes in Jewish history, 96ff.; Fast of the Fifth Month, 98; attitude of Judah the Patriarch to, 100; custom of going to the cemetery on, 105; a nature festival, N. 109

T'kufoh, observed as the New Moon, 275; announced in the Synagogue on the preceding Sabbath, 276; superstitions connected with the, 276

Trumpet, blown, 13, 14, 15, 53, 159, 181, 184, N. 169

u

Un'saneh Tokef, 118, 147–148, N. 135

w

Willow branches, 72, 78, 181ff., 186, 187, 188, 194, 195, 204, 205ff.

y

Yom Kippur, the beginning of the year, 121, 123; minor, 122, 143, 187, 194, 275; the Great Day, 125, 132–133; the day before, 151; linked with Chamishoh Osor B'Ov, 278; date, N. 143

z

Z'miros, 18, 24, 27, 35

OTHER Schocken Books

OF RELATED INTEREST

ON JUDAISM
by Martin Buber
Foreword by Rodger Kamenetz
0-8052-1050-4

THE SCHOCKEN PASSOVER HAGGADAH
Edited by Nahum N. Glatzer
0-8052-1067-9

JEWISH MEDITATION:
A Practical Guide
by Aryeh Kaplan
0-8052-1037-7

THE CHILDREN'S JEWISH HOLIDAY KITCHEN:
*70 Ways to Have Fun with Your Kids
and Make Your Family's Celebrations Special*
by Joan Nathan
Illustrations by Brooke Scudder
0-8052-4130-2

THE JEWISH HOLIDAY KITCHEN
by Joan Nathan
0-8052-0900-x

JEWISH INSIGHTS ON DEATH AND MOURNING
Edited by Jack Riemer
Foreword by Sherwin B. Nuland
0-8052-1035-0

LIFE IS WITH PEOPLE:
The Culture of the Shtetl
by Mark Zborowski and Elizabeth Herzog
Foreword by Margaret Mead
Introduction by Barbara Kirshenblatt-Gimblett
0-8052-1054-7

Available at your local bookstore,
or call toll-free: 1-800-733-3000
(credit cards only).